FR. TAYLOR REYNOLDS

NO LONGER *Strangers*

FINDING COMPANIONSHIP WITH THE SAINTS

Book 9798985443707
e-book 9798985443714
No Longer Strangers: Finding companionship with the Saints

Cover art: St Rose of Lima and the Child Jesus, anonymous artist

Imprimatur

+ Robert Marshall
Bishop of Alexandria, La
March 27, 2022

DEDICATION

In memory of my father, William F. Reynolds, who passed away April 11, 2022. Thank you for your blessings and for telling me I'll be "the best of the best"

This book is also dedicated to my mother, Agnes Reynolds who went into kidney failure as this book was beginning and who gave me an example of patience and long suffering.

I wish to also mention my spiritual sister, St. Rose of Lima who was the first saint to draw so close to me and has remained a loving and caring friend and companion

TABLE OF CONTENTS

Part II

ACKNOWLEDGEMENTS

It takes a village to write a book. In the case of this book, that statement is true from a couple of vantage points. On a human level, I could not have made the vision of this book a reality without the help of several individuals. It was a living testimony of the truth of communion and companionship in the Body of Christ which I outline in this book.

I wish to first thank Kirsten Fontenot Maslak who helped me with professional editing of both the grammar and the structural harmony of this book. She accepted the task while preparing for and celebrating her marriage and I am in debit to her for her gift of time and editing skills.

I wish to also thank Jenée Nagem who helped me with the formatting of his book, creating the cover design, and giving the final touches of taking this book from computer into the reader's hands. Jenée is a parishioner at the church of St. Joseph in St. Joseph, La which was my first parish as a pastor. It was great to work along side one of my parishoners and see this faithful mother and devoted wife using her gifts in collaboration with mine.

I want to offer thanks to the various people who read my chapters and offered advice and outside perspective. I really wanted this book to be something that could be read and understood by the everyday believer, while still offering something new for them to learn and a challenge to grow. I especially want to thank Teresa and Tim Strandquist, former parishoners of mine, who spent many hours reading through my chapters and offered grammar edits and critiques of statements. Teresa is a schoolteacher who has studied theology at University of Dallas and helped to offer a balance of truths and concepts, with ease of flow and comprehension for the reader. Tim, a green beret and a dedicated Catholic, offered an unbiased reading of some of the chapters to see if the average reader, who had no preconceived notions of the contents of the book, could understand it. I thank them for their friendship and service.

My talents as a writer are limited and even more as an artist. I wish to thank everyone who helped with the artwork that went into this book to bring the saints to life in a totally new way. For several saints, their depictions in this book are completely original and occur nowhere else. I thank all the local artists who gave their talents to this book and endeavor, especially Britney Brooks, Elizabeth Michalski, Mary Frank, Caroline Pellegrin, Norman Faucheux, Lilly Hidalgo, and Fr. Patrick Setto.

The very mission and purpose of this book could not be fulfilled were it not for all the various people who offered their testimonies and stories of the saints that interacted in their lives. These testimonies and biographies truly lifted this book from just a human work to a true cooperation with the saints. It was my encounter with these testimonies that drove me to write this book. Each of these individuals showed an excitement and energy caused by their love for their saint friends which transferring into their stories. I thank them for their honesty and courage in reaching out and offering their stories to be shared and experienced by others. Their testimonies also make this project a legacy that can't be found anywhere else. Thanks to Jeanette Adams, Fr. Patrick Setto, Katherine Ocello, Christina Brinson, Fr. Brian Seiler, Noah and Julia Hale, Kristen Dilion, Christina Branco, Bob Cash, Emanuela, Jessica Smith, Angelle Jeansonne, Vanessa Contreres and the Catholic group "Treasures of the Church".

Having just acknowledged the witnesses of our heavenly companions, I now thank the saints themselves. They are the heart and soul of this book. They helped to form this book not only in being subjects of biography but helping to inspire the writing of this book, in my life and in the lives of all the others who have written for this book. In many ways, I could claim that they are the truth authors and I am just the composer. I do not lay claim to any extraordinary gifts, no exalted level of holiness, no secret gift of clairvoyance, nor a special private revelation. What I have to offer in this book is simply a testimony for all on the road to heaven to share in. I acknowledge my unworthiness in claiming friendship with the saints, but also their unconditional love for us that reflects God's own love.

PREFACE

Writing a book can be a daunting task. Having never written anything other than assignments for classes, it was a bit intimidated knowing that what I write could potentially go into the hands of a vast audience of people at various states in life all over the word, rather than just a professor at a university. The first question I had to ask myself was, "what is something unique I can offer the world?" As a priest, I have the desire to share Christ with others; but writing a book is more than just sharing heartfelt passions, it means making that message 'immortal' so to speak. Not only will the message of the book be promulgated far, but also for years to come. Writing a book for me meant that I found a message worthy of that destiny. What that message is will be unfolded in the content of this book, but the discovery of that message and the road to writing about it I will disclose here.

I came across part of this message while in seminary when I was given a Medieval telling of the lives of the saints known as *The Golden Legend*, Unlike the more contemporary collections of the lives of the saints that are historically dated and chronologically organized to give an exact picture of the saints, *The Golden Legend* is filled with fantastic stories of saints battling dragons, fighting demons, enduring harsh tortures, converting hundreds of pagans at a time with sophisticated arguments, working mighty miracles, manifesting superhuman strength and true Christ-like poverty, and so much more. These stories have been collected and retold over centuries of Christians, passed down from one generation to the next, shared from the likes of priests and laymen alike until they were finally enshrined in this book. It was well known and perpetuated through a vast audience on times and situations: this collection is said to be what converted St. Ignatius of Lyola in the 1500s! I was always captivated by these stories and loved reading over and over about the various stories and legends of saints that influence the current lore surrounding the saints. Unfortunately, I think many modern readers would look at *The Golden Legend* with a lot of skepticism. It lacks a lot of historical evidence and proof, is very jumpy in its composition, and quite frankly seems to exaggerate the characters. Even the name 'Legend' would probably turn people off to reading it, believing it to be fictional.

However, the greatest message delivered from this collection of stories and legends wasn't the facts contained in the pages, but the testimony born from the hearts of believers. Each of those stories attests to generations of faithful believers who have been touched and inspired by the saints to the point of generating a true hero that lives in the imagination of the believer and carries them through their own struggles in the faith. The faith is not weak and the saints are not wimps. I used to read some of these legends to high school students and they always were captivated hearing these stories. Especially going over to Europe, it was amazing reading some of these legends and going out on adventures to find the source of these stories and monuments and shrines built around the fame of these saints. The true effect of the saints was tangible, almost physical, in its legacy. It was truly evident that the Legends had a lasting effect on the living believers.

The Golden Legend still holds a dear place in my heart and stands in many ways as the quintessential collection of the saints. When it comes to the saints, I see them as heroes, still alive in the hearts and imagination of believers. However, I would soon discover, as the Church has always taught, that its not just in memories that the saints still live.

It was thus with great enthusiasm that I started to see and recognize that still today, the saints were having living effects upon believers. Not just their stories, but the saints themselves are still present and working! I was blessed to find this reality in my own life with St. Rose of Lima, the story of which will follow later in the book. Then, like a set of Dominos, I started to come across a variety of people, many right in my own friend circle, who had testimonies of the saints coming into their lives with almost no invitation. As a fun fact, my original title for this book was going to be "Saint Stalkers", but I felt that gave a bit of the wrong image to the saints.

After coming across these testimonies, I realized I had a unique gift in my hands; I felt inspired to share these stories with the world and the truth that the saints are far more than we imagine. I started to put a plug out on different social media networks and forums, explaining my project and asking for people willing to share their stories. I found I wasn't lacking in responses: testimonies of saints, testimonies of Mary, testimonies of the angels all began to fill my email from people from all over. With all the various stories I had, I decided I needed to focus the scope of this book. I decided to take 10 saints who even in their earthly life attested to a connection with heaven and a promise to stay in touch with earth after their death. These 10 saints would form the core of this book and I would outline the testimonies of people concerning these saints. By and large, the majority of the stories that came in focused on several saints who had already promised in life that they would stay present in the Church such as Padre Pio, The Little Flower, and Maria Goretti.

Part II of this book was thus actually written, or should I say composed, first. Then, after I had seen the living message attested by these saints' lives and people's testimonies, I began to write part I of this book to give the groundwork. Part I of this book aimed to describe and give the basis for the relationship we are invited to have with the saints. Starting from the beginning of Christianity, and even going into Jewish and non-Judeo-Christian faiths, I outlined the principals and truth that communion with heaven has been planted in man's mind. I began to develop the understanding of the communion of saints as something that is very real and connected, that we see it and live it in the present. Not only did I read through many people's testimonies and personal biographies of the saints, I studied through various writings of the saints, Church documents, canonization materials, as well as spending much time in prayer with each saint.

Since I felt I had such a unique message to offer, I wanted to go the extra mile. I felt that several of the saints, when depicted in art, are either bland, or unrelatable. I also felt that a single image of a saint's face would not normally capture some of their wonderful personalities or the awesome events in their lives. I had been familiar with various young, Catholic artists who were skilled in drawing, painting and sketching. I told them of my project and offered them the list of saints and invited them to take the saint that spoke most to them and to depict them in a real, visual way that encapsulated their story. Several saints I had personal desires I wanted to see brought to life, others I left it up the creative genius of the artists. Their artwork is included in this book as well.

With all the raw material coming available for this book, I saw that there is room to grow: I am already planning to add a second and third volume- one for Mary and Joseph, another for the angels. Hopefully, in putting this book out, people will share more testimonies and stories so that this edition of the volume of the saints can be updated with more saints and testimonies, as well as more material for the other volumes.

I began compiling and crafting this book in the summer of 2019, but due to my duties as a priest, I had to shelve this project for about 6 months with the thought that I may not come back to this project. When the COVID-19 pandemic hit hard in March of 2020 and the world went on lock down,

I used this opportunity to go back into writing. Specifically, I focused on writing the biographies of the saints, which during a time of panic and uncertainty, offered to me a peaceful refuge. I also took some of the work I was doing and used it to create prayer cards of St. Martin de Porres and St. Rose of Lima during the various riots that were rising in parts of America. I used their intercession and friendship as an aid and a response to the hatred and violence taking place.

Part I took a lot longer to write since it was to provide the theological backbone to the personal experiences with the saints. It was beautiful to see that the richness of truth personified in the relationships the saints were making with the Church on earth, had laid hidden within the teachings of the scripture and tradition. Coming across and praying with scenes from the bible, teachings of the Catechism, even reflecting on the creed that I profess almost daily, I found the truth of communion with the saints as a bedrock of faith. Because it was a truth so central to the faith yet so misunderstood, I wanted to do a good job with it. I read multiple books, corresponded with the Congregation for the Cause of the Saints, explored the scriptures, and translated several primary sources. I became very pleased with the outcoming of research; something that was very catholic and orthodox, yet unique and personal.

I had hopes of getting a publisher to publish this book, but it seems that COVID did a number on publishers. I ironically thought more people would be writing during the lock down and publishers would be booming. However, many seemed to have lost a lot of employment and were understaffed. Being that this book is my first enterprise as an author, I did not have an establish relationship or portfolio of my own. Many publishers were uncertain of taking on a new author. After multiple attempts that all ended up with no success, I decided I would self-publish. I have enjoyed the exercise that self-publishing has provided and am grateful to have gone this path. I feel I can truly claim this project as my own. It has also brought me into close contact with several wonderful people who helped to make this work possible, and I believe the fruit of communion with others is something the saints would have willed to occur.

My prayers and best wishes go out to everyone who reads this book. You are invited to not just read, but to pray this book. You can hopefully take this book either from the trees or the forest: you can either begin with the saints(trees) in part II and then go back to part I(forest), or vice versa. Take a moment to pray as you enter in and ask the Lord to lead you and teach you through this book. This goal has been my prayer, I pray that it will be yours as well.

INTRODUCTION

The inspiration for this book started in 2019. I was living in Rome at a priest's residence for further studies. In the middle of my last year of Canon law studies, I decided to go on a mission trip to Perú. Easter break was approaching, and I figured that since I had two weeks off, I could embark on an adventure to boldly go to a place where no priest had gone before! Well, I certainly got what I asked for: I ended up in the village of Tupé which was some six hours away from Lima and about a mile up in elevation. I went there with a group of sisters, but except the one sister that I had met while in seminary, I knew no one. The culture was different, the language was one that I knew roughly, and the situation was dire. So much weighed on me as the only priest that had been to parts of this region! I expected the feeling of loneliness to hit me very hard. The odds seemed stacked against me as far as fitting in was concerned. My means of communication were nil and several thousand miles separated me from the nearest person I knew.

What I experienced, though, was starkly the opposite. I felt a great and powerful sense of belonging; this was where I was meant to be, and there was something strangely familiar about the place. I knew the liturgy that I offered backwards and forwards, but I even felt comfortable with the people, the culture. It was an experience of God, His love, His presence, and His concern that allowed me to feel like I belonged. I saw that within the Church there exists a unity of many cultures. Even here, in the jungles of Perú, where no modern tools or roads existed, the Church was as much present with the ministry of a priest as in the beautiful basilica of St. Peter in Rome. By taking the simple water from their streams and saying the words of baptism, these people are now as much Catholic as the Holy Father himself. Even though they are cut off from every other society and institution, they are as connected with the Pope and the seat of Peter as any prestigious family that lives in Italy. It was an overwhelmingly amazing experience to be able to see the dimensions of the Church so powerfully and vividly present. I remember coming back to Rome and talking with several students from St. John's University, where I was serving as chaplain. They were all very excited to hear about the cool mission trip (and the oddities of eating guinea pigs), but two students, a Jew and a Muslim, were most interested in hearing about the work of the Church. I was so on fire to tell them that the Church on earth had such care and communion with all her members. Every member of the Church was known and cared for. A bit deep for college kids eating gelato in Rome, but I think they appreciated the message.

God did something else that I did not expect; He gave me a heavenly sister to journey with me: St. Rose. I will share her story later in this book, but in a short time she has become one of the greatest gifts God has given to me personally since the priesthood itself. She accompanies me, encourages me, consoles and challenges me. I also found that as I shared my encounter with St. Rose, people from all over the world and from different walks of life had also experienced the saints as "stalkers", so to speak. The sense of companionship and the vividness of their stories convinced me that God was offering a unique message to the world about the saints: they are not dead. They are very present and alive. Sometimes, they are more active in the Church than we ourselves are!

Being a priest, with all the various duties that come with that role, does not give a lot of spare time to write a book. I found myself getting bogged down and had to put the work that was on my heart aside for a moment. Then 2020 came around. As the mandated quarantine was issued, I not only found that this time gave me an opportunity to write, it also gave me an inspiration. So many people struggled mentally, emotionally, and spiritually under the weight of isolation.

Depression increased, suicide became more prevalent, and crises of faith and identity were all around. People seemed to lose a certain sense of identity when they lost connection with others. People needed hope. They needed to know that God was still working and had always been working to draw near to them. The radical truth that a personal companionship was necessary became very evident.

God has a plan of salvation that entails not just white washing over our offenses, but a true and total incorporation of us all into something greater: a place of belonging. God wants to quench the aching heart of man that feels so alone and has been isolated through sin.

> So, then you are no longer strangers and sojourners, but you are fellow citizens with the saints and members of the household of God, built upon the foundation of the apostles and prophets, Christ Jesus himself being the cornerstone, in whom the whole structure is joined together and grows into a holy temple in the Lord; in whom you also are built into it for a dwelling place of God in the Spirit (Eph 2:19–22).[1]

Jesus, being "the way, the truth and the life" (Jn 14:6), is not only the end we seek, but the road we travel on. There is no holiness without Him. We cannot become holy, happy, or fulfilled alone. Holiness is not only an experience or a personal state, but a reality of unity. The truest peace, the most real sense of belonging comes from communion, from being a part of something or someone greater. In Jesus, we

1. All Biblical citations from the Revised Standard Version Catholic Edition.

discover and see the realization that true holiness cannot come about without drawing us out of our loneliness and separation and into true friendship with God. We can do nothing without God. Sin always means separation, and holiness always means unity.

God calls us to "be holy for I am holy" (Lv 21:4). Holiness and being holy is the goal of being a Christian, and thus being a saint (Latin *sanctus* meaning "holy") is the central goal of a Christian. Hence, it makes sense that those the Church calls saints, are those who not only are considered holy but experience the greatest nearness to God. Holiness is not just about moral perfection; it means being drawn into a true and full *communion*, which literally means "to become one with." The peak of this holiness in the Church are the saints. Moreover, the saints' most profound and central identity and reality is holiness and life as communion.

Even heaven itself, the greatest end we can achieve, needs to be seen as a unity not a division. Heaven is something that we know conceptually, but for now it is just a distant dream. Sometimes it takes a little nudge from friends in heaven to remind us how real that place is and how present it is. Sometimes, before we can go up to heaven, we have to let heaven come down; we have to discover that we are surrounded by heaven. I love astronomy, and sometimes the great mystery I discover by staring at the night sky is that I am just on a blue cork floating in an ocean of stars Just as you must first come to know the constellations to navigate the night sky, we must come to know the saint, those silent watchmen who become our guides and signposts for the spiritual life.

The saints have always been a point of curiosity for believers and non-believers. Rumors and speculations surround them.

Some outsiders will point at Catholics and see the saints as idols we place on the same level as God. Many insiders will see the saints as a nice garnish to add to the picture but really kind of an optional thing.

The center of Catholic belief is what Catholics actually profess when they say "I believe," and the ninth of twelve articles of faith is "I believe in the communion of saints."

However, it is not just the saints but the *communion of saints.* Our central belief is in this reality of communion and that the saints form this oneness in the Church. The great reality we shoot for is not just holiness but, in that pursuit, a true and full belonging—not just unity in a superficial way but a bond with something greater.

The Catechism says that the communion of saints is the Church in its deepest and most quintessential reality. It is what the Church is: the unity of those who are united in the Lord. Also, the respect and devotion Catholics show the saints are not just that of recollecting a memory but living an experience of unity.

> Communion with the saints. "It is not merely by the title or example that we cherish the memory of those in heaven; we seek, rather, that by this devotion to the exercise of fraternal charity the union of the whole Church in the Spirit may be strengthened. Exactly as Christian communion among our fellow pilgrims brings us closer to Christ, so our communion with the saints joins us to Christ, from whom as from its fountain and head issues all grace, and the life of the People of God itself." [2]

2. Catechism of the Catholic Church, 2nd ed. (Vatican: Liberia Editrice Vaticana, 2021), no. 957

Most often, we choose our favorite saint; whether it's a story that enchants us, a virtue we want to imitate, a situation we empathize with, or a hero we hope to become, the saints offer us no short supply of admiration. But do the saints choose us as well? My hope is that we can take a different look at the saints. I wish to address the forgotten reality that the Church is a community. Not just as a town or city where various people just so happen to have the same locality, but there exists something deep and more permanent, something that even those who have died still possess. In fact, those who have died and gone to be with God have the greatest communion with God, with each other, and even with us!

In this book, we will look at the understanding of this central Catholic belief in the communion of saints: who the saints are, why they are important, how one becomes a saint, what it means to be canonized, and so on.

I hope to address the true definition of the saints and the communion they form with each other, with God, and with us, which is the goal of the Catholic Church. Reaching that union with God is something that comes in tandem with union with others. The saints want us to be united with God, and their friendship is a means and assistance to that end.

This book will present the lives of the saints as a life of companionship. They, now in heaven, journey with others still on earth, and they live united with heaven while still on the journey. Each saint story in this book has been carefully crafted to highlight heartwarming moments and courageous and noble deeds, along with intellectually engaging lessons.

Also, each saint will be presented with a real-life testimony of fellow brothers and sisters of ours here on earth who have experienced in some way communion with the saints in heaven. These testimonies have been given in good faith and are meant to be a witness to the reality of this communion as something more than just an anecdote to entertain.

Every saint story contains a beautiful illustration of the saint that has been crafted by Catholic artists, making the faith alive again and visible to us.

As a priest, I hope to offer a unique perspective on the saints, not just of their lives but of the gift to the Church that the saints are. As a priest, it is my call from the Lord to share His gifts, including the richness of the saints, with all His children. Jesus in a special way entrusts the saints to His priests to share with His Church. In private revelation to a monk, Jesus related this in the famous book *In Sinu Jesu*:

> I never wanted to leave you alone on earth; this is why I have always surrounded you with my saints. I wanted and want still, that you should find in them a true friendship, a friendship that is all pure, a friendship that does not disappoint. Through the saints and by their ceaseless intercession for you before My Face, you will, at length, come to Me in glory. Do not cease invoking My saints and teach others to seek from them the help they need in the trials of this life on earth. In heaven, the saints will all be glad for having helped you make your way to Me in glory. [3]

My prayer, as a priest who wants to help people grow in holiness and closeness to God is that this book will not just be informative but reformative; may you take these saints on your own journey of life. I hope that you may find in them a true friendship and a support in hard times.

---

3. A Benedictine Monk, In Sinu Jesu (Angelico Press 2016), 7.

Finally, these saint stories cannot be read separately. Each one will share a different aspect of our Lord and God. However, they will also have a great common unity. Just as we are united together in this journey, so too are the saints in heaven. Their paths intertwined here on earth, for no saint is ever a saint alone. No one can be a saint without Jesus. Thus, Jesus draws to Himself and through Himself all those who are seeking holiness. All these saint stories must be read with one common virtue: love. The saints love Jesus and the saints love us. This is why they are part of our lives: they love Jesus whom we are all striving to serve, and they love us as their little brothers and sisters.

As you read this book, keep one point in mind: the saints love you in the present tense. They love and live in the Church of today. They see you and know you as one who has already walked the path you are on. But also, they love you with the great desire that you share in their joy in heaven. Nothing gives them greater happiness than for you to become a saint as well. God bless you on your journey through this book and in your own path to heaven. May you know that you are never alone. You are no longer a stranger.

PART I

CHAPTER 1

Who are the Saints?

"The saints found God. These men and women found what is essential. They are the cornerstone of mankind. The earth is reborn and is renewed by the saints and their unfailing attachment to God and to men, whom they want to lead to eternal salvation."[4]

Growing up in Central Louisiana, it was impossible to go to any Cajun festival without hearing a trumpet tout out the melody for "When the Saints Go Marching in." The jazzy refrain is almost seared into my memory: "Oh how I want to be in that number, when the saints go marching in!" Whether it be a New Orleans style second line, a wedding reception, or a south gospel funeral, that song picked anyone up on even the saddest of days, and it seemed to make everyone happy when they heard it.

Louis Armstrong certainly made this song popular in the early 1920s, and it became an anthem of Louisiana, especially as a rally cry for the New Orleans Saints. The NFL team took their name because John Mecom who was a native to Texas

4. Cardinal Robert Sarah and Nicholas Diat, *The Day is Long Spent,* (San Fransico: Ignatius Press, 2019), 29.

and Louisiana and a major stockholder, took ownership of the team in 1966 on, you guessed it, November 1, the feast of All Saints (as a fun fact, the colors of black and gold are a tip of the hat to Texas, home of many oil industries, since oil is known as 'black gold'). However, the song has an even older origin, with traces of certain southern gospel hymns, but the author is still unknown. But the song does beg a few questions: Who are the saints and where are they marching to?

So, who are the saints and why do we want to be in their number? As the song denotes, and as many people commonly understand it, the saints seem to be associated with memories, thoughts of a happier time, people who have gone on from us to somewhere better. Is this the exact definition of a saint?

'Saints' in Other Settings

As far back as can be traced, the experience of death has been a major factor in the development of cultures. Many historians date societies origins when they can document groups of people performing certain formal burials of the dead. The relationships and ties of life seemed to endure, and thus many societies built certain means of remembering these past souls. A certain echo of eternity existed in the way in which the memory and life of these past souls continued in their rituals, folklore, ceremonies, and marked graves.

Before the days of artificial city lights, the night skies glowed for the ancients with a mesmerizing light that awakened their minds to what was above and what was beyond. The early civilizations found themselves surrounded by the mystery of the world around them. In was in this setting that the ancients probed the mysteries of the world and tried to answer questions of life and death. Death offered another opening for man—a change in life that certainly marked something significant that must be anticipated but also recollected. Further, people noted for a more virtuous life than others were always cause for special remembrance. Particularly, societies have always given a certain immortality to those persons who were considered heroes. The philosopher Aristotle was the first to define a hero. He saw a hero in opposition to brutishness and considered him "superhuman," "men [that] are made gods."[5] But such a divine man is rare. The societies wanted the memories of their heroes to remain, to become part of something greater, be it a statue, a mountain, a lake, or the stars themselves. The enigma of the night sky soon became filled with the stories of epic figures and battles; some were so great that they became immortalized in the heavens. Of course, this doesn't explain how the stars appear, but it does give an organization, a purpose, and a meaning. It creates a connection and communion that spectators can still have with that hero's memory, with that virtue and strength. Their stories exemplified the power of virtue and gave meaning to the struggle men faced both inside and out. Simply put, the virtue of man was admirable; so admirable that he deserved a seat among the stars. It also pointed to the fact that man was not meant for the dirt; something called man beyond, into the great unknown, to an infinite reality. Man could see the shining light of a star at night, and such was the image of a person's virtue. The lives and stories of heroes also seemed to endure for all eternity.

The path for man to reach that status of immortality was different in different cultures. For some of the early societies, it was ironically by becoming more earthly: putting on animal skins, drinking the blood of a certain beast, placing animal bones on a necklace, and so on. All of these were attempts to somehow draw in the courage or power of the beast into

---

5. Aristotle, *On Man in the Universe* (Roslyn, New York: Walter J. Black Inc, 1943), 179.

man himself. Others tried to control unseen forces such as in voodoo or Hinduism, which saw a spiritual web of divinity all around man and within him. If man could harness that power, he could control his future and destiny.

The Greeks were the first to see that a certain relationship of virtue allowed man to escape his mortal state to reach an eternal home in the stars. Virtue is the highest and most perfect form of acting achievable. It was a certain perfection that man reached even while still on earth and made him like the gods. The philosopher Socrates spoke of the analogy of the cave, imagining man in a world (or cave) full of shadows, which represented this life. Man was called to break free from this imprisonment and make his way out to the realm of light above. This analogy was meant to summarize man's inner struggle to overcome the false illusions of emotions and pleasure and to grasp at a life of fullness that could only be arrived at through trials and by overcoming self.

There was one virtue possessed that, rather than being a product of man, was a gift of the gods: love. On certain occasions, the gods favored certain individuals with an erotic love that caused them to be housed in the heavens. This experience, as explained by Pope Benedict XVI, comes from the fact that love has the power to overwhelm man and transport him beyond himself. That love relates to divinity was apparent, and love's ability to move man beyond the mundane was palpable; but it had no direction or course and soon led to sin and the objectification of man. [6]

The cultures of the East developed with very different mind sets than that of our Western foundations. The East finds its identity in the group setting, in the unity of others rather than in personal goals. The East sees the spiritual

---

6. Pope Benedict XVI, *Deus Caritas Est,* (Vatican: Libreria Vaticana Editricia, 2005), no. 4–5.

and the communal life as very true and secure, unlike the West. Also, the East does not walk by the direct, blunt, confrontational nature of the West. Many in the East prefer a gentler, indirect approach, and the use of an intermedium or 'intercessor' is considered a powerful tool. Hospitality in the East is more important than timeliness. The power of intuition is as verifiable as the empirical.

Buddhism in the far East was one of the first religions to see that the way for man to go beyond his earthly nature was by annihilation of himself. They first strove through wisdom to acquire a certain purity as well as insight into the world. However, there existed another plan beyond just wisdom, beyond just information, that man was looking for. "Above the wise man, they place the saint or perfect man, who lives 'like the spirits' and practices, this time without effort, calmly and tranquilly, the law of heaven, which is perfection and truth unmixed with any alloy."[7] The Buddhist saint is one of the first examples of a man following a law that is beyond this world yet enlightens man's actions in this world. It is in the quest for Nirvana, which literally means the blowing out of the candle of man's desires, that he can follow this law perfectly and arrive at a state of peace.

However, just because this practice was novel and natural, does not mean it was correct. In Buddhism, Buddha is not their creator-god, just the enlightened one who has reached a god-like state. Reaching Nirvana is the end of the road. There is no greater life, and there is no greater other to which they journey; the reaching of the state above themselves is their goal. "The Buddhist saint thinks he is holy because he has suppressed or annihilated nature, but he stops at this and does not advance to union with a God who communicates

---

7. Henri Joly, *The Psychology of the Saints,* (Roman Catholic Books, 2006), 5.

to him a share in his own virtue."[8] The Buddhist not only does not see a concrete god to inform his path, but he also does not see afterlife as any real communion with anyone other than himself. He never becomes part of anything else, never becomes part of another. It is only while he is on earth that he is trapped in the circle of incarnation. Freedom from self becomes freedom from others. Nirvana is a breaking from the constant cycle of reincarnation and creation to enter a life separated from the earthly and those that are still living. The living simply look to their ancestors as examples. Their participation in this life has ended, and they now live an isolated eternity. *Karma* declares that their destiny is essentially in their hands, and it is determined by their actions; man makes his own fortune and is entitled to every punishment or failure: it is all his fault, in as much as he lives up to the great cosmic law. But men are very much alone in the struggle and destined to live out (and even relive) their mistakes.

In the Muslim tradition, there are many similarities with the Buddhist practice of self-denial and annihilation, but the end sought is different. The end goal is securing a comfortable place for oneself, the result of a certain karma in following what the law dictates. The Muslim counterpart to the monk is known as a *marabout* and normally lives out in the desert. "In India, the word saint means 'one who is delivered,' in Islamism the name 'marabout,'...signifies 'one who is tied or bound.' Tied or bound to whom? To God, for the saint or *ouali* is, properly speaking, the friend of God."[9] This notion shares the principal of familiarity with God that is further seen in the Christian concept of a saint. There is a permanent, central deity for the Muslim, and the *ouali* seeks

---

8. Joly, 7.
9. Joly, 11.

to be with him; he is then rewarded for all that he gave up on this earth. The believers can look to his example as well as ask for his intercession.

Saints in Jewish definition

The Jewish faith, which received a direct revelation from God, was the first to truly see and identify that God is the goal, the means, and the identity of man. The identity of man in God and God in man is the most fundamental identity for the Jewish believer. Man is destined for a relationship with God that is more than just an exchange of services, but one that endows man with a destiny, a likeness, and thus a dignity. When God created man, He made him in His image and likeness to show that this is man's greatest identity, and this impression is what gives man his dignity. Man's life was ruled by God, as the sun was created to rule the day. Man was created, which meant he was subject to the Creator. That relationship was seen primarily in the dependance on and relationship of the earth to the sun. Just as the earth relies on the sun for warmth, illumination, and all flourishing here below, so too does man rely on God for grace and life However, even at night, there were lights that shone in the heavens, and they gave light to those still below. A certain connection with light still existed and guided man at night. Even at the darkest moments of man's life, even in the great dusk that is death, man was never separated from light and companionship. God always provided light to guide and accompany. Man was created not just to be enlightened but to become light, that is, to share in God's very brilliance and goodness.

In a particular way, God invited his chosen people, the descendants of his servant Israel, to a deeper relationship with himself than had ever been experienced before in human history. It was a relationship that would forever change the way God's people identified themselves. To show man's destiny as likeness to the Lord, God called His people His *holy* people and commanded them, "you shall be holy, as I the Lord your God am holy" (Lv 19:2). *Holy* is thus a definition that is dependent directly upon God, His action and life, and is also the call and destiny of man. "As a nation Israel is holy, not on account of the magnitude of its virtues or of its superabundant merits, but because God has chosen it and set it apart for His service."[10] God's holiness is not just an example, but it is the life and love of God. The holy ones and the holy people are given life with God even here on this earth. This holiness of the Jewish people was almost seen more in a collective sense than it was in an individual. Man cannot just acquire that from God; he can only share in it with God. God and His people formed one and were united in the pursuit of holiness.

However, there were many accounts of those individuals that were exalted as holy men. Even when God first revealed Himself to Moses, He said He was the God of Abraham, the God of Isaac, the God of Jacob (Ex 3:6). God Himself is seen and honored in persons of holiness to the degree that these figures find their identity in God. Their lives and legacies live on in as much as they lived with and for God and now share in His life. The people can know God not just through messages and words but through the personal lives of those who went before them. The bonds that were formed with ancestors did not perish when it was the Lord who united them. God also shows Himself to be a God of communion, communion with the past and the present, communion with persons, families, and nations. It is through these figures and their legacies that God can offer a point of unification.

---

10. Joly, 13.

The prophets became for the Jewish people important intercessors with God in their day and situation. The prophet was a man informed by God to not only deliver a message of God, but to call the people who had strayed back to Himself and to the covenant through which they had union with Him. The medium is the message. The message they professed was the message they lived: holiness in imitation of God is not just eternal routine but a deep internal pursuit of the heart. With this understanding, many of the prophets showed that even as an individual, they could be holy and manifest some of the holiness of God by their actions, choices, prayers, and dedication.

A wonderful example is found with the prophet Elijah. When the rest of Israel had forsaken the covenant of God, Elijah, considered the last of the great prophets, was the only one to stay faithful to God. He went off and lived a solitary life with God by the river as God fed him; he challenged the prophets of Baal in their worship and called down fire from heaven to consume their altar; he had a certain apparition of God in the form of a still, silent whisper, and performed many courageous and daring feats. The first lesson that is learned from him comes not from his words but rather from the fruits born in the land of Israel: barrenness, drought, war. Elijah was fed and strengthened by God, but Israel had strayed from God, and it shows that "when God is got rid of, human nature is not emancipated."[11] Man tried and even today still tries to remove the overbearing God, but we end up losing more of ourselves. Elijah also showed how on many occasions the divine and heavenly entered and penetrated this world: from the providence of God to feed him, to the fire that came down on Mount Carmel, to the silent whisper,

---

11. Joly, 15.

God was present and palpable; the supernatural was no longer seen as something above and separated from nature but rather allpenetrating.

The end of Elijah's life gives almost as beautiful a lesson as his midcourse. As the Lord began to prepare Elijah to be called home, He gave him the accompaniment of another man named Elisha. Elisha began to pursue and follow Elijah, despite Elijah's wishes for him to depart. Elisha's persistence showed the yearning of man's heart for accompaniment; not just an emotional crutch but a true joining of spirit, where God can work and feed a man through the holiness of another. Their relationship soon reached an unprecedented climax:

> When they had crossed, Ë-lī'jah said to Ë-lī'sha, "Ask what I shall do for you, before I am taken from you." And Elisha said, "I pray you, let me inherit a double share of your spirit." And he said, "You have asked a hard thing; yet, if you see me as I am being taken from you, it shall be so for you; but if you do not see me, it shall not be so." And as they still went on and talked, behold, a chariot of fire and horses of fire separated the two of them. And Ë-lī'jah went up by a whirlwind into heaven. And Ë-lī'sha saw it and cried, 'My father, my father! The chariots of Israel and its horsemen!' Then he took hold of his own clothes and rent them in two pieces. And he took up the mantle of Ë-lī'jah that had fallen from him, and went back and stood on the bank of the Jordan (2 Kgs 15:9-13).

Elisha was able to ask for a great share in the virtues and holiness that he directly saw in Elijah. Elijah, moved by the petition and willingness of Elisha, was able to pour down that gift, an instrument of God. Even the very ascension of Elijah was something that first came down from heaven before going back up; heaven has the power to enter the midst of man as freely and powerfully as the wave of the ocean crashes upon the stones of the shore. Finally, even when the physical presence of Elijah is taken away, there remains with Elisha a presence of accompaniment and empowerment from Elijah although he is in heaven. If while on earth Elijah had worked such great wonders, Elisha begs, with expectant hope, that from heaven the spirit of Elijah could be doubled! It seemed that Elijah going to heaven provided a void in the prophetic mission. However, the contrary is true: his mission and power are doubled and lives in Elisha!

Holiness, as seen in the prophets, makes man more like God by opening him to the action of God in this life, sharing that life here on this earth, and calling him to share in it forever in heaven. However, differing from the pagan example, it is not an escape for the holy ones go up to heaven; rather, their ascension is fuller participation in the life of God.

Saints in the Christian Tradition

With the coming of Christianity, and the central belief that God took on a human nature in Jesus, there was not only a certain new revelation of God but something remarkable also happened to man as well. By taking on human nature, Christ made it into something sacred and holy. Jesus had already, to a certain extent, reconciled God and man in His Incarnation since He already united perfectly the fullness of His Divinity with the fullness of our humanity. Jesus is not just a model but He, the person of Jesus, truly is our salvation. With Him and what He brings to human nature, a renewal is given to human nature. In an ever more real way, the call to be holy as God is holy is more and more plausible and tangible in our ability to attain the likeness of God. God's life now abides in man's very flesh, making us truly holy.

In a most outstanding way, Jesus' death and resurrection has transformed the very fabric of man's destiny. Suffering, sorrow, pain, and death, which all became part of man's life after sin, have now been completely turned on their heads. Because Jesus endured all these realities in His flesh, He has taken in all that is to pass through man. However, these realities are now endowed with a salvific purpose; the resurrection has now granted a fuller promise and power to the body of man. The promise of the resurrection is not simply an emotional crutch in times of hardship; Christ has truly changed mankind. Pope Benedict XVI in his second book of Jesus of Nazareth compares it to an actual evolutionary leap in which mankind has been given the ability to pass over the limits once set in place by its former state of existence.

> It is a historical event that nevertheless bursts open the dimensions of history and transcends it. Perhaps we may draw upon analogical language here, inadequate in many ways, yet still able to open up a path toward understanding: as already anticipated in the first section of this chapter, we could regard the Resurrection as something akin to a radical 'evolutionary leap' in which a new dimension of life emerges, a new dimension of human existence. [12]

---

12. Pope Benedict XVI, *Jesus of Nazareth: Holy Week: From the Entrance into Jerusalem to the Resurrection* (San Francisco: Ignatius Press, 2011), 273–4.

Easter truly becomes for man a moment of unique grace and ability. As an evolutionary leap, it is a substantial change that takes place for the whole of mankind according to his nature. Man's nature now incorporates resurrection as his destination, rather than death. A new dimension in the frontier of the divine has been opened to man, and the very fabric of the human body is now open to a new realm of existing and living.

Christ's physical resurrection as an event for the whole of mankind is later articulated by St. Paul in one of the most powerful Christian images: "He is before all things, and in him all things hold together. He is the head of the body, the church; he is the beginning, the firstborn from the dead, that in everything he might be preeminent" (Col 1:17–18). The importance of Jesus' bodily resurrection was not just for Himself or His mission; but as He had assumed the whole of humanity (and in a deeper way, all of creation), He is the head which unites the body. Just as a body is destined to go where the head goes, so is the body of the Church destined to follow Christ!

The image of the body not only unites the believer with the promise of resurrection in Jesus, but also draws the members together into a certain unity with each other. Just as it could be said that Jesus' physical body was indeed holy (being He was God who is holy), we can see now how the body in its members is also holy. Thus, on many occasions the believers are referred to as *holy,* that is "sanctus" or "ἅγιος". The origin of the name *saint* is simply a reference made to the *holy ones.*

The reference to saints was quite prevalent in the early church. However, the use of the title develops overtime. We read in 1 Corinthians: "To the church of God which is at Corinth, to those sanctified in Christ Jesus, called to be saints." The term *sanctified* which literally means "to make holy" is one of the first times we see the term *holy* in the passive voice, i.e., it is something that happens to a person, something they receive. It is the holiness of Christ that they partake in as believers. Yet, they are still called to be holy, called to be saints, as in there is a further step or being they must arrive at. Regardless, the Second Letter to the Corinthians is addressed "with all the saints who are in the of Achā'ĭa," indicating the identity of a permanent stable group, a certain status already gained, which becomes a common greeting in many of Paul's other letters as the identity of the Church.

Paul makes an interesting reference in the Letter to the Colossians where he begins as usual by addressing it "To the saints and faithful brethren" and then includes a further reference to "the love which you have for all the saints," showing a certain communal bond and love they have amongst the Church members that are not present with them. This sentiment is extended in an interesting way later when he says, "giving thanks to the Father, who has qualified us to share in the inheritance of the saints *in light*." Here there is a unique distinction, not in the term *saints* but in the modification έν τώ φωτί, "in light." It is a bit ambiguous at this point to tell specifically what group Paul is referring to or where they are. However, it can be imagined that by evoking the terms of inheritance and being in light, these saints are those who have passed from this world to the eternal light of heaven and obtained a certain treasure. For Paul, and for the growing theology of the Church, distance, location, even death itself does not seem to determine separation in reference to the Church. "But now in Christ Jesus you who once were far off have been brought near in the blood of Christ" (Eph 2:13). The distance experienced by members is not a physical location, but a separation due to sin that alienates from God as well as others. In Jesus, all are seen to become one and find reconciliation not only with God but with others. Thus, Paul can famously say, "So then you are no longer strangers and sojourners, but you are fellow citizens with the saints and members of the household of God" (Eph 2:19).

Paul's use of the term saint makes the believer, along with other believers, sharers in a common destiny and place of common orientation as citizens of a common city. They belong to something greater. The title of citizenship can exist and persist, even when they are not present in that city. Paul is not referring to an earthly city but to the heavenly city. There are thus those who are not only citizens but are potentially already abiding in that heavenly city: the saints "in light." We also heard in his Letter to the Colossians that we share in the inheritance of these saints in light; inheritance is understood as a sharing not just in a good but in a status, as part of a family. God, who is the great Benefactor, has given a promise to share in a certain treasure and community to which the saints in light already experience and form a part of. These saints in light seem to be those who have gone before us and have passed away in death. Paul underlines in Ephesians that, through Jesus, all the saints are brought into one, almost regardless of the status of their progress, for the only true progress is becoming one with Jesus. After the victory of Jesus in the resurrection, death no longer holds power over the Christian; it does not change or mark man as it had before. Therefore, death has no power of separating or dividing the body of Jesus. As it had no lasting power over the body of Jesus the first time, it has no power even now. There is thus a distinction between the saints on earth and those of heaven, but not a separation.

In St. Paul's writings, we find a universal or horizontal definition of the term saint; it unites the members of the Church together as one, regardless of heaven or earth: all are one and all are equal members of the Church. St. Paul used the term almost ambiguously, not to confuse the term or to belittle its importance, but to show the great power that the Church has of uniting its members into one, both on earth and in heaven. However, in St. John's writings, we find the development of the distinctive character of saint and the deep destiny and tie with heaven. All the holy ones, that is, all the saints, are destined for heaven. God's will and the work of sanctification is to ultimately bring a person to heaven.

The book of Revelation is one of the most mystical and intriguing books of the Bible; yet, for all its mystery and suspense, it can be surprisingly simple and straight forward on some teachings. At the opening of the book, John addresses the different church communities in some of the major areas of Asia Minor and uses their lifestyles as a message for the entire Christian community. The universal Church and all her members are being addressed in the true image for the Church, seen not as a conglomeration of various scattered communities but as a unified force reflected in heaven. The reader is taken at different times to the very throne of God and the interchanges that occur in heaven. Chapter 4 begins the view into heaven and the heavenly worship of God around His throne. There is then a powerful insertion: "And when he [the Lamb] had taken the scroll, the four living creatures and the twenty four elders fell down before the Lamb, each holding a harp, and with golden bowls full of incense, which are the prayers of the saints" (Rev 5:8). As we have seen, the prayers of the saints could refer to the prayers of the saints here on earth, which are being raised up to God by means of members who are already in heaven. The heavenly dwellers have a connection with the faithful on earth; they are not simply praising and adoring God alone but are assisting those on earth.

St. John gives the clearest and most quintessential definition and distinction to the saints in heaven that we find in Scripture:

> After this I looked, and behold, a great multitude which no man could number, from every nation, from all tribes and peoples and tongues, standing before the throne and before the Lamb, clothed in white robes, with palm branches in their hands, and crying out with a loud voice, "Salvation belongs to our God who sits upon the throne, and to the Lamb!" And all the angels stood round the throne and round the elders and the four living creatures, and they fell on their faces before the throne and worshiped God, saying, "Amen! Blessing and glory and wisdom and thanksgiving and honor and power and might be to our God for ever and ever! Amen." Then one of the elders addressed me, saying, "Who are these, clothed in white robes, and whence have they come?" I said to him," 'Sir, you know." And he said to me, "These are they who have come out of the great tribulation, they have washed their robes and made them white in the blood of the Lamb" (Rev 7:9–14).

It is worth examining in detail this beautiful image presented by St. John. There is no specific identity given to these individuals. Their identity is less understood by personal qualities but rather by a single, unifying factor: victory! Though there is clearly a great difference and distinction among all these individuals, they are all tied together in the single reality of having passed through great trial and are now united by their status with the joy of victory they share together. They are "washed white," an image of having been purified by the one uniting bond of the Lamb, who is, of course, Jesus. They are purified and made ready for heaven; though from various places and cultures, they are made one in the same destiny.

In St. John's vision here, the saints have not only been sanctified, but also raised to a state far above what any man can do alone. Hence their great song of praise shows that their achievement of victory could not be done without Him. This is confirmed by the final part of the verse:

> Therefore, are they before the throne of God, and serve him day and night within his temple; and he who sits upon the throne will shelter them with his presence. They shall hunger no more, neither thirst any more; the sun shall not strike them, nor any scorching heat. For the Lamb in the midst of the throne will be their shepherd, and he will guide them to springs of living water; and God will wipe away every tear from their eyes (Rev 7:15–17).

This verse is the image of a central truth of our faith: to be holy is a gift received and cherished but is not one's own merit; it is from God and calls to God. This image now bestows upon the Church its grand finale. Those who have been members here on earth, those who have been drawn together, who have suffered much and endured much, are now given a perfect image of where they are promised to arrive. There is closure given to all that occurred while on earth, and heaven is not only an end to the trial, but a reward and a new life! The work begun on earth by God Himself giving and sharing with them some of His own life and holiness is finished, but not ended, in heaven as God allows them to experience the great rest and peace of His own life.

Though they have rest and reward, Scripture does not divorce that reality from them continuing to share in God's activity. The souls in heaven are still involved in raising the prayers of the faithful on earth up to God, which not only creates a connection but also magnifies the heavenly saints in heaven's praise. This final image offered to us by the New Testament sums up and clearly defines what has come up to this point in the Christian's understanding of what a saint is: the saint is one who has actively received the Lord's action of sanctification, becoming more like God and more united to the body of Christ, as they endured the struggles of this world and achieved the grace of perseverance won through Jesus' resurrection, to finally arrive at a place of peace and enjoyment in the next life.

Saints in the Catholic Church

As the definition of the early Christians becomes more refined, we begin to see the vision of saints carried on by the Church. The Catholic Church has received the fullness of faith from Jesus and His revelation given to the Apostles. As time went on, the specific details and qualities became more articulated and accentuated as the Church herself moved through the ages. Like a statue in a block of marble is present in the block but over time is made clearer and more defined through the work of time and sculptors, so too is the image of the saint.

Lex Orandi, Lex Credendi is a basic principle in the Catholic Church that says "the law of praying is the law of believing"; as the Church has prayed, so she has believed. All the Church's beliefs she upholds, defines, and protects are born out of a living relationship with her God. Every principal of belief in the Church is not just an intellectual matter but are born from the encounter with the Living God. The beliefs and principals of the Church are not and cannot be understood outside of a living relationship with God because they were born from a living relationship with God and express that reality. It's been said that the greatest way to understand and hand on the faith is not on a university desk but on one's knees and before the Church can raise up a teaching, she must first go down on her knees. The belief in the saints, those dearest friends of God, are no different. The Church upholds the teaching of the saints because the saints uphold the Church. The heavenly saints are not just a static belief but true pillars that have carried and continue to carry the believers on their journey to heaven. They are also the living embodiment of God's plan for man to live in heaven. Some have said that the feast of All Saint's Day is greater than Easter since it completes the mystery of Easter by celebrating the resurrection of the entire body of Jesus, which was celebrated on Easter primarily in Christ the Head.

We now see that the fullness of the climax but also the starting point of holiness in the Catholic Church are both personal and active, as well as communal and passive. The saint relates to the communion of saints as a member of the body, but the saint also manifests the full presence of God in his unique gifts and mission. Each saint becomes an image and model of what the entire body is meant to be. And thus, the way that saints are admired in the Catholic Church becomes an image for the entire Church seen through an individual member. The call to holiness is personified. The holiness shared in by one can become a benefit to another. The Catechism of the Catholic Church declares, "Since all the faithful form one body, the good of each is communicated to the others.... We must therefore believe that there exists a communion of goods in the Church. But the most important member is Christ since he is the head" (CCC 947).

Even in death, the saint shows a great example as a member of the Church. The Catechism says, "So it is that the union of the wayfarers with the brethren who sleep in the peace of Christ is in no way interrupted, but on the contrary, according to the constant faith of the Church, this union is reinforced by an exchange of spiritual goods" (CCC 955). The saint sleeps in the peace of Christ and now lives with

God in heaven. However, this resting in death does not make them any less bound as brothers or members of the body. Their death has been marked by Jesus' death, and thus the hope of their resurrection is a keystone in the Christian's view of the saints: they are not truly dead. Jesus promised that those who live and believe in Him shall never die (Jn 3:16); they even now share in the glory that is to come. This hope is offered to all, and the Christian can see already in the saint's life and death the power of Jesus' resurrection. The saints can share with the wayfarer a taste of the rest to come. The saint makes the hope of the future something of the present for the faithful on earth. Their lives not only offer us examples, but they give hope that the end goal is possible.

The Martyrs

"Blessed are you when men revile you and persecute you and utter all kinds of evil against you falsely on my account. Rejoice and be glad, for your reward is great in heaven." –Matthew 5:11

We saw in Revelation the multitude beyond counting, dressed in white robes. It was said that these are those that endured the great time of tribulation; they have been washed by the Lamb's blood but also have been strengthened to endure great hardships on this earth. Jesus is one and His gift of salvation is offered equally to all, but some have had a greater share in the lot that Jesus Himself endured. One of the great marks of Jesus' ministry was that He was persecuted, suffered, and put to death. It was by that road that He reached the resurrection, which is the promise held for all men. Those who follow the same road as Jesus did were more certain of arriving at the same end that He did.

Not only did they stand strong in the face of difficult trial, but the faith they had in the power of resurrection and new life was so strong they knew that even the loss of their very life through torture and hardship would not overcome the promise of Jesus. These witnesses to the resurrection who had died were honored by the other Christians as one of the first acts of public veneration. The martyr's testimony of faith was an incarnational response of faith in the face of the opponent; in the face of torture, persecution, even physical death; the natural response of the Christian endowed by faith was one of complete trust in the power and promise of Jesus. Jesus walked this path of death and taught with His very life that it is nothing to fear, for death is not as strong as God. The martyr's faith was what strengthened them, not just by giving them a finish line to aim for, a treasure waiting for them, but their faith gave them already in the present some of that new life to come. Pope Benedict XVI articulated this power of faith very beautifully.

> Faith is not merely a personal reaching out towards things to come that are still totally absent: it gives us something. It gives us even now something of the reality we are waiting for, and this present reality constitutes for us a 'proof' of the things that are still unseen. Faith draws the future into the present, so that it is no longer simply a 'not yet'. The fact that this future exists changes the present; the present is touched by the future reality, and thus the things of the future spill over into those of the present and those of the present into those of the future.[13]

13. Pope Benedict XVI, *Spe Salvi* (Vatican: Libreria Vaticana Editrice, 2007), no. 7.

Thus, the entire faith in Jesus and the promise of new life through hope was able to change the present trial befalling the Christian. Even as their bodies were being put to death, by faith they already possessed the new life within them. While not leaving earth yet, they already had the life of heaven. Those who died by terrible means were already a message, a living proof of what was to come. It was the hope of resurrection that was obtained by the martyrs' faith. So great was this hope in the resurrection promised by Jesus that in the face of their torment and anguish, they celebrated; victory was proclaimed even as the mortal body lay dead because victory was already possessed. By experiencing a death like Jesus', they were also able to give the evergreater certainty of union with a Resurrection like Jesus. Death and resurrection are two great cosmic powers that were facing off, and life had already shown it was victorious. The martyrs' faith gave them not only that strength, but it drew them out of the suffering by drawing the power of the resurrection into them! Their experience of death was forever changed because the reality of resurrection was so real. The faith of the martyrs then were not just models of faith, but as Pope Benedict said, their faith gave something greater to the Christian community: it gave hope that allowed the Christians on earth to share in that victory of heaven.

The martyrs are not just witnesses of hope, but they are also witnesses of fortitude. They show forth, not the strength of man, but the strength of God in man. It is a strength that loves its enemies, that is gentle in the face of hatred yet immovable in the face of opposition, and a fortitude that stands strong in its convictions. The fortitude the martyr shows is more than just willpower; rather its anchor is in God Himself.

> The testimony of the martyrs makes manifest a message: the salvation of Christ. In the testimony of the fragile creatures such as women, children, and elderly, shines forth the omnipotence of God. The martyrdom becomes, therefore, a proclamation of the hope in God, whose power sustains the humble and is therefore victorious. The martyr, moreover, is not a loser but a victor. [14]

Not just hope, but the fact that our faith is in an allpowerful God rings out all the louder when a strength beyond their nature holds the martyrs up. Only God could allow them to endure what the very nature of man trembles before. It is a message and testimony beyond words, written with the very body of the martyr. Originally meaning simply "a witness," the martyr was soon connected with the action of martyrdom or martyred.

It is not until the Christian persecution in the second century AD that we find the earliest examples of the term μάρτυς, 'martyr' and μάρτυρειν 'to be martyred', specifically referring to those who give their lives for Christ. . . . the verb to *martyr* is in the passive voice shows us that it cannot be intended to mean simply testifying as a witness; something clearly was done to these Christians and not merely *by* them. [15]

---

14 . My translation: "Le testimonianza dei martir rende manifesto un messaggio: la salvezza di Cristo. Nella testimonianza di fragili creature come donne, giovanni, anziani, risplende l'onnipotenza di Dio. Il martirio diventa, quindi, una proclamazione della speranza in Dio, la cui potenza sostiene gli umili e che è comunque vicente. Il martire, infatti, non è uno sconfitto ma un vincitore." Congregatio de Causis Sanctorum, "Le Cause dei Santi: Sussidio per lo Studium," (Libreria Editrice Vaticana, Quratra Edizione, 2018) 76.

15. Cathy Caridi, *Making Martyrs East & West* (DeKalb, IL: Northern Illinois University Press, 2016), 13.

There is now a deeper, more internal reality to be looked at rather than just being killed or dying. It was in perceiving the deeper message and testimony of life beyond just the physical passing of death that made the early Church to designate some as truly a martyr. Only those who were actually and truly martyred bore witness to the other Christians of the power of the resurrection over death and thus were celebrated and honored by the Christian Churches.

The basis of the specific veneration of the martyrs is another truth inspired by Revelation.

> When he opened the fifth seal, I saw under the altar the souls of those who had been slain for the word of God and for the witness they had borne; they cried out with a loud voice, 'O Sovereign Lord, holy and true, how long before thou wilt judge and avenge our blood on those who dwell upon the earth?' Then they were given a white robe and told to rest a little longer, until the number of their fellow servants and their brethren should be complete, who were to be killed as they themselves had been (Rev 5:9–11).

This vision gives a clear image of God's care and acknowledgment of those who have suffered for the faith, His desire of their ability to rest, and His promise that they should not be alone. There will be many who join that mission of being put to death for the Word, as well as those who will receive a similar crown and be recognized as a witness. It is also a powerful strength for the faithful to honor and look to these martyrs on their journey.

The context of martyrdom arose principally in the face of the Roman persecution. In the Roman Empire, it was said that the emperor, and the empire itself, was not simply a terrestrial authority, but also divine. The emperor was considered the *pontifex maximus,* the great bridge between the gods and man, since he himself was a god. Thus, he held a certain religious jurisdiction and demanded a religious subjection from the people of the empire. All those in the Roman Empire were allowed to keep their religions, but they had to also offer religious honor to the Roman emperor/state.[16] The Roman Empire thus established a certain communion between all people spread in the different provinces, between the different cultures and races as well as with the divinity above.

The Christians held that such an act of honor to the emperor was not acceptable with Christian beliefs. It was considered idolatry to revere any human on the same level as God and to give them the same treatment. Thus, Christians refused to offer such worship and were ironically charged as atheists!

In the second century the persecution becomes more targeted at Christians for their beliefs, and many Christians died at the hands of those who sought to kill them out of malice and hatred of the Christian faith. Since Rome was considered a sacred city, when Christians were killed, they were brought outside of the city wall, meaning they had left the sacred city.

The martyrs slowly became known and recognized through their individual testimonies, qualities, and unique traits that they offered and how they each made real the message of Christ. The local communities thus see the martyrs in their unique, individual paths and the variety of testimonies they offer the Church in the present but also the future. The

16. In Rome, the famous building of the Pantheon is the circular structure that used to house a statue of every religious figure from the different Roman provinces, with the god of the Roman state at the center and all the other statues facing it.

Christian communities are now able to highlight by name, by story, and even by date these witnesses in their lives. It was a living experience of encountering these martyrs' strength as they were plucked from their very midst, and they truly became witnesses before their very eyes of the power that hope gave to them. There was no mistaking their ability to face death in that way: it was something supernatural; it was something worthy of veneration. That general and universal belief in the resurrection now became concrete and particularized. Into every member and cell, the resurrection of the body has endowed its power.

As time went on, the definition of a martyr became finetuned in the face of false martyrs. What does it mean to be a false martyr? Someone who was not a true martyr! The early Christians did not have well drawnout definitions; their faith and prayer informed them, and they knew a martyr when they saw one. For some, this option seemed too good to be true: be killed by the enemy and you are set for heaven! Even criminals of the state could essentially find an easy way out by being a martyr. Things were bound to get bad really fast.

Around the year 300, the worst persecution of Christians was enacted under Emperor Diocletian. The persecution was direct and widespread; not only were Christians persecuted for refusing to worship the Roman state, but also for possessing specific items, such as Christian books. There existed around this time a heretical sect known as Donatists who believed that by handing themselves over to be martyred they were assured of heaven and that they could enter paradise by an essential suicide.

> In response, Mensurius, bishop of Carthege in the early 300s, formally condemned those Donastists who voluntarily turned

> themselves over to their persecutors. . . . In the midst of this conflict, Gratus, presiding over the Council of Carthage in about 348, successfully argued that misuse of the word was causing suicides and those who had simply died a violent death to be venerated as martyrs. Canon 2 of this council thus helped to refine the definition even more, by indicating that someone who had killed himself, or who had been killed in the act of committing a sin, could not be considered, much less venerated as, a martyr.[17]

It is in these moments that the Church began to see her mission as not simply a place of sanctification, but also a place of guiding and teaching. In fact, to fully and properly help her members become sanctified, it was necessary for a certain teaching office to develop. The Church had to define herself by teaching, and teaching was also a characteristic of the Church. Thus, an organic development began to occur in the Church; to better assist her members and to make them holy, she must become a teacher and guide for her followers. Being a teacher, like Christ the Master, became a central element of the Church. In a slow process the Church, building upon the lived faith that she handed on, formed her beliefs; they were the fruits of the Church living out her mission in the midst of the world and truly being who she was as the body of Christ. It was not an authoritative declaration that dictated the Church's beliefs, rather it was the Church's beliefs that stood in prime of place, and the authority stepped in to protect what is believed from error.

---

17. Caridi, *Making Martyrs,* 14.

Concerning martyrdom, there must be the material element, which is the action performed on the martyr (torture, killing, imprisonment, et alia) and a formal element on the part of the martyr, that of willingly accepting the action out of love of the faith. This acceptance had to come as a voluntary acceptance of the treatment as a gift from God and not a manifestation of a person's own will or strength; the will must be to love God above death, but not to provoke death. Then there must be present the formal part from the persecutor, that is an odium fidei or hatred of the faith (which could also be for some aspect of the faith); this must be the true cause of the death. All these elements are important, but love is most important. It not only is what unites the Christian most with God (1 Jn 4), but it also gives them a concern for the persecutor; anyone who sought to be put to death was failing in charity since it meant leading the persecutor into committing a sin.[18]

Slowly, those who had obtained these internal conditions and had witnessed to the hope, charity, and faith that was seen at an extreme level in the martyrs were also considered to be honored in the same way as the martyrs were. Though they did not die at the hands of wicked foes, there were some who were seen to have battled fiercely against the devil and won. They gladly gave up their lives through the works of love and charity, as well as selfdenial and penance. One of the first was the bishop St. Martin of Tours who lived shortly after the time of great persecution. He is reported to have had many battles with the devil, as well as being man of great penance and charity.

This then leads to one of the great climaxes of the Catholic understanding of a saint: one who is canonized. This point

---

18. Congregation of the Cause of the Saints, "Le Causa dei Santi," (Vatican: Libreria Editrice Vaticana, 2011), 81–85.

will be covered at greater length later but essentially a canonized saint is a person who manifests holiness in almost every sphere of life and witnesses, from a variety of vantage points, an image and example worthy of respect and even imitation. Basically, a canonized saint witnesses to every level and form of holiness from every vantage point and to every type of man who may look to their life. They are said to be saints, or holy, not just because of an internal spirituality or because of an adherence to generic Church teaching and God's commands, but also because of their human qualities, their psychological soundness,[19] their altruism, and so forth. To every man in every situation, they present the image of the truest man: Jesus Christ.

Also, the process of canonization did not come together all at once (more in chapter 3). Just as we saw the slow development of the definition of a martyr, so too the development of canonization took a great deal of time. Again, the reason it was so formulated came because of, or more of a response to, the changing situations of the time and as a manifestation of the Church's teaching office. As the Church leads people along the path of sanctification with the tools God gives, the Church also teaches the means of salvation and holiness.

In summary, a saint in the Catholic Church is an equal member of the body of Christ who, having been a recipient of God's gift of holiness, not separated by death but rather triumphing over death, are in heaven where they give intercession, companionship, and example to the members who are still passing through the time of great trial. In the

---

19. This does not mean that some, if not many, of the saints dealt with certain health issues or some mental or psychological condition. Many saints bore terrible suffering of mind and body; however, they endured and carried the condition with courage and strength to the point of being worthy of emulation by others. Despite great weight from human weakness, they were supported by grace to be able to overcome what nature was not strong enough to.

following chapters, we will look more in depth at the saints in the Catholic view: why they are important, what they can teach us, what the exact union we have with them looks like, and then how one becomes a saint, and how and why saints are canonized.

CHAPTER 2

Why follow them?

The intercession of the saints. "Being more closely united to Christ, those who dwell in heaven fix the whole Church more firmly in holiness. . . . They do not cease to intercede with the Father for us, as they proffer the merits which they acquired on earth through the one mediator between God and men, Christ Jesus. . . . So by their fraternal concern is our weakness greatly helped."

Do not weep, for I shall be more useful to you after my death and I shall help you then more effectively than during my life.I want to spend my heaven in doing good on earth
–CCC 956

As we set out now to understand the place and role of the saints in the present-day Church, I'm reminded of the great physical church of St. Peter's in Rome and its square. To be fair, it's not a square at all, it's a large ellipse surrounded and enclosed by colonnades or a series of immense white columns. It is encompassing yet welcoming. There is no wrong way to enter the square: whether coming from one of the sides and passing through the colonnades, wrapping around from behind near the Vatican Museum, or, my personal favorite, the long straight drag from Castel Sant'Angelo all the way down the Via Conciliazione straight to the front. On an early Saturday morning, the sky would be painted with a bright blue glow like the ocean and the dome would stand straight and tall like a light house. If a pilgrim arrived there at the right time, they could catch the first rays of the sun hitting the top of the dome before it slowly slides down to paint the rest of the basilica in gold.

Once inside the square, you are drawn into the controlled chaos that is found only in St. Peter's square: huge lines of foreign tourists following a guide waving a flag, a group of religious sisters weaving their way in and out of the enormous line to enter the basilica, a newlywed couple staging a windblown photo, teenagers trying to take the perfect selfie with one of the fountains or catch the exact moment of them jumping in the air, and hundreds of other visitors, pilgrims, and inquiring minds with no idea why they are here in the first place. Thousands upon thousands of people pass over the polished cobblestones, slick from years of hurried feet shuffling over them. Every so often the little blue police car will pass through and remind people to not jump a barricade, a few vendors will wander around trying to sell you a rosary or an unrealistic bobble head of the pope, maybe a seagull or three will try to land and eat some food that a rushed kid dropped on the ground. It's a place you could just sit and people watch for hours. As a priest in clerical attire, I would be approached often by a tourist trying to manage a huge, disordered map who would speak in slow, determined, English (presuming me to be an Italian I suppose), "Vatican . . . Museum?" To which I respond in fluent English, "Well you want to go out that way and hang a left at the end of the wall and stop to get a gelato at 'Old Bridge.'"

The square itself forms an analogy for the Church on earth: the gathering of various peoples, cultures, and languages at different stages in life, all into the embrace of mother Church, symbolized by the sweeping arms of the colonnades. Everyone on their various journeys of life can find a home in the Church. But the image does not stop there. All these vagabonds in the square pass not only through the Church, but also under it; high up on the tops of the columns, lining the entire inner ring of St. Peter's square, stand colossal statues of 140 saints, teetering right on the edge of the colonnade. The exhaustive list includes a variety of saints from different time periods: apostles, martyrs, missionaries, and many more. Many of the statues have an old crumbly look to them, whereas some are white and pristine. One detail that underlies them all: they appear to be drawn upward into something else. The architectural design makes it seem that they are standing with almost no visible support from below at all. It's a very compelling image showing that the saints' anchor is above rather than below them. Yet, their position there above is not to distance themselves from the crowds below. In the very language of their bodies, their gestures, their gaze, they are being directed and guided to a life beyond them and a destination unseen. Their overall place in this physical building is to be watchmen to guard as well as guideposts to direct. The statues' attention to the beauties of heaven remind us that something greater is out there.

The saints on St. Peter's colonnade, despite that they are above the pilgrims, are companions and guides for the pilgrim. No matter where in the square you find yourself, you are equally close to the saints above. Their position above actually gives a closeness to the pilgrim: by being above they are unaffected by the longitude and latitude of those below. In the square, you are closer to the saints above than to another person on the opposite side of the square. This image reflects that the saints in heaven are never distanced from us on earth by location or position in life, be it geographic, moral, or spiritual. In fact, their presence in heaven allows them to remain closer to the Church on earth then when they were on earth.

The preceding chapter aimed at defining just who the saints are, in other religions and in the Catholic Christian belief. What we have found is a definition of the person of a saint, but also a web that seems to string all saints together with each other and even with us in today's time. However, when it comes to the saints, something more than a diagnosis is needed. After all, haven't we said this point is a center of our faith? That the saints, or the communion of saints, is the truest definition of the Church? It is a truth of faith that has a bearing on our lives, it is a truth that bind us with them, and we should understand exactly what that means and how to do it. For many people, the thought that the belief of the saints means something for them and their relationship with God, that it is not just garnish but can actually impact our walk with God, gives them pause. Very rightly, it is a point that one should not adopt lightly.

Understanding the saints means something for our walk with God. The saints are not standing in front of us, but on the side of us. What binds people together, is ultimately the common goal we share, the shared end we both are looking at. Going back to the image of St. Peter's square, it takes a very keen and educated eye to look at each statue and identify who it is. Some clues can be gathered by what they are wearing or what they are holding, and several can be easily mistaken for another saint. However, it's in raising our eyes upward not just to them, but with them, that we know them to be saints. So too for us now, an intellectual diagnosis or historical biography of the saints can provide good insight into their story; but they remain prisoners to the past. We can only understand a person to a certain point by looking at their face; rather, when we put ourselves shoulder to shoulder with them, see to what goal they gaze, lean on them, and walk with them do we discover their truest identity. C.S. Lewis says, "You will not find the warrior, the poet, the philosopher or the Christian by staring into his eyes as if he were your mistress; better fight beside him, read with him, argue with him, pray with him."[20] All the more is this point true with the saints: the true definition of a saint does not come from what we can see as we stare at their images and stories; rather their identity is found in that communion we are invited to share in: following them, praying with them, sharing their hopes and joys. In fact, what sets the saints apart from just memorials is not just what we can take away from looking at them, but what they want to share with us and how they want to be involved with us, sharing our struggles, praying for our needs, offering their rewards and strengths to us.

Having reached heaven does not damper but increases their ability and desire to be near us. We see through them the common work that is for the Christian to perform. There has recently been a lot of study into the effects of space travel on astronauts when they return to earth. Much of this research is covered in the book *The Overview Effect* by Frank White who interviewed many of the astronauts who spent time orbiting the planet. All of those interviewed conclusively shared this 'overview effect' where, even thought they were distanced from the earth, experienced a greater unity with Earth, that seeing the entirety of the planet from above, they saw the oneness that exists that many of us below cannot see. They felt compelled to share this experience and bring an end to the division on the earth. Their shared stories have been fundamental in shaping a more unified identity as people upon earth. If this effect can be had and shared by astronauts traveling a few hundred miles above the earth, how much more by and with the saints who have reached the heights of heaven with God, become ever more bound with the Body of Christ and filled more than ever with the charity

20. C.S. Lewis, *The Four Loves*

of God?

To begin journeying with the saints it is important to see what we all share: a nature that yearns for communion. Knowing how the nature of man is created plays into how God redeems man and thus how salvation will look. Understanding the role the saints have in our lives comes from understanding the role that others have in our lives.

Man as a Relational Being

A common (and sometimes comical) social experiment is to ask children who their role models are. The answer can vary on a spectrum from a singer to a celebrity, an athlete, a comedian, or a family member. The choice is based largely on how much of a connection they feel with a person or on the discovery of a certain trait they want to imitate. Regardless of who or why they look to a certain person, the fact of the matter is that we are changed, and continue to change and form ourselves, from encounters with others. Our identity, our world, progress, goodness, freedom, pretty much every concept of truth we form comes from the impact or influence of other people. The family is a perfect example of how we are formed by persons and relationships. Man is destined to form and create his own identity, not in isolation, but with others. Even the fact that man himself is created, or rather, loved into existence by two people who choose to live in a relationship of love together for life reveals that man is relational. The family is then bound together for life to provide for the upbringing of man. Since man is more than just flesh, man needs the informed example and guidance of others to form and know who he is. It is in being loved into existence that man also comes to know that he is more than just flesh in blood, but something deeper, something more.

This experience of forming or *finding* our identity in others, is founded on the basis of creation itself. In fact, it's found in the simple reality that we are created, that we are not just the produce of ourselves, but bound in a relationship with God. Pope Benedict XVI expresses this beautifully in an address to seminarians in Rome:

> Therefore, this is the first point: to be a creature means to be loved by the Creator, to be in this relationship of love that he gives us, through which he provides for us. From this derives first of all our truth, which is at the same time a call to charity.
>
> Therefore, to see God, to orient oneself to God, know God, know God's will, enter into the will that is, into the love of God is to enter ever more into the space of truth. And this journey of coming to know God, of loving relationship with God, is the extraordinary adventure of our Christian life. . . . There is no freedom in opposing the other. If I make myself the absolute, I become the enemy of the other; we can no longer live together and the whole of life becomes cruelty, becomes a failure. Only a shared freedom is a human freedom; in being together we can enter into the harmony of freedom.[21]

From beginning to the end of man's existence, his identity and destiny is bound up with otherness. The fact that we are a creature means there is a Creator we are intimately bound to; the fact that who I am comes from another, speaks to the fact that the identity of myself is found outside of myself.

---

21. Pope Benedict XVI, "Address to the Community of the Roman Major Seminary for the annual feast of our Lady of Trust," February 20, 2009.

We then are led through family and friends to the discovery of ourselves in the other person. We learn that the definition of ourselves is more than just 'me.' God made us for more than ourselves alone because He made us in His image and likeness and made us for Himself! It's no surprise then that the final place of man is a destiny not of solitude and self-absorption but rather a kingdom of God filled with others of a great diversity.

Here on earth, we are made to prepare for that reality by entering into relationships. Our being is even in a temporal relationship with the past: ancestors, family lineage, and cultures are all linked to the formation of man today. Our identity is based very much on our pasts and where we have come from. Our identity stretches forward to the future as the call to continue to build the future comes from us. Societies form and identify themselves when many people come together to form a unity and establish goods common to all that can be shared by all, benefit all, and are protected by all. *Common goods* are goods that all people can share without making them less but actually increasing them by sharing. Such examples are education, defense of life, promotion of family, and protection, etc.

The happiness of heaven is also a reality that the more we here on earth share in it by faith, the more it grows and increases for all, especially for the saints who already experience it fully. Preparing for and understanding heaven can be hard because perfection is something we are not accustomed to on earth. It is easier to understand and imagine hell at times than it is heaven. Thus, understanding the perfection of communion in heaven that we prepare for here is difficult. However, understanding the opposite reality, the loneliness of hell, is easier. We are all accustomed to loneliness. Not just the absence of people, but the sense of not belonging or being cared for. Have you ever had the uncomfortable experience of being lost? Have you ever been separated from a child, a friend, your homeland, or the people you know? Amid a huge crowd of people, you can feel totally alone. The sense of being alone or belonging is more fundamental than just the physical; it points to a moral and spiritual sense of our presence.

Man is so familiar with his fallen state of loneliness that becoming accustomed to the state of salvation and heaven as communion is hard. Many times, we feel that we can achieve peace on our own. We both love and hate being isolated from others. This is clear in the fact that we like things done our way, the way we are familiar with. We are very used to being the drivers of our own progress and reliant on our own skills and plans. It is a double edge sword that cuts us as it cuts us off from others.

This miserable experience can be imagined as a slow drive down a long highway. We take it as loners. Our end, our road, and our final destiny are all our own. We need no one else and we want no one else. We want it to be our journey and we want the goal to be authentically ours. This reality is the heart of sin: separation from God, wanting our own heaven apart from God and in spite of God. This precisely is the experience of sin and the temptation of the flesh that St. Paul talks about. Pope Benedict in the same address elaborates further:

> The absolute "I" who depends on nothing and on no one seems to possess freedom truly and definitively. I am free if I depend on no one, if I can do anything I want. But exactly this absolutization of the I is "flesh", that is a degradation of man. It is not the conquest of freedom: libertinism is not freedom, but rather freedom's failure... Because in reality it is not so: man is not an absolute, as if the "I" can isolate itself and behave only according

> to its own will. It is contrary to the truth of our being. Our truth is that above all we are creatures, creatures of God, and we live in relationship with the Creator. We are relational beings. And only by accepting our relationality can we enter into the truth; otherwise we fall into deception and in it, in the end, we destroy ourselves.[22]

Man must understand his own nature to progress toward God. In fact, many have fallen away from God because of a misunderstanding of man's nature. Martin Luther, father of the Protestant Reformation, can trace the roots of his thoughts back to a lack of trust in the inherent goodness of human nature. His foundational 'protesting' was an attack on the Catholic Church's authority to make certain teachings and declarations regarding faith and moral. This distrust was built on the belief that the Church can't be a trusted authority because *man* can't be a trusted authority. Man's nature is inherently faulty and is flawed to the point of being incapable of rising above himself and so his judgments can't be trusted. Thus, the promise of "faith alone" and *sola scriptura,* or "scripture alone," proposed by Luther as the only firm basis of truth in this world comes in opposition to man's ability to be a judge or authority. Man is not able to know God alone by his nature. Man is not able to discover or formulate truths by his own power. Only faith, only the pure action of God upon man, is what saves and allows him to know God. This tenet was highlighted in Martin's famous image of human nature represented as dung upon which snow, representing Jesus' blood, falls and covers the ugliness of the dung. When

---

22. Pope Benedict XVI, "Address to the Community of the Roman Major Seminary."

God from heaven looks down, He only sees the snow, the blood of His Son, and not the dung of man's filth. And so that was how he believed man was saved: man's nature is dung and will forever remain dung. Jesus came to die, and His blood poured out for us has become the snow that covers our nature, and so the Father looks down to see no longer the dung but only His Son. Much of Protestant tradition was based on this belief that shaped how they saw man himself. The view of Church authority was brought into question, and especially the view of man's role in salvation and call to holiness shifted. Finally, the example and honor given to any man was underrated and the aid men offered one another was minimized. Men, who were meant to support, guide, and build up each other by God's design had lost their influential power.

The goal of this book is not to offer a complete reply to all the thoughts of Protestantism. However, it is important to see the attacks made upon the truth that man is fundamentally good and the need to restore hope in man's nature. Man was made in the "image and likeness of God" (Gn 1:27). This dignity, though affected by the fall of man, was not taken away entirely. We see throughout the Old Testament the teaching of the goodness of man's nature and God's love for His people, even in their sins. I call to mind particularly Psalms 8, 51, and 103; the prophet Jeremiah as he proclaims how he was known by God before he was conceived; and much of the wisdom literature. In a beautiful way, we see Jesus, the Way, the Truth, and the Life, the Savior of the universe, desired to save man by becoming man. "God became man so that man could become God," was a central truth held in the early Church. God could have saved us by any means, in any way He wished. However, in His wisdom He saved man in the most perfect way possible, and His decision on this matter cannot be questioned. The central reality for our salvation is that Jesus became one of us. St. John wrote in his letter, "By this you know the Spirit of God: every spirit which confesses that Jesus Christ has come in the flesh is of God, and every spirit which does not confess Jesus is not of God" (1 Jn 4:2–3). God wanted to save all of man. Jesus' birth, life, passion, death, and resurrection were means of uniting the divine life of God with our humanity and sanctifying, or making holy, all that is man and all that he experiences. Man's nature now has the infusion of grace, which is God's life, added to it, to allow his nature to go beyond its limits. All men at all stages are sacred because of what (or who) they bear in their nature.

Jesus, taking on the whole of mankind, makes Himself not only the perfection and model of each individual man, but of all men in Him. He is the great "other" who is the bridge of man to God in Himself. He becomes a brother to us and in that journey calls us to each other. Jesus calls us to love of others here on earth not only in imitation of Him but also because they form part of Him. What we do to the least of our brothers, we do to Him (Mt 25:40). This shows that Christ is in all men because He has taken all into His nature and destines all to be with Him. The kingdom of heaven, He says, is like a mustard bush, or a net of fish, or a wedding banquet, or a great feast! Heaven is a place of perfection; it is a place of communion and communion shows the full image of what God's life is. Hell is a state of the margins; it is a state that is lived not as much in a place but as separation and loneliness. Heaven is not private, but it is personal; it is full of persons. Sainthood is not only conformity with Jesus, but in that, a unity with others. Jesus gives the image of the vine (Jn 15) showing that our union with Him is a flourishing vine of branches, leaves, and fruit, each producing from and with Him. Jesus again calls all of us to be members of His body. Each little cell not only builds up the greater whole which is Jesus, but benefits and builds up each other. All parts of the body, no matter where in the body they are, are connected to each other. The inner organs are connected with the external members. All are together and united by the person of Jesus.

We now turn our attention to this role the saints play in our lives. We who are members of the Church, seeking and following Christ, are being offered a gift by the saints. What exactly is the call we find in the saints? Why should we look to the saints? These answers should rightfully call us to delve into the mystery and in seeking to understand them more, we can discover we are led closer to Our King.

The Place of the Saints in the Lives of Believers

For many believers, the personal act of accepting the truths of the faith and making God central in their lives is the quintessential act of being a Christian. This task is paramount for the believer and should not be second-guessed; it is critical that Christ, who wished to save all, should establish with all a personal relationship and a unique bond. However, our distrust of human nature makes us dubious of the role others can play in this relationship, and we often fear that others could be a barrier. People cannot come between us and our God. Certainly, there can be dangers and temptations to allow almost anything to take the place reserved to God alone in our hearts and minds. Christ is the only mediator with the Father. However, we know we are called to fellowship with others. We know there are those who are already in some way rejoicing with Christ in heaven. If they are in Christ, what does that mean for my relationship with Christ? "That they may be one" (Jn 17:21) was Jesus' prayer. We are bound with them, but how do we relate to them? What is the appropriate role and what exactly does *communion* mean? The word communion literally means "one with." How does this relationship with the saints look in prayer, and how do we always keep God at the center? We will examine what the Church believes are the saints' greatest gifts to us on earth. These 'gifts' form the heart of their relationship with us. Though the gifts they share and the relationships they have are manifold, we can categorize them into three areas: example (the life they lived that we can read about and learn from), intercession (the prayers in heaven they make for us now) and companionship (the support and love we can experience now that comes to full fruit in heaven). These gifts are summed up in the prayer of praise the Universal Church offers to God in honor of the saints: "For you are praised in the company of your Saints and, in crowning their merits, you crown your own gifts. By their way of life you offer us example, by communion with them you give us companionship, by their intercession, sure support, so that, encouraged by so great a cloud of witnesses we may run as victors in the race before us and win with them the imperishable crown of glory through Christ Our Lord."[23]

Example

Be imitators of me, as I am of Christ. –1 Corinthians 11:1

"Lead by example" is an axiom underlining the power that a person's life, character, habits, responses to circumstances, etc. can have on others. Many a parent has told their child a fable, a fairy tale, or a legend, not in the hopes of making the child believe in the actual passing of events, but to teach them a lesson through the story. G.K. Chesterton, the famous Catholic author from England, once said, "Children don't need fairy tales to tell them dragons are real; children know dragons are real, but fairy tales tell them that they can be slain." In other words, some of the most important

23. Preface I of Saints. "The Glory of the Saints." The Roman Missal. English Translation according to the Third Typical Edition. London, The Catholic Truth Society, 2010.

lessons we can learn, don't come from calculations and cold hard data, but from a living example of the message seen in a person's life. It's the story of the knight's courage and the journey he goes on that gives an example of bravery for the children. Many times, calling to mind the lives that people have lived in the past instructs man in how he is to live today.

In addition to teaching a lesson, memories serve as the basis of hope. When we see and remember by looking back at what has happened in the past, it gives a certain assurance and strength for what may come. We can almost predict what comes next. We can learn from mistakes. We can repeat a formula. When we see the lives of people who we say are now at peace and have reached a place of rest, it gives us, who are walking a similar path, an image of where we want to be in the future. So, even though the virtue of hope is oriented to the future, its root is found in the past, in a promise that has already (but not yet) been realized in an event and gives us that sense of confidence. The saints offer to the world that living example of what man wants to reach. The memory of saints can be a source of hope for man.

Even the secular man can reflect on and admire the saints. Saints were always people of their times. Though they are people of prayer and people centered on the Lord, they were not people of idleness. They worked in this world, and they worked well. They responded to each opportunity with enthusiasm and magnanimity. Many times, their mindfulness of heaven kept the saint from getting caught up in the common snares of sensuality and self-absorption that can slow down and inhibit true progress. They also teach that any position in life can be considered worthy and venerable and that no occupation, whether meek or lowly, is an obstacle to greatness. Henri Joly beautifully reminds us that the saints, in their spiritual pursuits, were not cut off from external good works.

> When the interior is filled with the spirit of Christ, exterior action flows from it, as from its true source and, sometimes in another, fertilizes the field of this world's activities, for the benefit of mankind . . . It will in no way surprise those who are accustomed to recognize the handiwork and influence of the saints in the evolutions and revolutions through which the human race has passed. The saint, although he is a man of God, is still a man, and a man who has not developed and raised himself under the influence of grace, in the direction of the supernatural and eternity alone.[24]

The life of prayer that the saints had, though it was a refuge from the hardships of this life, did not distance them from the concerns of bettering this world. Many of the greatest kings, queens, teachers, doctors, and scientists are saints. Prayer allowed them to see the world as a whole. Speaking to God allows man to judge according to His standard and can give to our view a more objective scrutiny. So, the saints' prayers allowed them to be more invested in the good (Gn 1:10)

However, it's not equivocal that a life of progress makes one a saint; saints want to see the world make true progress. Saints such as Mother Teresa, John Bosco, Elizabeth Ann Seton, Frances Cabrini, Elizabeth of Hungry, and Louis of France can all be praised from a secular perspective for the good they did for the world. They saw the world from

---

24. Joly, *The Psychology of the Saints,* 23.

God's eyes but worked in the world with man's hands. Saints can offer to people a new way to view the world in hopes of making true progress. Astronauts admire that one of the great gifts they bring back to earth from space flight is a new perspective of earth, a certain overview effect. They consider this new perspective as one of their greatest gifts back to mankind since it gives mankind a new view on themselves. The saints receive a similar but superior effect from their prayer by allowing them to bring back to men the view that an all-loving God has of mankind.

The saint, thus, can never be simply a social servant or philanthropist. What it is that gives their life and example its luster is also that which is most central to the saint: their relationship with God. What we see and admire in them is not just them, but God. In the example of the saints, we recognize that it is not simply human achievements that we admire, but how God is able to work and be manifested in various kinds of people's lives. In the wonderful work *The Noontime Demon,* which treats on the sin of sloth, the power and magnitude of man's actions are calculated concerning our call to reflect God's action:

> For Saint Thomas, human acts are a preparation and even more an anticipation: we already see God in human activity. We have a marvelous example of this in the lives of the martyrs. The activity and the witness of the martyrs are already a revelation of the face of God: in their lives we see God. . . . The activity of man—particularly the activity of the saints—reveals a true reflection of God's face. There is an original character to the lives of the saints in which the mystery of God is reflected. [25]

The character of the saints' example is that is goes beyond just them. It is not just an example of how a singular person lived, or even how a good person lived. Because God is the basis of their life, their example can be applied to a universal level. Their life lived in God takes on an almost immortal quality. It is one that is continually able to give life because it is modeled on Christ who constantly gives life. The example of the saints is a living example. It is not just a remembrance of past events or stories but is one that is truly formative and lifegiving.

The memory of them thus evokes a true hope—a living hope of what is to come since their lives already experience the fulfillment of that promise that God gives to man. Reading and knowing the lives of the saints gives a certain power to our lives; it encourages us by showing how the various injustices and sufferings we experience can lead to a level of holiness and peace that the world does not give. Not only do their lives teach us how to overcome trials by exemplifying strength in difficulties, but how every circumstance of life can be transformed. It demonstrates what St. Paul said, "Now I rejoice in my sufferings for your sake, and in my flesh I complete what is lacking in Christ's afflictions for the sake of his body, that is, the Church" (Col 1:24). Not that Jesus' life or suffering was insufficient, but His life desires to be lived in our lives. In the saints we see how each in their own regard reflect the suffering and life of Christ.

This brings us to the final thing the saints' example offers us: a living translation of the will of God. The ways God speaks to us are many and various. Knowing what God asks of us here and now and how to do it can often be difficult. The saints show us not only what His will is but also how He asks it of us. The universal call to holiness is made clear

---

25. Jean-Charles Nault O.S.B., *The Noonday Devil: Acedia, the Unnamed Evil of Our Times* (San Francisco: Ignatius Press, 2015), 75.

in the way each of them lived it in their lives. They express the teaching that all people are called to holiness by being a living and breathing demonstration of that teaching. Even the more difficult teachings—the revelations of God, the mysteries of who God is, and His plan of salvation—is seen, known, and lived by the saints. Thomas Dubay, the great spiritual writer, details that even the most silent, unnoticed saint offers a great work for us: a living translation of the biblical message:

> They not only lived the revealed word well; they also have lived it heroically well. Both the biblical word and their lives are inspired by the one Holy Spirit. While scriptural commentators often contradict one another in their explanations (and as logic points out, in a contradiction one of the two parties must be mistaken), saints do not contradict one another in the ways in which they concretize the Gospel. True enough, each is unique, and all together they present a multifaceted and complementary diversity in their various life situations. St. Thomas More lived Gospel poverty as a husband and a father, in a manner different from that of St. Francis of Assisi or St. Robert Bellarmine. This kind of complementarity enriches, whereas the contradictory type is damaging to the mistaken party, for error puts one out of touch with a given reality.[26]

---

26. Thomas Dubay, *Fire Within* (San Francisco: Ignatius Press, 1989), 13.

The truest and deepest messages of God are lived out in the various lives of the saints. Jesus, who Himself was the full revelation of God, was incarnate in a human person and as much as the saints live in and with Jesus, they help to make the revelation flesh again in their very lives. Even the most difficult of mysteries has its truest meaning in the saints. The sometimes-mysterious designs of God's will are made clear for us when we look at the way in which the saints lived in response to His call. Many of the saints not only taught with their lives but with their writings and preaching as well. However, one thing that makes their teaching so powerful is that it was tied to and reflected in their lives of prayer, charity, penance, and simplicity. If someone has trouble understanding Scripture or the teachings of the Church, the saints give witness to the true meaning.

Intercession

"Therefore confess your sins to one another, and pray for one another, that you may be healed. The prayer of a righteous man has great power in its effects." –James 5:16

Intercession is a great act of charity where we plead before God on behalf of another person. In the end, God is the only one who has the power to answer and grant prayers. However, God calls all of us to be His instruments. The Bible cites many times that patriarchs, prophets, and leaders prayed on behalf of other people and God granted the request. We know the story of Abraham who interceded for the sinful city of Sodom and the Lord spared the city, even when He had planned otherwise (Gn 18:16–33). Moses interceded to God after the Israelites had turned from God immediately after being freed from Egypt and had sparked God's anger[27] (Ex 32:7–14).

In the New Testament, Jesus calls His disciples to radical

love, and one of the ways He teaches them is to "pray for those who persecute you" (Mt 5:44) "so that you may be sons of your Father who is in heaven" (Mt 5:45). Our Lord shows that intercession is not only a means of gain for the believer but also extends outward in charity toward others. At the center of Christ's mission was intercession, to stand between God and man and pray on our behalf. Throughout Jesus' ministry He retreated to go pray. On the Cross, He prayed for those who killed Him and from heaven He intercedes for us before the Father (Heb 7:25). Thus, being a true follower of Jesus means to imitate His love and His intercession.

Our role in interceding for others is necessary in our call to follow Christ. One of the consequences that arises from the Protestant understanding of the faulty, unworthy nature of man is a false belief in man's incapacity to truly and fully be used as an instrument of God. In interceding for another, man acts as an instrument of God cooperating with God, who is all good and all powerful. The Protestant thought is that man will ultimately be a barrier to another if he tries to mediate or intercede for him. However, the goodness of man and the sacredness of man's nature, derived from Jesus uniting our nature to His, is that man is not a barrier but, because of the inherent worth and sacredness of our nature, he is a bridge to God. St. Paul underlines this principle again by telling us that "the body is not for immorality but for the Lord...your bodies are members of Christ...your body is a temple of the Holy Spirit within you..." (1 Cor 6:13, 15, 19). The temple, especially for the Jews, was a place where

---

27. The Old Testament's reference to God's anger and wrath as described in these scenes should be understood in its proper context: these stories were written long after the events took place and were addressed to Jews probably living in pagan lands and constantly tempted to being unfaithful to the covenant by pagan religions. Idolatry needed to be shown as sinful but God also as forgiving. It was an image and revelation that demonstrated the motif: love the sinner, hate the sin.

the presence of God dwelt. The temple was not a barrier to meeting God but rather a place to facilitate that encounter.

On multiple occasions in the Gospels, Jesus underlines and showcases how beautiful and powerful intercession is and how it in no way presents a barrier. Throughout the Gospels Jesus shows Himself to be God by being the one true author and cause of miracles in our world. He calls us to be in the union of charity with others by praying for one another. This does not distance Him from the one being prayed for but draws Him nearer in love. There is a great example of this from the Gospel when a master comes to intercede for his servant before Jesus. Note well how Jesus responds:

> As he entered Cą-pêr'ną-ųm, a centurion came forward to him, beseeching him and saying," Lord, my servant is lying paralyzed at home, in terrible distress." And he said to him, "I will come and heal him." But the centurian answered him, "Lord, I am not worthy to have you come under my roof; but only say the world, and my servant will be healed...". When Jesus heard him, he marveled, and said to those who followed him, "Truly, I say to you, not even in Israel have I found such faith…". And to the centurian Jesus said, "Go, be it done for you as you have believed." And the servant was healed at that very moment. (Mt 8:5–8, 10, 13)

"He marveled": Our Lord showed awe and wonder at this man's intercession! This man knew that Jesus alone had the power to heal; he knew that Our Lord did not even need to be present; Jesus did not even need to see and address the servant. Our Lord marveled and was moved by such an act of faith: the master's belief that a simple prayer of intercession sufficed. Jesus did not argue; He did not say that He was distanced from the poor servant because of the master's intercession. His heart was moved by the charity and faith of the master and allowed this master's intercession to be an instrument of a miracle. This event was not an isolated one either. At another point in Scripture, Jesus encourages the act of intercession and calls for believers to be instruments of His miracles. We can see this dynamic being played out in the Gospel of John:

> And at Cą-pêr'ną-ųm there was an officer whose son was ill. When he heard that Jesus had come from Jű-dē'ą to Galilee, he went and begged him to come down and heal his son, for he was on the point of death.... Jesus said to him, "Go; your son will live." The man believed the word that Jesus spoke to him and went his way. As he was going down, his servants met him and told him that his son was living. So he asked them the hours when he began to mend, and they said to him," Yesterday at the seventh hour the fever left him." The father knew that was the hour when Jesus had said to him, "Your son will live." (Jn 4:46–47, 50–53)

Far from Jesus discouraging mediation, He is moved by the humility to believe and pray for another person. He even challenges us to be greater believers by trusting that He calls us to be instruments. Being an instrument means relying on Him as the cause but trusting that He acts through us, incapable as we may be. This participation is the true power of intercession: we can be instruments of God through our faith, humility, and charity.

Since the work of intercession is something that all

followers are called to do, it was and is also accomplished by those who are the greatest followers of Jesus and have now joined Him in heaven, the saints. Truly, Jesus has said that "he who believes in me will also do the works that I do; and greater works than these will he do, because I go to the Father. Whatever you ask in my name, I will do it" (Jn 14:12–13). This promise of Jesus is seen in a remarkable way in the saints, firstly because they followed Jesus in such a heroic way that it can't be argued that they did not believe in Him. The saints follow Jesus not just in this life but to an even greater extent in heaven, where their faith and trust in Him has come to perfection. Their charity and care for the rest of the Church has also reached its level of perfection.

One of the greatest ways they participate in the Church is through intercession, still acting as instruments of God by showing His care for the Church as well as the fulfillment of His promise that He has a place in heaven prepared for us. It is from that place in heaven, distinct but not separated from us, that they fulfill Jesus' promise of performing greater works through their intercession. As Jesus in heaven still has a role of intercession, so too the saints in heaven are still able to plead for us, who are not able to be as close to Jesus as they are in heaven. They act as those figures in the Gospel who intercede for others, and Jesus, in like manner, is moved by the faith of the saints, as well as their charity for us fellow members. God is always the first cause and the end of all prayers of intercession and answers given, but the saints participate as instruments for us. Because the saints also endured in their own lives many of the same things we are currently enduring, they have a deeper compassion for us. The same compassion that God has for us is shared in by the saints and manifests in a larger, more various degree the depths and intentionality of God's care for us. Far from the saints being a barrier between us and God, their intercession, understood not as an end in itself but as an instrument, manifests all the greater the power and care of God the Father. A father is one who draws his family to work together and to love each other as he first has loved them. When saints show care and concern and a certain ability to help others, it is a greater proof that God is a good Father, who is imitated and reflected by all His children even more. Just as a flower is known by its scent or the sun by its rays, so is God known and His goodness spread and diffused more by the saints.

The next chapter will cover more in-depth how becoming or making someone a saint was a work with and for the Church. The journey everyone makes to be closer to God affects the entire Church. Part of the proof of a person's sainthood is the effect they have upon the Church. In a most remarkable way, miracles are a supernatural effect upon the Church of the person's sainthood. They manifests a closeness to God as well as a charity in listening to the pleading of the faithful.

Seeking a saint's intercession thus has three ends: first, it glorifies God, the principal author of all good works, which He manifests through various instruments as a conductor's skill is augmented by guiding a variety of music into harmony; second, it confirms a person's place in heaven. When someone intercedes for us after their death, the resulting miracle shows that the person invoked is close to God, since God is the origin of miracles. Third, it gives great help to us here on earth. The faithful on earth are called "Militant," meaning they are in a battle. On our own, without the grace and help of God, we can't reach the end. We need many eyes and ears to help us and to give the reinforcements we need to engage in this battle, which is more spiritual than it is physical. Our prayers to the saints give them permission to pray for us and to look after us and offer us the help that often we don't know we need at the time. It is also true sometimes that the natural world reaches its limit, and we need an extra assistance. Right at that time spiritual aids supply for us in our need, as St. Paul tells us, "Likewise the Spirit helps us in our weakness; for we do not know how to pray as we ought, but the Spirit himself intercedes for us with sighs too deep for words" (Rom 8:26). Hence, those who were totally possessed by this Spirit in this life and are now fully live in the Spirit in heaven can't help but intercede for us.

Companionship

"Therefore, since we are surrounded by so great a cloud of witnesses, let us also lay aside every weight, and sin which clings so closely, and let us run with perseverance the race that is set before us."
–Hebrews 12:1

Companionship with the saints is not only a culmination of what we have already discussed, but it is the most powerful gift the saints can share with us. The companionship of the saints is not only the gift of their living example and their intercession, but it is something more: it is a vivid, active presence. In fact, it's only by the saints being a living and active agent in the Church that their examples and intercession can have any power or meaning for us. If the saints are dead and gone, then their example is little more than an encouraging story and their intercession is superstitious murmuring. It is important again for us to remember who the saints are to give definition and reality to their participation. Who they are not only reminds us that they are members of the Church in heaven who are present in a spiritual way, but it reminds us they are persons, true living subjects with minds, hearts, and souls. They remember the trials of this earth; they know us as friends and our unique situations; they love us in the most perfect way. They love us because of a certain familiarity with the life and events we go through. Hence there are patron saints who offer a certain assistance and accompaniment to specific individuals or situations that those saints were familiar with. Just like us on earth, when we see someone that we identify with, whether it be a situation we have found ourselves in, a trial we have gone through, or a passion we share, we can't help but share in the desire for that person to overcome and achieve. Because grace builds upon nature and holiness makes us more truly who we are, not less, the saints have kept their personalities and the passions they had on earth. More than just conserved, they have been perfected! Also, their closeness to God makes them have a special love for the things God loves. Henri Joly details this point:

> St. Catherine of Siena use to say: "The reason why God's servants love creatures so much is that they see how much Christ loves them, and it is one of the properties of love to love what is loved by the person we love." . . . Many other saints whose lives and actions were more hidden than hers, have said the same thing, that when Christ crucified takes possession of a soul He inspires it with a very great tenderness for the humanity for which He died. Sanctity demands complete detachment from all pleasures which are derived from self-love. . . . Once self-love is destroyed, the barrier is done away with and not only is there no law of detachment from all things, but the soul is enjoined to love everything, provided that it does so 'for the love of God.'[28]

The saints, having been possessed by Jesus to an extreme level while on earth, have been fully and completely possessed by Christ in heaven, in the fullness of Him taking them to Himself. Because of this complete possession, they can't help but love in an identical way the people that Christ loves. As much as we know God to be active, present, compassionate, and near us, so too the same must be argued for the saints. The truest reality of heaven is union with God and to see His face, it thus means that the saints are ever more united with the love of God and see Him in the person of the other.

Saints worked with grace while on earth and were able to do what seemed impossible. In heaven, the barrier has been completely broken. They can achieve the highest level of accomplishment imaginable for a creature because of their incorporation into the life of God. What this means is that the vision and desire of the saints has been freed, but so has their potential to be made present and to offer help. Without being omnipotent or omnipresent as God is (since only God is a perfect being), their nature is freed from the influences of this world and their nature has been elevated to share life with God and thus participate in and reflect His life. Every love on earth is subject to error, weakness, and exhaustion; not so for the saints. While on earth, God equipped each of the saints with a certain set of gifts, talents, and graces to accomplish the mission He called them to. The richness of God never expires, diminishes, or is taken back, even when their mission on earth finishes, "For the gifts and the call of God are irrevocable" (Rom 11:29). No, the richness of God grows richer: "For to him who has will more be given, and he will have abundance" (Mt.13:12). The reward of man's labor is not to have the richness of grace and virtue taken away but to have it increased! The mission given on earth is rewarded by giving a share of more, not less.

Heaven then becomes a place of simultaneous reward, enrichment, and rest. Jesus reminds us, "You have been faithful over a little, I will set you over much; enter into

---

28. Joly, *The Psychology of the Saints*, 160.

the joy of your master" (Mt 25:21). It is important to pay attention to the sequence Jesus gives: faithfulness over the little that the master gave is rewarded with stewardship over much; they are then able to participate in the joy and rest of the master. What else could this mean but that the saints who were faithful with a small task on earth, are then, upon meeting the master in heaven, given stewardship over more of the flock on earth? They are then called to share the Lord's own rest and joy. The rest of God in heaven is not idleness; it is overflowing abundance. The saints are rewarded by being enriched with more gifts and graces; the talents that they watched over while on earth are increased in heaven. This stewardship is seen in the saints' continued role and activity in the Church and in our lives. Now in heaven they are ever more empowered to watch over more of the Lord's beloved than they ever could while on earth.

While resting with the Lord, they are never idle; they are stewarding and helping us to reach the same goal which is heaven. The saints, while sharing in the great prize that is the victory of heaven, find themselves drawn closer to us not as a duty but a true joy. Jesus Himself promised that "there will be more joy in heaven over one sinner who repents than over ninety-nine who need no repentance" (Lk 15:7), revealing that heaven is not only attentively watching the progress of us here on earth, but is actively engaged in our fulfillment of the final joy. The more we can share in the joys of heaven, the more the saints enjoy its fullness. So it is their great joy to assist us and journey with us. The fullness of what they have is not lessened by us sharing it, and their ability to participate in God's heavenly rest is not dampened by watching after us and being our companions.

Though the saints may not be seen as physical companions are, their presence is no less real. Their presence in heaven allows them to be made present spiritually, if nothing else, in every place that we find ourselves. They share a certain timelessness that allows their gifts and personalities to be ever fresh and new. In the true Christian perspective of charity, they can be fully present to us. Many people who knew saints like John Paul II and Mother Teresa said they treated every person with so much care and attention. The saints see the image of Christ in us more clearly from their place in heaven and are more devoted to us because of that vision.

Their companionship gives us the assurance and knowledge that we are not abandoned, but also confirms that we belong to a greater community that hopes for our success and holiness and desires what is truly our greatest happiness. The saints give us a sense of belonging, as if we were part of the kingdom of God even though we are not yet in heaven. Through the saints, we are given a foretaste of the great friendship and community that will be heaven. Also, they offer us a share in the graces and gifts they possessed on earth as well as those they are rewarded with in heaven. The gifts they had on earth have now multiplied and the stewardship they now have is shared with us. Acts 2:42 speaks of how the early Church shared everything in common as they shared the teaching and the great sacraments together. Indeed, the entire Church, both on earth and in heaven shares all her goods in common. The Catechism declares:

> "*They had everything in common*" "Everything the true Christian has is to be regarded as a good possessed in common with everyone else" . . . *Communion in charity.* In the sanctorum communion, "None of us lives to himself, and none of us dies to himself." "If one member suffers, all suffer together; if one member is honored, all rejoice together. Now you are the body of Christ and individually

> members of it." "Charity does not insist on its own way." In this solidarity with all men, living or dead, which is founded on the communion of saints, the least of our acts done in charity redounds to the profit of all (CCC 952–53).

The identity of the Church is a place of oneness in Christ where all share in the gifts of each other since they are all participating in Christ. Therefore, the saints seek to offer us a share in their gifts and good works. This fact is not only because of the communal nature of the Church but also because the gifts that the saints receive are given by the Holy Spirit, and "the Holy Spirit 'distributes special graces among the faithful of every rank' for the building up of the Church. Now 'to each is given the manifestation of the Spirit for the common good.'" (CCC 951). The specific destiny of the charisms of the saints is for the rest of the Church and since God does not take back His gifts but rather calls them to a greater stewardship, those gifts are now offered to the rest of the Church in her need.

> In the communion of saints "a perennial link of charity exists between the faithful who have already reached their heavenly home, those who are expiating their sins in purgatory and those who are still pilgrims on earth. . . ." In this wonderful exchange, the holiness of one profits others, well beyond the harm that the sin of the one could cause the others. Thus recourse to the communion of saints lets the contrite sinner be more promptly and efficaciously purified of the punishments for sin (CCC 1475).

Though the charisma and gifts are possessed by the saint, they are ultimately Christ's and thus belongs to the entire body of Christ. Therefore, because the saints are given this stewardship over them, they have a greater duty to be near us and share their gifts with us. The gifts given to the saints, though given to them as an individual, were given to them as an instrument for the Church. As our companions, they allow those gifts and their intercession and charity to journey with us while we are still on earth. This common sharing is the identity of the Church, the body of Christ's union of the members as one. We are "no longer strangers and sojourners, but you are fellow citizens with the saints and members of the household of God" (Eph 2:19). As fellow citizens, not only do we abide together, but we share goods in common. Francis Spirago, in his commentary on the Catechism highlights this shared treasury of the saints that we have access to:

> In a similar manner all the people of the country have a share in the institutions supported by the country, such as hospitals, asylums, wall courts, etc. So also, in the family circle all the members have a claim to share in the common goods such as riches or honor. . . . there is the same sympathy as in the human body, where a strong member comes to the help of one that is weaker, the possession of good lungs, a sound heart, or healthy stomach may help the body to recover from what might otherwise have been a fatal illness. The eye does not act for itself alone; it guides the hands and feet.[29]

The saints accompany, guide, and assist us. From their place in heaven they are appointed with this stewardship, not for themselves or to lord it over the other members; their place in heaven is as much a responsibility as it is a reward, and the assistance we have is as much ours as theirs. We thus can lean upon them not only for moral support and assurance that we are not alone, but also so that they can make up where we lack and allow us to share in the gifts and talents they had on earth. At the same time, these gifts act as means of intercession to God on our behalf. Spirago further relates:

> The saints must know much of what happens on earth, for their happiness consists in the complete satisfaction of all their desires. The devil knows all our weaknesses, as we know from the way in which he tempts us. The prophets of the Old Testament sometimes fore-told future events, and knew the most hidden things; is it likely that the saints are less fa-vored than they? They rejoice when a sinner is converted (Lk 15:7). "What can escape those," says St. Thomas Aquinas, "who see Him Who sees all things?" [30]

Much of the saints' care comes from their watchfulness over us. They are ever vigilant for our needs and our pains and make them known to God. It is also this watchfulness that gives us great comfort in knowing we are not alone and assurance that our steps are being watched and guided. As the saints know God's great desires, they also know our needs, as well as where we are, and where we need to be. They constantly let us know that we are not alone. In very simple and beautiful ways the saints make their presence known to us. I love to

---

29. Francis Spirago, *The Catechism Explained* (Post Fall, ID Mediatrix Press, 2020), 224.
30. Spirago, *Catechism Explained* 225–26.

hear the stories of little children; their simple, sweet faith allows the saints to make themselves more present. I know several stories of little children who feel saints squeeze their hand or hear the voice of a saint speaking in their head, and others have reported they even see saints. Their childlike faith is very inspiring. In part II you will be invited to read the stories of saints while they were on earth and the various ways they reveal their companionship with us here and now.

It is thus by means of example, intercession, and companionship that we have seen the reason for the saints in the Church. In some way, the saints are the truest identity of the Church as well as her greatest gift. They fulfill man's natural identity; they show forth his great call above nature. Their power of intercession and accompaniment is a great treasure that is handed down by Church to every Christian of every age. There is so much joy and comfort in knowing that the saints are alive and active. They have been with the Church from its beginning and will be with it until the end because they *are* the Church. Now it is time to see how the Church has come to know which people are saints and what the process for becoming a saint is in the Catholic Church.

CHAPTER 3

Oh, How I Want To Be in That Number

The Church is not a democracy in which the majority ends up making the decision. The Church is God's holy people. In the Old Testament, a little nation that was always persecuted ceaselessly renewed the holy covenant by their holiness of its everyday life. In the early Church, Christians were called the 'saints' because their whole lives were imbued with the presence of Christ and with the light of his Gospel. They were in the minority, but they transformed the world. [31]

Louisiana has been blessed to continue to live with a rich Catholic heritage and tradition. Maybe that is because Louisiana has held on to the old world a bit tighter, maybe because its culture is rooted in French-Catholic origins, maybe it is the more rural, natural setting of the state. Regardless, my younger days were filled with culturally Catholic mementos that pointed to the primacy of faith in all aspects of life. When I was a boy, my mom gave me a small prayer cloth from a little girl named Charlene Richard, who lived in South Louisiana and died very young. She was affectionately known as the Cajun Saint because so many people visited the tomb of this little girl who had died of leukemia. Though she was only twelve, she showed a great spirit that resembled St. Thérèse and she offered up her

31. Cardinal Robert Sarah and Nicholas Diat, "The Day is Long Spent" (Ignatius Press, 2019), 30

suffering daily for various intentions. She was buried in the cemetery in the tiny, backroads town of Richard, Louisiana. Very soon, thousands of people began to flock to this little girl's tomb to pray, to seek healing, and to find something that was captured by this twelve-year-old girl. Every year on the anniversary of her death (August 11), hundreds of people would gather at the nearby church for a mass honoring her.

Charlene was named Servant of God at the beginning of 2020, an awesome moment for the community of followers. However, what exactly does it mean to be named a servant of God? Some of us would probably figure it has something to do with becoming a saint. Is it a step to becoming a saint? What is the difference between a servant of God, a blessed, and a saint? Why is there so much distinction if heaven is a place of oneness with God? Certainly, all of these are valid questions. Quite frankly, I had been a priest for five years and had gone back to Rome for further studies before I really learned and understood the process for canonization. I was blessed to finish my two years in Rome by taking a course from the Congregation for the Cause of the Saints and I was able to sit down and study the entire process that someone must undergo to be declared a saint.

We have seen in the past few chapters that the saints in heaven have a very involved role within the Church on earth. In many ways, the understanding and development of the Church on earth has occurred in tandem with the journey of the saints. The saints have built up the Church as the Church has sanctified the saints. The two go hand in hand. The process for someone to become a saint is reflected by, witnessed by, and verified by the Church. God wills that as He raises one member of the body up the whole body be raised up, and thus the goodness He pours out multiplies on earth!

What it Takes To Be a Saint

I was the youngest of all my siblings and when there would be parties or celebrations, I normally just did my own thing, ate my own food and drink. On a few occasions, my siblings offered to give me a taste of some alcohol to see what I thought. They would hand me a red Solo cup filled with ice and a colored drink. Before the drink even reached my mouth, I would smell something like mouth wash or cologne in the cup. The second it hit my mouth I would spit it out; it tasted horrible! I loved eating and drinking sweets, but this tasted bitter and strong. Why would adults drink this stuff? I couldn't understand. As I got older and was introduced to alcohol again, I remembered this experience and figured, "Why bother with it?" I was told that it's a taste you must get used to, an acquired taste. It's hard at first but over time you learn how to sip, not gulp, and how to enjoy the greater experience it brings. My taste as a child had become so accustomed to sweets that the taste of something like alcohol was repulsive at first. Over time, I saw that after getting use to it from incremental exposures, I was able to appreciate it more and discover the greater experience that could be offered from mature balanced drinking.

Several Christian authors have said that heaven is "an acquired taste." Heaven is something we anticipate here on earth; we begin to experience it and live it here and now through prayer, sacraments, works of charity, and other devotional acts. However, like children, we aren't used to it and it takes much virtue and intention to acquire this taste for heaven. When Aristotle wrote about the various causes that give identity to an object, he said that the most important was the final cause, or the end that the object sought. The end or final goal is only last in a chronological sense of execution. However, the end forms the principal and starting point in reference to purpose and intention. Imagine the fisherman:

the fish is the end of all his labors, but from the moment he wakes up, to the efforts to load up his boat, get the tackle together, and endure the waiting at the lake, the fish forms the purpose and driving force of his whole endeavor and gives him an identity. The end has its anchor at the final point, but it exists from the beginning in the intention and pushes all the actions towards that end. Because of this, it informs everything else that the object does. Heaven is the final cause for the saints while on earth: it is ever in their intention during their life, something they slowly learn to become familiar with and to seek. Even though they don't arrive there until they die, they have already become acquainted with heaven on earth and have gained that acquired taste here and now.

The more I see the various exercises of the spiritual life and spiritual direction, the more I recognize them as training. We many times say, "hell is only for those who choose hell." Really, hell is for those who *condition* themselves to choose it. By their life's desires and actions, they become the kind of people who would choose hell, even though if asked directly they would probably say 'no.' Heaven is a similar reality. On the road to heaven, Christians make mistakes and fumbles; they often fail and sin. However, we can always get back up and persevere. What is important is that in getting up, they are motivated by that drive for heaven; they are slowly overcoming the accustomed taste of earth and being trained for the greater benefits that heaven promises. A Christian should not get upset or despair because of a failure here and there; ultimately, the overall line graph of their life ought to have an upward direction while along the line there may still be some peaks and valleys. At the end of our lives, our actions will form a definite shape, either of a saint or not.

Our entire life, with its ups and downs, are in God's hands. He alone sees everything from the big to the little and He alone makes the goal possible. God alone can make someone a saint. He alone is the one who can sanctify a soul, He alone is the final judge of souls, and He alone is the life of heaven that is desired. However, here on earth, the Church has learned the effect that a saint has through their example, intercession, and companionship. These realities are real, tangible, and quantifiable. Those who have already acquired that taste for heaven while on earth are recognizable even during their journey. Once the saints reach their destination, the Church can verify that reality too.

Sainthood requires the full action of God but also the full involvement of man. It is an incredibly simple, yet at the same time, an incredibly challenging task. It demands all of man's life since it is living in the full life of God. Saints' lives are radical, but they are also clear; it is not hard for people to discern a true saint. They can see the radical way they live, which is so different from the ways of this world. Maybe not immediately but the fact of their sainthood comes out in the saint's lives and their effect on others. There is a sense, the *sensus fidei* or 'sense of faith' as the Church calls it, that the entire Church has concerning certain truths of the faith. Though it is God alone who judges and brings someone to heaven, when an individual's sanctity is true and certain, it has a visible and palpable effect on the Church. As we read in 1 Corinthians 12:26: "If one member suffers, all suffer together; if one member is honored, all rejoice together." The Church, the body of Christ, feels the sense of joy and reverence when one of her members is recognized to have been counted among the saints in heaven. The effect of one member can be witnessed by the rest of the body.

The canonization of saints is thus the Church recognizing saints as they build up the Church, both on earth and in heaven. The canonization process has more to do with the growth of the Church on earth and heaven in holiness, merit, and memory than it does with judgment, jurisdiction, and authority. Canonization is not a magic wand the Church waves to create idols; it is an organic practice of the believing community. We will now see how the canonization process is a recognition of the journey the saints continue to take with the believing Church, each benefiting and honoring the other.

The Christian Case of Canonization

Despite the very elegant, elaborate, and even at times grandiose structures and procedures in the Church that we see today, their origins are found in a very organic and human root. The Church appropriately sees the mustard seed as the image of herself: although small and seminal in its beginning, over time and with growth it forms a much larger organism. With the Church, her full grandeur of development was present in the beginning in potency. The same is true with the canonization process. Looking back at the original belief of honoring the saints, we see the core belief that still motivates the Church's activity and forms the fountain for further growth and expansion. The practice of honoring the saints started off simple, yet within that simplicity was contained all the potential we see flourishing today; and it all started with the martyrs. Originally, Caridi describes, it was not a difficult or artificial process to declare someone a saint:

> Acknowledging that a Christian had died a martyr's death initially required little more than some common sense and a right understanding of Christian theology. But rules and regulations gradually developed, for the precise reason that all laws generally do: (a) gray, borderline situations arose that required both clarification and the development of official, consistent definitions of the terminology in use, and (b) perceived

> abuses cropped up that had to be checked. It was theology, not canon law per se, that required church officials to act.[32]

"Spontaneous" is a perfect word to describe the developments in the Church, especially concerning canonization because it signifies a natural immediate response. Spontaneity was thus how the Church on earth responded to situations. Much like a river that forms beautiful curves and banks because it must adjust to avoid obstacles in its path, so too is the Church's development formed from her steering her course through the terrain she encountered.

Suffering and death were the first and longest lasting experiences for the Church to respond to. Jesus had promised again and again that those who believed in him would never see death. Thus, it was a saddening reality when the surviving members saw Christians dying as martyrs, but faith drove them to give a response full of hope. They came to understand death as a doorway to heaven, which was a cause of rejoicing.

The Cult of Martyrs

In chapter 1 we defined what a saint is, and further what a martyr is. This chapter will focus on the historical development of the honor of martyrdom and why that was influential for the Church. For the Christian, being a testimony of Christ was the center of their faith. After Jesus' ascension, the witnesses of His life, death, and resurrection held the greatest testimony for belief in Him. The influence of a witness was as important then as it is today; it is the greatest teaching tool. A witness testified to Christ not

32. . Caridi, *Making Martyrs,* 10.

only with their words, but with their good deeds and their charity—their whole being was transformed into a living testimony. The greatest witnesses were those put to death for their beliefs. Not only was their testimony strengthened by showing the power of their conviction, but their death also immortalized their witness.

> The extreme witness of faith brought about by the outpouring of blood relates directly to the teaching of Christ, which was very much alive in the early Church. In the preaching of the apostles, largely reflected in the Gospel accounts, there are numerous references to the disciples' conformity to their Master even at the moment of persecution and death suffered in his name. The disciples were therefore aware of the sacrifice that was required of them. [33]

Someone who died as a martyr was thus seen as someone who had completely synthesized the teaching of Christ in their life and with their blood. Honoring the martyrs was not a coping mechanism to get believers through hard times, rather it was recognized as the greatest act of service someone could offer Our Lord. On this account, great honor was given to their buried, both to the body itself and its arrangement, and the account of their death.

As with many other cultures and religions, the Christians

---

33 . My translation: "l'estrema testimonianza della fede attuata con l'effusione del sangue si colega direttamente all'insegnamento di Cristo, che era molto vivo nella Chiesa primativa. Sono numerosi nella predicazione degli apostoli, riflessa poi nei racconti evangelici, i riferimenti alla conformita dei discepoli al loro Maestro anche nel momento della persecuzione e della morte subita in suo nome. I discepoli quindi erano consapevoli del sacrificio che veniva loro richiesto." Le Causa dei Santi, 168.

had specific funeral customs for their dead that incorporated aspects of their beliefs. One of the more outstanding at the time was that Christians buried the entire body intact rather than cremated because of their belief in the resurrection of the body. This practice was very different than the usual practice in Rome at the time and ushered in the usage of the catacombs, which were underground tombs in the firm yet absorbent soil outside of Rome.

Not only was the place and method utilized by Christians unique but also the roles of those who participated in the burial. The right to bury a supposed martyr was reserved to viri timorati or "pious men," based on Acts 8:2 of the burial of St. Stephen, the first martyr. Rather than the families, it was these designated men of the community who buried the martyrs because "the martyr began to belong to the community and always assumed more for the entire community the significance of 'testimony' of the death and of the resurrection of Christ."[34] Thus it was important the burial be carried out by holy representatives of the community to honor the testimony the martyr gave and to underline the universal importance for the entire community.

The next major development in honoring the saints came with the death of the bishop Polycarp. The celebration of his death and burial is remembered more than anything he did in this life. Besides offering a beautiful and stirring account of his death, a written record describes the solemn transfer of his body. The actual remains of his body were a treasure for the Church that became a source of strength for believers and encouragement for those undergoing the test.[35] Not only the immaterial witness and memory, but even the physical remains and location became a gift for the community of believers to cherish. There was a closeness to the Savior in

34. Le Causa dei Santi, 168.
35. Caridi, *Making Martyrs*, 17.

the martyrs' bodies since they suffered like Him and were promised to rise with Him.

The reverence given Polycarp also showed that the Church believed that the place where the martyr was buried was sacred. Gathering at the tomb was an opportunity of joy as the community joined each other in celebration and tasted a bit of the happiness the martyr was experiencing in heaven. The celebration was a communal event not just because Polycarp was honored by the community but also because honoring Polycarp developed the community in a special way: it gave the community on earth an identity and a destiny beyond just the endeavors of this life on earth. Such gatherings of faith, hope, and joy began to mark the community of the Church with its identity.

The celebration of the martyrs also gave a rhythm to the Church, not simply a rhythm connecting persecution, suffering, and death to resurrection, but also to the community's own reckoning of time and memory. Marking the anniversary of the day of martyrdom gave the community an opportunity to gather, celebrate, and rejoice. This gathering was no day of sorrow, but a joyful day. The day of their death was called the *dies natalis* or "day of birth" because this anniversary marked the day they were born in heaven. The celebration not only gave encouragement to the militant Church but also reminded them of the martyr's new life that they shared in through the celebration.

> Their tomb was the point of convergence of the cult of their honor, constituted by the celebrated remembrance of the anniversary of the martyr as *Dies natalis*, which memory constituted a celebration for the entire

> community, it was animated by prayers aimed at the communal exhortation and the living encouragement for persevering in the battle of faith.[36]

These feasts were recorded and passed down not just through time but to different communities as well. Not only did the Christians join with their brothers in heaven in celebration but also with all the other Christians throughout the different lands. The record and account of the martyrs' death and the date of their death were recorded and then passed to other communities. Slowly, a calendar of reference was made, formed from various communities observing the martyrs' death, producing concrete records and lists of their own martyrs, and celebrating their witness together as a communal church both on earth and in heaven within the liturgy (which literally means a public service for the people).

This practice produced two important historical and liturgical centerpieces: the *acta* and the *diptycha*. The acta was simply a record of the events that transpired from the arrest of the Christian all the way through their death. It became the written witness that was read and spread to other churches to share the example and give encouragement to those gathered in the liturgy. It became the focal point of the celebration and the anniversary. The diptycha or "tablets" served more of a functionary role but had a long-lasting impact. These were the actual lists of names that were noted, conserved, and passed down to form a rhythm throughout the year. These formed the basis for the first liturgical calendar and later the martyrologies.

---

36. My translation: "il loro sepolcro era il punto di convergenza del culto a loro tributato, costituito dal ricordo celebrativo dell'anniversario del martirio come dies natalis, la cui memoria costituiva una festa per tutta la communità ed era animata dalla preghiera finalizzata all'esortazione comune e al vivo incoraggiamento nel sostenere il combattimento per la fede." Le Causa dei Santi, 170–171.

These tablets also have names of bishops who had died but not necessarily as martyrs, as well as people who were still alive at the time the tablets were written. While this practice may not make sense to us now with our desire to categorize and create clear lines of distinction, it was a practice that underlined the great unity that these Christian communities had during the celebrations on these days: the entire Church was one and was existing as one. Even though Christians recognized distinctions between praying for a person who had not died and commending themselves to the prayers of a martyr, the liturgical celebration united all together as one. "Prayers on behalf of the faithful (both living and dead) and prayers glorifying the martyrs were all included together. . .. the fact that all names were listed together in the diptychs indicated the communion and love that united all the members of the church, triumphant, suffering, and militant."[37] So these tablets, and the general act of celebrating the memories of the martyrs, gave rise to a deeper identity of the Church's unity on earth and in heaven.

None of these practices were the result of an arbitrary design or an authoritarian scheme. Rather, they arose from the Church living as the Church. These practices not only grew spontaneously and organically but, because of that organic reality, they reflected and strengthened the identity of the Church. They were not only created by the Church but were also helping to create and craft the Church herself. The practices that honored the saints helped the Church create and form an identity that was not only vertical with the saint but also horizontal with the other members. Part of the organic reality of this devotion was that each community had their own list of martyrs that they celebrated. However, over time each community began to share some of the more

---

37. Caridi, *Making Martyrs*, 22.

outstanding martyrs and their lists with other communities to form an even greater and more universal list or *canon* of saints that the entire Church recognized. The common memory and communal celebration of these martyrs served as the canonization process at the time, since, as the meaning of canonization indicates, they were listed in a table or calendar of saints to be remembered and celebrated together. Thus, the process of declaring someone a martyr or a saint did not occur in one central location, but rather took place wherever the Church was alive. As a result, some martyrs were venerated and recognized in one location but not yet in another. This spontaneous, organic development lent itself to a very natural sense of the faith, but also left room for certain abuses and disagreements to arise.

The Controversial Case of Canonization

From what we have seen, the original practice of honoring martyrs was simple, yet influential, spiritual, yet with a palpable communal effect. Basically, the saints were being set up as role models with a huge public following. Though the Church saw this effect it is spiritual supernatural light of preparing for heaven, it can't be ignored that sainthood was an attractive reality. Not everyone who wanted someone on a list for admiration did so as a fruit of mature Christian faith.

We saw in Chapter 1 that the presence of false martyrs, or those giving their life for somewhat selfish motives, became an issue the Church had to deal with. The dilemma of the false martyrs, though it was a contentious moment in the Church's past, did help to define why someone should be considered a saint. Thus, many of the liturgical and juridical practices served two roles: spiritual edification as well as historical certitude. This principal is especially true with the writing of the acta, as Caridi relates:

> They [acta] ultimately would be written not simply for the spiritual edification of the faithful, nor in order to preserve a truthful historical account for posterity; rather, the purpose of writing the account would be to convince church authorities that the person in question did indeed deserve to be recognized as a saint. [38]

As the Church began to move out of the persecutions of the third century, Christians began to have more freedom and more openness to express their beliefs. The Church was now tasked with vindicating the beliefs and practices that were based on her faith in the Lord but were being challenged by unorthodox practices. This included the honoring of martyrs, as Causa points out:

> Between the end of the III century and the beginning of the IV century there was a tendency to perform in the church a true vindication of the martyrs, that is, a vindication and a defense of their authenticity. In other words, a sort of ordinary preliminary process was carried out by the competent authority with the aim of approving and then introducing the cult of a martyr who until then had not been recognized or venerated as such. In the previous periods, the condemnation for the faith in Christ and the execution of martyrdom were a public and notorious fact, which did not need to be accepted and demonstrated; for this reason. [39]

---

38. Caridi, *Making Martyrs* 31.

The toleration of Christianity during this period was refreshing and certainly gave a new dimension and enrichment to the faith, but it also meant that the veneration of the martyrs was now taking on a new dimension as well. The Church needed to establish firmly verified and true facts about the events as well as a clearer definition of what made someone a martyr and worthy of veneration in the first place. Each person whose name was inscribed in those tablets, had their feast day remembered, or had the events of their life and death recalled at a liturgical assembly needed to be verified first.

One of the final, great seals of approval for veneration was the transfer of the martyr's body to a more dignified location for veneration. As was said earlier, the tombs themselves became a cause of assembly, but as Christianity began to come out in the open more, the ability to decorate and even form shrines and churches around the tombs marked a physical development in encouraging veneration. The laying of a martyr to rest and the location of their tomb were very sacred and formed a crucial part of the forthcoming veneration to the saint. Hence, the practice of moving a person's body made a huge statement about the person's status and approval for veneration. Only the tombs of fully approved martyrs were allowed to be venerated and the same principal applied later with the moving of their body.

---

39. My translation: "tra la fine del III secolo e l'inizio del IV secolo si tendeva ad operare nella chiesa una vera vindicatio dei martiri cioè una rivendicazione e una difesa della loro autenticità. In altre parole si operava da parte della autorità competente una specie di processo preliminare ordinario allo scopo di approvare e quindi introdurre il culto di una martire fino a quel momento non riconosciuto e non venerato come tale. Nei periodi precedenti, la condanna per la fede in Cristo e l'esecuzione del martirio erano un fatto pubblico e notorio, che non aveva bisogno di essere accetato e dimostrato; per questo." Le Causa dei Santi, 171.

The Confessor's Case for Canonization

Even though a deeper examination of the lives of martyrs was used primarily to distinguish a true martyr from a false, it did bring up the reality that there could indeed be some people who, not dying a martyr's death under the established criteria, could still be honored for living a martyr's life, so to speak. As mentioned earlier, many other people's names were listed on the tablets in addition to martyrs, some living and some dead. Many good people were honored and prayed for on the list, but it wasn't until this process of examination started that the early Church began to consider them to be of a similar status as the martyrs. One of the first manifestations of this practice arose because of the holy bishop Martin of Tours, France who died around the year 380. Though Martin did not die as a martyr, he led a life filled with virtue and was an example that inspired the Church as she was seeing her faith and holiness lived out openly. Martin was the first of what the Church called the cult of confessors. What raised him up was not so much his difference but similarity to the martyrs:

> The decisive and fundamental factor that induces the veneration of confessors is very similar to that found for the martyrs: it is based on the testimony of their extraordinary life, both at the pastoral level for bishops and at the ascetic level for monks, a life that is normally known and esteemed by their contemporaries. [40]

40. My translation: "il motivo determinante e fondamentale che induce alla venerazione dei confessori è molto simile a quello riscontrato per i martiri: esso è basato sulla testimonianza della loro vita straordinaria, sia a livello pastorale per i vescovi, sia a livello ascetico per i monaci, una vita che normalmente è conosciuta e stimata dai contemporanei." Le Causa dei Santi, 177.

Martyrs and confessors differ in the means of their death, but they are united in the same extraordinary holiness through their charity, their faith, and their witness to Jesus. Though the cofessors lived the same lives as others, they lived with such heroic virtue that their lives and those they impacted were transformed. The confessors also thus began to receive the same veneration, including annual commemorations, as the martyrs.

The cult of the confessors soon had a great effect on the Church, especially affecting the way in which saints were viewed. Though given the same honor and attention as the martyrs, the confessors were honored for different reasons. We have already said that their merit and honor was based on their life rather than their death, but the evaluation, discernment, and even the proposal of their possible sainthood were all fruits of the new development and growth in the Church. For the martyrs, their canonization was simple and straightforward: did they die in witness to the faith at the hands of an unjust aggressor? This criterion was not only easy to evaluate, but the final judges were clear. The Congregation for the Cause of Saints relates:

> While for martyrs it was sufficient that their names were written in the diptychs or in the local calendars so that they may be considered saints and thus to be remembered annually on their dies natalis with the liturgical celebration, for confessors the situation was more difficult and more complex: for them it was not enough to present one single act, that is, their martyrdom, officially recognized, but there had to be considered and examined their entire life and above all to judge if it should be truly worthy of being proposed to the admiration and the example of present

> and past with the veneration of their tribute by means of the liturgical cult. [41]

It is easy to say that a martyr was made a saint by his death and a confessor by his life, but that is missing a crucial development in the Church. The very body of believers who had already been inspired by the confessor's life were promoting them! While questions had been arising about which criteria a bishop or the clergy should use to examine and judge whether they should put an individual on the list—since it was the clergy who had done the inscribing and celebrating of the martyrs—the process was now reversed; the people were promoting, and the clergy were following after. This shift is indicated beautifully by the Congregation:

> It was originally the *vox populi* [the voice of the people] that pushed for the veneration of a confessor from the influence of their own sentiment, enthusiasm, and of the admiration of their virtues and from the miracles attributed to them without a previous examination or control. In other words, the *life* of the confessor, as it was known and judged by the people, constituted the foundation and the root of the canonization; the veneration that a confessor received during life continued

---

41. My translation: "Mentre per I martiri era sufficiente l'iscrizione del loro nome nei dittici o nel calandario locale perché fossero considerati santi e quindi essere ricordati annualmente nel loro *dies natalis* con la celebrazione liturgica, per I confessori la situazione era piú difficile e piú complessa: per essi non si doveva tener presente un solo atto cioè il martirio, ufficialmente riconosciuto, ma doveva essere considerata ed esaminata tutta la vita e sopratutto giudicare se essa fosse veramente degna di essere proposta all'ammirazione e all'esempio dei presenti e dei posteri con la venerazione loro tributata tramite il culto liturgico." Le Causa dei Santi, 179.

after death and thus signified and constituted
a true canonization. [42]

Here we see the true communion of saints coming into greater focus: the confessors, while alive, inspiring their brothers and, after death, leading their brothers and sisters on earth to greater holiness, raising them up to God, and desiring to have them as fellow companions. The believers on earth were no long simply admirers of the saints but were now, through their own lives and holiness, being personally touched and led by the saints. It was thus the people whose lives were being changed who were lifting their companions up. This phenomenon began to form the heart of the belief and practice of the communion of saints: a belief that was performative in the life of the Church and practiced through the lives of believers. The Church triumphant in heaven and the Church militant on earth kept an intimate tie despite the separation through death.

It was not only the common aspect of the confessor's life that was raised up, but primarily the more extraordinary, the parts that drew the most fame and attention, even if it was only a normal task done just with extraordinary devotion. Various authors collected and wrote about the events of the confessors lives to serve as a fount of knowledge. Miracles and extraordinary works during their lives were enumerated and highlighted; these became not only the most unique events but one of the most crucial to examine for their canonization. As with the martyrs, the confessors' bodies

---

42. My translation: "Era originariamente la *vox populi* che spingeva alla venerazione di un confessore sotto la spinta del proprio sentimento, dell' entusiasmo e dell' ammirazione per le sue virtú e per I miracoli a lui ascritti, senza un previo esame o controllo. In altre parole, la vita del confessore, cosí come era conosciuta e giudicata dal popolo, costituiva il fondamento e la radice della canonizzazione; la venerazione che un confessore riscuoteva durante la vita continuava anche dopo la morte, e ciò significava e costituiva di fatto una vera canonizzazione." Le Causa dei Santi, 179.

were taken as a beautiful treasure and found a worthy place of veneration and soon became a location of pilgrimage and intercession. Because of this increase in intercession, miracles after their death began to take place. Though miracles did not originally mark a needed step to secure canonization,[43] they gave assurance and proof of their life in heaven.

Thus, we now see a great power in the living voice and faith of the Church in the canonization process. The saints are from the body of Christ and for the body of Christ. The growing spirit behind the developments in the canonization process shows again and again the organic spirit of devotion that has sprung up in the Church throughout her various seasons.

The Centralized Case of Canonization

The Church was experiencing a true expansion of the faith in the third century. The faith was spreading in various forms of life, prayer, ministry, and work; the faith was developing the understanding of the Church and of the human person. The Church took a long and winding journey over the next few centuries to arrive at the canonization process that we know today. From invading barbarians to plagues and new religious orders, the Church was responding to a lot of developments in her life! The saints, being a crucial pillar of the Church, were also carried through and developed in response to these changes. It would take another book to detail the entire history of the Church and the evolution of canonization. For brevity's sake, I will only highlight a few of the more salient events throughout the Church's history.

At the beginning, the canonization of saints was still

43. In some of the Orthodox Churches in the East, primarily the Russian Orthodox, miracles through the intercession of a saint were always considered part of the canonization. See Caridi.

primarily in the hands of the local churches and bishops but was starting to swing more into the hands of the pope. One of the most important (and somewhat humorous) moments in the process of this transfer took place around the year 1170. Pope Alexander III (the first pope to use the verb "to canonize") got wind that the people of Sweden were venerating as a martyr a man who had gone out with friends for libations, became drunk, and then was beaten to death by his own drunk companions! He was being hailed as a martyr and there were even reports of miracles taking place through his intercession. Clearly, there was cause for concern with raising up this man as a saint. So, the Pope had to act fast and forcefully. In a formal decree, which later became the bedrock for future Church law, the Pope told them, "Even if many miracles take place through his intercession, it is not licit to publicly venerate someone without the authorization of the Roman Church."[44] Just goes to show, getting drunk really does cause memory loss. This decree laid out that calling someone a saint was a very serious matter that had bearings on the rest of the Church. In this regard, it was necessary that the Pope himself be aware and give approval before someone is canonized and that not just miracles, but quality of life was necessary to guarantee a person's status as a saint.

Later, in 1198, as Pope Innocent III was preparing to canonize a layman who was not a martyr, he sought to establish great certainty of the man's holiness. "Innocent III made a statement about the elements needed for canonizations in general: 'Two things are required, so that somebody may be considered a saint in the Church Militant, namely works of piety during his life and miracles after death.'"[45]

45. Caridi, *Making Martyrs,* 123.

44. My translation: "Cum etiamsi signa et miracula per eum plurima fieret, non liceret vobis pro sancto absque auctoritate Romanae Ecclesiae eum publice venerari." Le Causa dei Santi, 199.

While still upholding the primacy of Church authority, Pope Innocent saw that the sign of merits and miracles was the only true guarantee in the fullest sense that a person was truly and full a servant of God and now shares in God's reward. While the research into miracles was still young and developing, this moment did show an interesting new development in the canonization process. Innocent even went so far as to require that "Catholic officials investigating a potential saint at the local level [are] to submit two, three, or four miracles, indicating that the lesser number would suffice if they were more obvious." [46]

In 1234, with the help of St. Raymond of Peñafort, Pope Gregory IX promulgated the Church's first centralized list of laws and decrees. Among them was a law that the only valid form of canonization was celebrated by the Holy Father. Soon after, Gregory famously canonized one of the most wellknown and important saints in the Church: St. Francis of Assisi. His canonization was important not only because the entire process, from the beginning examination and investigations to the final ceremony, was completely intact but also because the Pope himself celebrated the entire ceremony. The Pope made the proclamation, "We have decreed that blessed Francis, whom the Lord glorified in heaven and we are in debt to honor here below, with the council of our brothers and other prelates of the Church, should be inserted into the catalog of the saints and the festive day of his death should be celebrated"![47] With some adaptation, this declaration is the same used even to this day in the mass of canonization.

---

46. Caridi, 125.

47. My translation: "abbiamo decretato che il beatissimo padre Francesco, che il Signore glorificò in cielo e noi veneriamo con debito ossequio sulla terra, con il consiglio dei nostri fratelli e degli altri prelati della Chiesa, sia inserito nel catalogo dei santi e sia celebrato il giorno festivo della sua morte." Le Causa dei Santi, 203.

1588 saw some major developments that centralized and formalized canonization. Pope Sixtus V made some major headway by moving to Rome all the various ministries and functions that the Church was linked to and giving them stable, permanent offices to survive the changing of persons and times that would come. He made about fifteen Congregations, among which was the "Congregation for the Sacred Rites" (that later would split and one half would form "The Congregation for the Cause of the Canonization of the Saints") that organized and handled everything from liturgies and sacraments, to canonizations and ceremonies. Because the final step of canonizing a saint is that they are remembered and honored in the Church's universal prayer, the congregation in charge of sacraments and liturgy was tasked with helping in the evaluation and discernment process, although the ultimate decision remained the Pope's. This Congregation accompanied the saint through the various phases and gave their final assessment to the Pope. The congregation also instituted some guidelines for the canonization process. For example, concerning miracles, when a person's martyrdom was absolute and without a doubt, no miracle was needed, but for more dubious cases, miracles acted as confirmation. Though later legislation made more hard and fast rules, miracles were still a bit of a negotiable area.

The institution of this congregation was the final keystone in centralizing the canonization process in Rome under the power of the Pope. However, it does not mean that the development of the process is at an end, or even what we see today.

The Current Case of Canonization

The Canonization process as we see it today has developed over a long series of processes, controversies, and miracles.

At the heart of it, though, is still the desire to encourage and empower the Church on earth through fellowship with the saints in heaven.

The canonization process is composed of two main steps: an initial local process and then a final, more universal stage in Rome. At all times, there is a constant dialogue between Rome and the local area where the person died. [48] The local process is a beautiful manifestation of the Church's duty to judge her members. The Church does not rule only in disciplinary measures, but bishops are also judges over their own flock as to the merit of their lives and whether others can follow them as examples. Even the local, particular Church of the bishop and his diocese possess the full power to teach, sanctify, and govern her flock and to guide the course of their entire lives, from birth on earth with baptism until birth in heaven with death, the Church guides conversion from sin to reparation and conversion from disciple to saint.

Fama Sanctitatis

Among the first things examined, as well as the most central to the canonization process, is the presence of a *fama sanctitatis* or a "fame or reputation of sanctity." This term refers to the presence of a true, organic, and communal recognition of a person's holiness. This fame at times can manifest while the person is still alive, but it certainly skyrockets after they have died. Such fame exists because holiness is not only easy to recognize, but it is also contagious and attractive. The very life of a saint becomes a light and testimony for others. Others are inspired to be saints and are drawn closer to the saint. This element is of central importance in the canonization of a saint, because it determines what effect the saint is having

48. *"Mater Sanctorum"* Instruction for conducting Diocesan or Eparchial Inquiries in the Causes of the Saints, (Vatican: 2007). Art. 21.

on the faithful, as we read from Vatican II's declaration on the Church as the light of all nations, *Lumen Gentium:*

> When we look at the lives of those who have faithfully followed Christ, we are inspired with a new reason for seeking the City that is to come and at the same time we are shown a most safe path by which among the vicissitudes of this world, in keeping with the state in life and condition proper to each of us, we will be able to arrive at perfect union with Christ, that is, perfect holiness. In the lives of those who, sharing in our humanity, are however more perfectly transformed into the image of Christ, God vividly manifests His presence and His face to men. He speaks to us in them, and gives us a sign of His Kingdom, to which we are strongly drawn, having so great a cloud of witnesses over us and such a witness to the truth of the Gospel.[49]

The truest reality of this fame of holiness is thus not just the holiness of the saint that is witnessed by the people, but how it impacts others. People who are drawn to venerate a person that has died and to admire their holiness are ultimately drawn by the authentic and deep thirst they themselves have for God. His Face is manifested through them. The saint's holiness is not manifested as a vision or a teaching but above all as a palpable reality. People know someone's holiness because of an experience they have with the person, either before or after their death.

---

49. *Lumen Gentium* Dogmatic Constitution on the Church, (Vatican:1964) 50.

The real effectiveness of this fame, which is different from the fame experienced by the memory of something past and gone, comes from the saints' continued, living witness to the believers in the Church. As companions in the Church, they pray for and assist those who, inspired by their lives or encouraged by their faithfulness in adversity, seek solace and help in their own lives. The realities of the saints' presence in heaven, and thus their confirmation as a saint, comes from their assistance to those who draw near to their life and example. Hence, it is important to consider whether this fruit is present when considering someone for canonization. Jesus reminds us that we know a tree by its fruits and that we glorify God in bearing fruit. The presence of this fame is not only that which begins the cause but is the entire reason for canonization: that people are led through veneration to grow in holiness. The fame is a reputation of holiness that also engenders holiness in others.

Thus, before any steps can be taken, it must be found that "among a significant portion of the people of God, the Servant of God enjoys an authentic and widespread reputation of holiness or of martyrdom as well as an authentic and widespread reputation of intercessory power."[50] As already mentioned, this devotion, to prove that it is inspired by true holiness, "must be spontaneous and not artificially produced. It must be stable, continuous, widespread among trustworthy people, and existing among a significant portion of the People of God."[51] As from the beginning of the Church, it is always something organic, something that is truly ecclesial and permanent. Since the saints assist the Church's mission, if the effect of the saint is not known or experienced palpably by the Church, the Servant of God's

50. Mater Sanctorum, art. 7.
51. Mater Sanctorum, §2.

sanctity would be hard to verify. For example, if a certain monk were alleged to be a saint, having had visions and such, but his own local community or superior does not seem to recognize it, the claim would not stand. Or, if a lay person in a small town is proposed as a saint, but the local pastor has no clue who she is, then it would seem to be a farfetched cry. Normally, among the first witnesses looked at, are those who lived with, worked with, and were in direct contact with this person, including family. If these people cannot testify, then it is very doubtful that other supporting claims could be found further out.

Again, the heart of canonization is the recognition that someone, for the good of the Church, is a saint. If the natural effect of someone being in heaven—i.e., a palpable effect on the community of growing in holiness and an already established honor for their holiness—is lacking then the title of a canonized saint should not be granted them. This reputation of holiness becomes the golden thread throughout the entire process and is finally extended to the entire Church at the canonization of the Servant of God.

Recent or Ancient; Martyr, Confessor, or Oblation

It is important for the petitioning diocese to establish if the person being considered for canonization died within a recent period, and thus eyewitnesses still exist; or if they died at an earlier period, and thus all examinations will be conducted on writings and historical information.

Next, they must know if they are dealing with a case of martyrdom or heroic virtue (confessor). If it is a martyr, the process is a bit easier since they simply must look for the necessary conditions of martyrdom. When dealing with a confessor, who is examined for a life of heroic virtue, it is necessary to examine the entirety of their life, their writings, and their death to see if they lived and exemplified the cardinal and theological virtues to a heroic level and how they progressed and grew in virtue and faith throughout their entire lives. This procedure will entail a great many more witnesses and a more in-depth examination of their inner intentions and faith amid the various challenges throughout their life, namely whether they responded in an expedient, quick, and loving way, especially in the acceptance and carrying of suffering, in love for the poor, and in devotion to Our Lord. In dealing with someone considered a martyr, the primary focus will be on the criteria of their death—whether they suffered a violent death, voluntarily accepted death for love of the faith, and were intentionally killed out of hatred for the faith or a practice of virtue connected with the faith. The servant of God considered for martyrdom needs to witness not only to faith but also to charity, not just in the reason for their death but in how they showed love for their persecutors, forgiving them, and even wanting to avoid death so that their killers would not be guilty of sin! It is not as essential that the entire life of a martyr be examined, but it must be seen that they did not lose the faith or die in any grave sin; rather, the act of martyrdom was the crowning act of their life.

On July 11, 2017, Pope Francis in *Maiorem hac dilectionem* opened up another procedural path to canonization for those who, "following more than closely the footsteps and teachings of the Lord Jesus, have voluntarily and freely offered their life for others and persevered with this determination unto death."[52] It is a path for those who, not being killed by a violent death from a persecutor out of hatred for the faith, followed a path of charity and love for others to the point of death. It is a true manifestation of love of neighbor and of God that calls for virtue and a voluntary offering of one's life. For this path to be considered it must be shown that the

52. Pope Francis, *Maiorem hac dilectionem* Motu Proprio (Vatican: July 11, 2017).

person's life and death presented "a free and voluntary offer of life and heroic acceptance *propter caritatem* of a certain and untimely death; a nexus between the offer of life and premature death; the exercise, at least as ordinarily possible, of Christian virtues before the offer of life and, then, unto death."[53] Basically, they either offer a gift of self out of pure charity for another or a good cause that results in untimely death, or they habitually give of themselves so generously that it even leads to their death. An example is St. Damien who went to the island of Molokai, ministered to the lepers there, and eventually contracted leprosy and died. His death was thus a direct effect of the charitable work he was doing.

On the occasion that a group of people is being considered for sainthood, the circumstances of the examination are important because if they all died at the same time as martyrs, then they are considered as one communal sign of martyrdom; thus, they only need one major petition and are examined as a group. However, if they are not martyrs then every person being considered must be petitioned and examined distinctly, even if they are being examined at the same time.

Once all the preliminary information is gathered, the diocese simply asks Rome for permission to begin the examination process and the person formally becomes a Servant of God.

Process of Examination

At this point, the cause reaches the stage of full, open dialogue concerning the Servant of God. The door is wide open for people to bring forth all evidence, testimonies, correspondence, or concerns to the bishop. At this time, intercession to the Servant of God is encouraged and

---

53. *Maiorem hac dilectionem,* Art. 2.

miracles begin to be examined and publicized. The bishop assigns various offices and people to push forward with uncovering proof and testimony; to promote the cause and raise awareness; to ensure objectively that everything coming forward is just and unbiased; to conduct a theological study of the cause itself and the real proof of virtue, martyrdom, or oblation; and to study the historical dimension and circumstances. Various notaries are employed to offer certification to the documents. In addition, a medical witness who can offer testimony and proof to miracles of healing is needed as well as a specific committee dedicated to studying all writing and correspondence of the Servant of God for any theological errors or doubts or lapses in faith. The certification and documentation are central to the canonization because it gives verified proof of holiness that stands the test of man and proves in all spheres of nature that the saint is worthy of reverence.

Miracles

Miracles are an essential step later in the process of examination, but I wanted to speak on the general understanding of miracles now since often they are a manifestation of the fame of holiness. Additionally, they get most of the local Church involved with the Servant of God.

First of all, we must remember that God plays the central role in every miracle: God is the ultimate author of all miracles, and His glory is the final end of all miracles. God does, however, use instruments in His great works. Jesus Himself promised that those who follow Him will do greater works than He did (Jn 14) and thus miracles through a Servant of God's intercession can not only attest to the reality of their being a true follower of Jesus but can also act as a sort of divine seal on the judgment rendered by those looking at their life. Miracles, of course, also empower those who receive them to do what they normally can't and inspire us to turn to God in greater faith.

Miracles during a person's life can attest to the level of holiness they possessed on earth, but miracles after death are a deeper confirmation of their place in heaven. There can be various signs that happen after the death of someone who is considered holy: conversions can take place, people can be moved to holiness, a certain sense of peace can dwell around their tomb, etc. All of these are important witnesses to a fame of holiness, but these are not the specific kinds of miracles that are looked for in the cause of canonization. Firstly, the examiners look for miracles that are a direct answer to a specific request asked of the Servant of God and given in proportion to what was asked. For all miracles to be officially considered, they must be direct, intentional, rapid, complete, permanent, and unexplainable. *1) Direct:* a direct connection must be drawn between the intercession of a Servant of God and the granting of the miracle. If someone was doing a "shotgun" method and asking intercession from many saints, then it is hard to claim that the cause was this Servant of God. *2) Intentional:* a person must have clearly invoked a Servant of God for the specific miracle that took place. *3) Rapid:* there must be a relatively quick connection between the time of intercession and the resulting miracle. While the change doesn't have to be immediate, it must clearly rule out natural or progressive change over time. *4) Complete:* it must be a fully answered prayer, and the miracle must be in proportion to or greater than what was asked. *5) Permanent:* the effect brought about by the miracle cannot revert to the condition that existed before the intercession was sought. This condition applies primarily to medical healings and conversions. *6) Unexplainable:* it must be clear from every natural angle that this miracle took place outside of the natural realm. A miracle, to be clear, is not something that goes against the natural order but is above it. It is out of the realm of possibility as determined by nature. Miracles are not just healings, but anything that goes beyond what physics or the physical order dictate. For example, one miracle occurred in 1988 when a submarine began to sink off the coast of Perú. The commander sought the intercession of Venerable Maria of Jesus Crucified and with extreme ease was able to open the hatch and save the crew. At the depth they were at (roughly 15 meters or 50 feet down), the pressure of the water would have been comparable to about 4 tons![54] However, the commander and those on the submarine not only attest to his ability to open the hatch (which was beyond any man) but also say that it was done with ease.

During the process, a separate community is tasked with examining the veracity of the miracles, especially if the miracles deal with medical healing. The reports of the miracles should be directed to the postulator, who collects all documented information and then sends them off to be examined by either medical commission or theological investigators.

Proofs

For any cause, whether martyr, confessor, or oblation, the process will be determined by the ability to gather and present verified proofs, both for the Servant of God's holiness and that their life and death matched the type of cause being promoted. Everything will need to be documented or documentable. Of first importance are direct writings, both public and private, of the Servant of God. Writings given for public use will be verified based on the amount of orthodoxy, courage, and clarity in speaking on the faith and teachings of the Church. However, even in private writing a certain authenticity, in which their faith and morals remain and are

54. Le Causa dei Santi, 117.

not compromised at any point, must be apparent. An in-depth study of the writings by experts who are knowledgeable of theology and history is needed to give a clear image of the Servant of God. Their opinions will be recorded and submitted as well.

Eyewitnesses will always offer a key testimony. To better interpret their testimony considering the other proofs and the general flow of the cause, it is important that there be certain individuals to listen to and guide the flow of their story so they can give credible and accurate accounts that build a strong foundation for the case. Generally, these are gathered after the writings and historical documents are compiled, but if there is a danger that these crucial sources may be lost, the eyewitnesses can be heard first.[55] If the case is recent—that is, people are currently still alive who were contemporaries of the Servant of God—there must be an eyewitness who can testify about the martyrdom or virtue of their life; this includes family members.[56]

A medical expert who can give a testimony about any healings must also be examined at this stage. Mostly, they are examined at this point so that, later in Rome, this miracle will have more weight and its veracity will be more certain. It should be noted that the medical expert or physician is not giving testimony about the Servant of God, but about the miracle in a very objective way. If the person who was healed is still alive, they are examined again by another team that the diocese has established to see that the permanence of the miracle is in place.

Finally, an investigation and declaration should be made that there is no unlawful or unorthodox practice of the faith taking place in regard to this Servant of God.[57] Examples

55. Sanctorum Mater, Art 82–83.
56. Sanctorum Mater, Art 98.
57. Sanctorum Mater, Art 117–119.

of this malpractice may be masses offered with their names mentioned in the Eucharistic prayer, superstitious practices taking place, any malpractice using the Servant of God for secular purposes or gains, or any other gatherings that either are contrary to the Catholic faith or have not been approved by the Church and give the impression that the Servant of God is a saint already. None of these instances are the same as the fame of holiness that we mentioned must be present. The fame of holiness always leads people into greater personal holiness and docility toward the Church; it is simply the organic manifestation of holiness that takes place when it is truly present in a person. The "absence of cult," as it is called, is more to prevent the faithful, as we have seen in the history of the Church, from engaging in any excessive, hasty, or inappropriate celebrations and gatherings concerning the Servant of God.

Relics

Although relics are not venerated yet, at this point that the bishop must verify the relics of the Servant of God. Relics have always been a very contentious reality in the Church, and so when someone is a Servant of God, on the road to being named a saint, their body must be carefully examined, and all parts of their body accounted for in an appropriate manner.

The basic devotion of relics has its roots in the truth of the resurrection. The final resurrection, which we call the resurrection of the body, will take place at the end of time, before the final judgment. Every person's body will be resurrected and glorified, those who have already died and have had their particular judgment as well as the living. All will receive their original body in a glorified state. God created the human person to be a soul and body unity, and our greatest perfection will be in the end when the soul and the body are together. Our soul is made and destined for this body. It will be the body we have for all eternity. The saints, those who we believe have already been personally judged and see God already in their souls, wait to see Him perfectly with their body at the final resurrection. We believe that the body they had on earth will be resurrected, glorified, reunited with their soul, and then privileged to see God for all eternity. Hence, their bodies even now are a small promise of what is to come, and honor given to their bodies is a foreshadowing of the great honor that will take place in their bodies at the end of time. Therefore, it behooves the bishop to assess and know the situation of the Servant of God's body. [58]

Further, the faithful feel a deep connection with the saints through their relics. It is literally part of the saint and can be evidence that holiness is indeed tangible and something that abides in our world. Scripture tells several times of the shadow of St. Peter falling on people and healing them or the cloak of Christ touching someone and bringing healing. Relics can be an amazing benefit for people and, in certain instances, the cause of a miracle (e.g., someone touches a saint's tomb or a relic is touched to them and they are healed). Since relics will play a bigger part later when the Servant of God is a blessed, it is up to the bishop to examine and ensure that all relics truly belong to the Servant of God and to record and list where these relics are preserved and venerated.[59] This information will be documented, certified, and stored.

Off to Rome!

Eventually, the Servant of God's case is sent to Rome for

---

58. Note: some saints experienced a certain gift of being incorrupt or having a fragrance around their body. As amazing as these signs are, they are not necessary for moving forward with canonization.
59. Sanctorum Mater, Appendix Art. 2–5.

the Congregation of the Cause of the Saints to examine. The Congregation makes what is known as a positio, a large file that keeps all the documents and the current position of the servant of God together. It's like a case file for the Servant of God that is constantly updated with new information and can also easily testify to the Servant of God's merits. The Congregation uses this positio make an objective and unbiased evaluation.

After an extensive examination of the Servant of God by the Congregation and the careful crafting of the positio, the Congregation presents to the Holy Father a decree authentically declaring that the Servant of God's virtue is heroic or his martyrdom bene esse probato, "has been well proven." [60] It is interesting to note that the Church does not say "perfectly," to prevent any form of unrealistic or exaggerated view of sainthood. It simply says, "well proven," that in a sufficient and clear way, they have seen the reflection of Christ in this person. After viewing this decree, the Holy Father, recognizing this Servant of God's merit, can now give him or her the title of Venerable.

The Blesseds

In 2010, when I had first arrived in Rome for my major seminary training, I was privileged to attend a beatification within 3 months of my arrival. It was the beatification of a young Italian girl named Chiara 'Luce' Badano. It was beautiful, it was exciting, it was . . . in a field. Also, the Pope was not the celebrant. It seemed like a big deal, but at the end of the day, although I was in my first year of theology and halfway done with seminary, I could not tell you about the importance of beatification or what it really meant to be beatified.

---

60. *Codex Iuris Canonici* Pius X, Benedict XV, 1917, Citta Vaticano. Can. 2115 § 1.

Many Catholics generally understand that being named blessed (being beatified), is one step before you are canonized a saint. However, many are unsure what that means for the person being named blessed. For some, including my young, naive self, it means that they are right at the door of heaven but have not yet entered. For others, a blessed could mean that they are partly a saint, but they still don't have everything they need.

Theologically, there is nothing different between a saint and a blessed. The term blessed is interchangeable with the term saint in the Scriptures and much of the Church's tradition. The final status of a person's soul is known only to God, who alone can bring a person to the beatitude of heaven. The way in which the Church has related with saints and blesseds has been mostly the same. Both categories describe someone who enjoys the life of heaven and either led a life worthy of admiration or were martyred. Thus, both saints and blesseds are seen as great supports and companions to the Church on earth. The difference stems from the scope of influence given to the public veneration and devotion of that holy person.

Hence, a blessed is the same as a saint in the view of theology and ontology or 'what' they are: someone in heaven. To become a blessed is thus the same status theologically as a saint. The way someone becomes a blessed in the Church's eyes is through recognition of the Church of their path to sainthood as the Congregation relates:

> From the point of view of ecclesiology, it [beatification] is a fruit of a solemn and definitive declaration from the Pope and therefore engages pontifical magisterium; from the juridical point of view, it receives the canonical approval of one miracle; from

> the liturgical point of view, others are given the right of a prescriptive cult in the universal Church. [61]

So, a blessed has been recognized as the instrumental cause of at least one miracle, has been solemnly declared by the Holy Father, and has been given formal liturgical recognition and devotion within a specified and limited sphere of the universal Church. Their lives and memories can still be shared and admired by the universal Church: the only limit is placed on the official acts of the Church in the liturgy offered to the blessed. This prescription should not be seen in a negative light, as if they are not good enough to be on the same level as a saint. It should rather show that all saints, members of the Universal Church, are also members of a particular Church, their diocese, a religious order, etc. The Universal Church is also formed by and present in the particular Church. The full life of the Church is expressed completely in each diocese. Hence, granting to a smaller sphere of the Universal Church the ability to honor this Servant of God, is for the growth in faith, holiness, devotion, and miracles on the local level. It shows the vitality of the entire Church in its individual and specific members, as well as the entire body; it underlines the unique charisms with which God has adorned the members of the body for the building up of the Church. It also helps to gather the individual cells of the body around the central lifegiving force of the Eucharist at Mass. Thus, the blesseds already offer support to the Church by calling the individual cells, which together built up the whole body, to greater unity and strength.

---

61. My translation: "dal punto de vista ecclesiologico, è frutto di una dichiarazione solenne e definitiva da parte del Papa e quindi impegna il magistero pontificio; dal punto di vista giuridico, riceve l'approvazione canonica di un miracolo; dal punto di vista liturgico, gli viene concesso il diritto di un culto precettivo nella Chiesa universale." Le Causa dei Santi, 146.

Hence, we see that beatification is a permission given to the smaller segment of the Church that is custodian of the cause declared by the Pope and prompted by an officially recognized miracle.

As explained earlier, the miracle must be verified, using the categories mentioned above. On top of that, it must be examined by certified experts and given their unbiased opinions. The collection of these miracles normally takes place through the postulator or the office set up by them for collecting these answered prayers. However, at this stage they may also be sent directly to the Congregation. When a miracle comes in, it is voted on first by the experts and then the Congregation if this miracle seems to fit and is worthy to move forward the process of beatification. The Congregation then presents the miracle and request to the Holy Father. The request to investigate beatification and the investigation of the miracle should come through the postulator, whether directly or indirectly, and should be connected to the Ordinary of the diocese in which the Servant of God died or which has his remains. In so doing, this also designates where the cult is strongest and where the permission for veneration should be sent. Many times, it is a religious order that is seeking approval for one of its members and so the beatification grants permission to all members in the order, wherever they are in the world, to offer the full memorial and devotion to this Blessed on their feast day. The feast day is normally the same day in which the person died, unless there is another day which seems more appropriate or it falls on the same day as a major feast (Christmas, Annunciation, Sts. Peter and Paul, etc.). For the area or community granted permission, the blessed may be honored with a mass using proper prayers and even mention of their name in the Eucharistic prayer (Eucharistic Prayer III) and the Liturgy of the Hours.

The crowning moment is the beatification ceremony itself. It is a moment of unique importance not only for the

Servant of God but for the community receiving permission to venerate them. Traditionally, the Pope himself celebrated the rite of beatification. However, Pope Benedict XVI chose several times not to preside over the beatifications but to delegate. Either way, it is a beautiful and powerful ceremony. Often, the ceremony takes place in the diocese that is being given permission for the cult, which is the diocese that began and moved forward with the cause. This practice again gives a moment of rejoicing and union to the particular Church. It is also meant to keep them united with the Universal Church through the presence of the presider, either the Holy Father or the President of the Congregation for Saints or another delegate. The ceremony consists in the presentation of relics, the official granting of the feast day, and the solemn proclamation that the Servant of God is within the book of the blessed.

The Road to Canonization

In May of 2014, just one month before I was ordained a priest, I was able to be a deacon at the canonization of St. John Paul II and St. John XXIII. Two years later, in September of 2016, I returned to Rome to attend the canonization of Mother Teresa of Calcutta. These two ceremonies were two of the most magnificent celebrations and gatherings of people in the last decade, firstly because of the sheer number of people present at these celebrations, close to a million people at each one! Traveling from various countries, cultures, and backgrounds, they descended upon the city of Rome, hoping to get as close to St. Peter's Basilica as possible. They came for various reasons: some because the saint being canonized was from their homeland and they wanted to celebrate and honor the achievement of one of their own, others were touched by the saint at some point in their lives and wished to give thanks, others were just drawn and attracted by the power of their lives and examples. Mankind feels like it's a part of something greater than almost anything man has achieved before. Truly, there is no greater title someone can receive than "saint." Being a true citizen of heaven is the greatest joy anyone can have. Also, being canonized by the Catholic Church means that their life is held up to all men of all times as an example.

It is a very powerful and moving experience to be present at a canonization: knowing and even sensing that one of your brothers or sisters in humanity has reached this exalted point. They have gone to the highest level that a human can reach. To put it in simple terms, they have become a hero. I remember right after the ceremony of St. John Paul II's canonization, as the mass was ending, I was told as a deacon to go back into St. Peter's, divest, and leave before the mass ended. However, I looked across St. Peter's and saw the altar of John Paul II with the newly engraved title "Sanctus," ablaze with candles. I could not miss out on this opportunity; I ran to the altar and knelt before this newly named saint. I knew that in a few minutes thousands of people would line up to pray here. Masses would be held here almost back-to-back for years. I hardly knew or admired this man while he was pope on earth. Granted, I was a little kid for most of his pontificate but even as a teenager I was not attentive to him. However, after he become a saint, I really felt a deep love and closeness to this man. I remember crying at his beatification for an unknown reason! The fact that I was at his canonization just weeks before my ordination to the priesthood I knew was telling. And now, being at his tomb and calling him a saint, I felt more love for him and love from him than I ever had! Such amazing graces are poured out on the Church as a whole and individuals by canonizing someone! However, despite these fruits, it's still not an easy process to canonize someone.

Many religious communities choose to stop the process when their brother or sister has been declared a blessed. That step gives them permission to celebrate their beloved fellow Christian in all the liturgies and to spread devotion to them through their story and example. To be honest, it is not a cheap endeavor to go through the canonization process: helping to pay for all the people involved, for advertising and materials to promote the cause, travel, and other expenses can all cost a lot. For this reason, many communities stop at beatification.

So, what more is involved to canonize? Primarily and mostly definitively, the Holy Father himself must give a solemn proclamation. The technical definition of canonization is "the solemn act with which the Holy Father declares in a definitive way that a Catholic faithful is actually in eternal glory, and that for people on earth is an example to learn 'the most secure way among the various things of this world, that we can reach perfect union with Christ, that is, holiness.'"[62] The act of canonization is said to be an act of the Holy Father's the charism of infallibility whereby the Holy Spirit guides the decisions of the Pope to not err. Because the status of a person's soul is known to God alone, as well as because it is such a high proclamation about the central mystery of salvation, a declaration of sainthood must come from the agent on earth promised not to err in judgment. During the ceremony the Pope states: *Sanctam esse decernimus et definimus,* "We discern and define [them] to be a Saint." Infallibility is not a manifestation of autonomy or some gross excess of power that the Pope has, but rather is a gift whereby he can work with and be led by the Holy Spirit in a greater way on earth. The final discernment and decision on sainthood has been seen and witnessed to by

---

62. My translation: "l'atto solenne con cui il Sommo Pontefice dichiara in forma definitiva che un fedele cattolico è attualmente nella gloria eterna, è per noi ancora sulla terra un esempio per apprendere 'la via piú sicura per la quale tra le mutevoli cose del mondo possiamo raggiungere la perfetta union con Cristo, cioè la santità'" Le Causa dei Santi, 505.

the whole Church, and it is the guidance of the Holy Spirit which prompts the Holy Father in this proclamation. In fact, the entire evaluation is "the process of discernment from the Church of how much the Holy Spirit is performing in the Church and in the world."[63] It is a discernment of the saint's presence in heaven through proof of life and miracles, but also how the Spirit, during different times and circumstances, moves through various individuals and makes them brilliant with the light of Christ. Thus, the Church must always read the signs of the times to know not only the struggles facing the Church in every age but also how God raises lights fashioned for each moment.

To assist in this discernment process, the Pope needs a seal of approval in the form of another miracle. This miracle should not only contain all the essential elements discussed earlier and be verified as authentic, but it must also take place after the Servant of God has been beatified. Even if many miracles took place before beatification, there must be at least one miracle after they have been beatified to offer assurance of their presence in heaven and the effectiveness of their intercession. This miracle is then properly documented, and the recipient of the miracle notified and examined. Traditionally, if they can come to Rome, their presence at the canonization is a powerful testimony to the Universal Church of the reality of the miracle.

Finally, as said before, the actual efficient cause of the canonization is the ceremony of canonization celebrated by the Holy Father himself. Traditionally it takes place in St. Peter's Basilica (recently, because of the popularity of the canonizations, they have occurred in the square). Catholics from all over are invited to be witnesses to this most gracefilled moment in the Church's life. Since it is the saints

---

63. My translation: "il processo di discernimento da parte della Chiesa, di quanto lo Spirito Santo stia effettuando nella Chiesa e nel mondo." Le Causa dei Santi, 506.

who help build and guide the Church, it is right and just that the Church body be present to give thanks and invoke their aid on the Church below. The ceremony opens with the rite of canonization. It begins with a petition from the Prefect of the Congregation for the Cause of the Saints to the Holy Father asking that this blessed be inscribed in the catalog with all the other saints. This request is primarily a liturgical inscription, but it reflects the moral certainty, as much as is humanly possible, that this Servant of God is indeed united with the other saints in heaven. An appropriate next move is the invocation of the litany of the saints for the Pope's judgment but also to turn the Church's focus to the union of the heavenly Church with the earthly and the role this blessed will have in the greater communion of saints as a companion.

The Holy Father acts as the guide for the entire universal Church in a truly universal celebration that extends the memory, example, and merits of this Servant of God to all times and places. The ceremony, as well as the Servant of God's life, becomes a living message to the world about how to overcome the evils of our time and how to find holiness. The ceremony is not only liturgical in that it offers thanks and honor to God on behalf of this Servant of God and unites the faithful around God's altar, but it is also a solemn public proclamation that has legal and juridical effects. Their name truly becomes canonized, which means placed in the canon or list of other saints. They are now to be recognized and honored throughout the ages.

After the prayer, the Holy Father makes one of the greatest declarations of the Church: the formal act of canonization. I here offer an English translation:

> To the honor of the Holy and Individual Trinity, to the exaltation of the Catholic Faith and the growth of Christian life, by the authority of Our Lord Jesus Christ, of Blessed Apostles Peter and Paul and ours, after mature due deliberation and imploring frequently divine help, as well as council of many of our brothers, we discern and define Blessed N. to be a saint and we inscribe them into the catalog of the saints, placing them in the Universal Church amongst the saints to be recalled with holy devotion, in the name of the Father. [64]

The Church then bursts into a joyous cry of "Thanks be to God!" as "Iubilate Deo" is sung, and the relics of the newly canonized saint are presented to the Pope to be venerated and incensed. It is an emotionally powerful moment as the banner holding the image of the saint is unveiled and the entire congregation of thousands of faithful begin to shout and cry, giving thanks to God. It is one of the most powerful moments for a Catholic to be a part of, as well as one of the most Catholic actions to take place. The prefect then offers thanks to the Holy Father, and the Church enters her divine worship and thanks God in the celebration of the mass, starting immediately with the "Gloria." The mass traditionally ends with the Angelus, the Holy Father's address to the people about the new saint, and the declaration of the

---

64. Original Latin: "Ad honorem Sanctae et Individuae Trinitatis, ad exaltationem fidei catholicae et vitae christianae incrementum, auctoritate Domini nostri Iesu Christi, beatorum Apostolorum Petri et Pauli ac Nostra, matura deliberatione praehabita et divina ope saepius implorata, ac de plurimorum Fratrum Nostrorum consilio, Beatam N. Sanctam esse decernimus et definimus, ac Sanctorum Catalogo adscribimus, statuentes eam (eum) in universa Ecclesia inter Sanctos pia devotione recoli debere. In nomine Patris et Filii et Spiritus Sancti."

saint's established feast day, which is normally around the time when the canonization is celebrated.

Conclusion

The canonization of a saint is very beautiful and moving, but is only one element, a key element, in the entire story of sainthood. The canonization process does not make somebody a saint. It is a process of examining and verifying, as much as humanly possible, the belief (and hope) that someone is in heaven. The formal act of canonization gives permission to the Church to act upon the inspiration and example the fellow Christian has given to them by their life, death, martyrdom, and charity. The canonization process creates a list of the official saints that the Church has verified and confirmed and extends the fame of their holiness to the entire Church. At this point, the saint's journey has just begun in the Church! In really, as we discussed with the fame of holiness, their work in the Church has been taking place from the moment they died, and the canonization is a recognition of the role they play in the Church.

Even if many Catholics are unable to go to a canonization ceremony, pray at the tomb of a saint, or visit places they lived and work, we are not deprived of a closeness to the saints. The greatest connection we can have with them comes from a daily walk with the saints, sharing that communion with them in their example, intercession, and companionship.

Our focus now shifts from the Church and her work with the saints to examine the saints and their work with and in the Church. We will now look at how the truths we have examined in these first three chapters, particularly the communion of saints discussed in Chapter 2, is lived out in our lives here today. It will be an invitation to you to take new courage and understand the faith we profess in the communion of saints.

PART II

THE SAINTS

Up to this point, we have studied the definition of a saint, we have examined the principles of communion with the saints (example, intercession and companionship), and we have delved into the process by which the Church lists those who are known to be saints. Now in Part II, the principles laid out in the first half of the book will be made concrete and personal through the saints. What we have learned so far about the saints is highly theological and historical and may seem a bit distant and foreign to us. However, if the point of communion with the saints is true, it will effect that truth in the life of the Church. One of the greatest proofs for the truth of the communion of saints will come from contemporary, real-life examples of the love and companionship of the saints coming alive. In the following pages, you will learn about 10 different saints through biographies and testimonies from everyday people who have found saints to be their companions, many of whom found the initiative was on the saint's part.

The biographies I have written may not list historical facts and data and or follow a chronological scheme. I have structured the biographies to give background and insight into the saint's life, but I have highlighted the characteristics, qualities and attributes that were most foundational to understanding their life and identity, to aid us in the first gift the saints offer us: example. The personality they had on earth is enriched in heaven, so learning about their character, helps us know them now in heaven. It can also aid us in finding connections we may have with the saints: overlapping in experiences, shared difficulties, common hopes, and dream. I also lay out situations of the world that they responded to and answers they can provide for us in our daily struggle with the elements of this world. I offer lessons that can be taken away from each saint, either from the story of their life on earth or their role in heaven, and how they embody different virtues or patronages in a heroic way. Then, I detail the great experiences the saints had of heaven, the love they expressed on earth, and relationships they had with friends on earth and other saints in heaven. Finally, I write of their great familiarity with God, God's interaction in their lives, and how they lived a spirit of prayer on earth and continued to have a contact with us in heaven showing their power of intercession. Much of these biographies have been written using direct writings of the saints themselves. Several have been written by people who have become dear friends with the saints and so the saint becomes not a strange concept to explain but a dear friend to share.

Finally, each saint story contains a testimony of how the saints have drawn near to various people in various situations and have formed lasting friendships. Far from being simple anecdotes, these stories are living testimonies to the vitality of the saints and how they have led many into a deeper relationship with Christ. The saints can and do leave lasting and palpable impressions on the Church and their activity in the Church is so forceful that it is awe-inspiring.

In the beautiful and marvelous story of *I dared to call him Father*, Bilquish Sheikh details her conversion from a very prominent Muslim in a high, official family in Pakistan to the Christian faith. Her entire journey occurred in a land without the usual presence of Christianity; she had to hunt down a Christian family to ask them about the faith. The catalyst for her journey was almost completely supernatural. She highlights how an unknown man that she had never seen or heard of before became her guide on this journey:

> I found myself having supper with a man I knew to be Jesus. He had come to visit me in my home and stayed for two days. He sat across the table from me, in peace and joy we ate dinner together. Suddenly, the dream changed. Now I was on a mountaintop with another man. He was clothed in a robe and shod with sandals. How is it that I mysteriously knew his name, too? John the Baptist. What a strange name. I found myself telling this John the Baptist about my recent visit with Jesus. "The Lord came and was my guest for two days." I said: "But now he is gone. Where is he? I must find him! Perhaps you, John the Baptist will lead me to him?"[65]

John the Baptist indeed became a guide for her and led her to encounter various Christian missionaries. He not only led her to read the Bible, but he stood at the crossroads of her life and pointed her toward baptism. His intervention into her life came from the saint's own heart and desire for the salvation of her soul. He was no idle observer, nor was he simply an inspiring story that she heard one day and wanted to imitate. He was a dynamic and driving force in her conversion. As on earth he was the precursor to Jesus,

65. Bilquis Sheikh, "*I dared to call him Father*" (Grand Rapides: Chosen Books, 2003), 30.

the one who constantly pointed the way to the Lord, so he continues this role in heaven as is testified by her story.

Just like with Bilquish, the saints stand at a crossroad in our lives, pointing us to Christ. But they don't just stand at the crossroads, they walk it with us. They already have walked it and have much to share with us about the walk. They offer us their stories, they offer us their prayers, they offer us their gifts and talents. It is now my joy to offer the saints in turn to you.

"St. Rose Meeting With St. Martin"
Original Hand Drawing by Elizabeth Michalski

ST. ROSE OF LIMA

To open this section of the book, I want to take the lead and share with you one of the dearest friends I've ever had: St. Rose of Lima. She has helped inspire and encourage me to write this book, but she has also been such a wonderful friend, that it's not a task, but a joy to reveal to you the wonderful companion I've found in St. Rose. She has helped me to dissolve the imaginary barrier we make with heaven and see how easy it is to reach heaven if we just live close to heaven now. She has shared much of her own gifts and virtues, as well as accompanied me along many of my own journeys here.

Her life reflects what her name suggests: nature, beauty, and growth. Its inspiring to see that her identity, her appearance, and her life had such a beautiful harmony and transparency. We are accustomed to encountering deception in this world; a twisting of the truth that the devil, the father of lies, introduced to us in the garden. We struggle to see things as they are, and many times we are disappointed.
Not with Rose of Lima. As a saint, she entered into harmony with the God who is simple, true, and good. Her relationship with God created harmony throughout her life, so that the name she bore, the beauty she reflected, and the inner life she lived, were in complete sync with one another. She truly lived as a rose in her beauty, her spirit, and her personality; she mimicked the rose's life.

Rose, born Isabelle Flores de Oliva, was the first canonized saint of the new world. As the new colonies and families began to grow and flourish in Perú, so did new life in the Spirit. People had been seeking the New World in hopes of happiness and peace, free from the corruption of the Old Europe. Rose would be destined to take root here and give evidence through her prayer, penance and charity that the greatest destination man should seek is heaven, the new world of everlasting peace.

Perú was a new Spanish colony and a chance for a new start in a virgin land. However, Perú had already been occupied by the Incas. The first colonization of Perú led to bloodshed and discovered paganism at the roots. However, many families came to Perú with great success in laying a stable foundation. The Flores family owned property in the middle of Lima, the capital, and they planted one of the first rose gardens; they were the caretakers of some of the first Spanish roses to grow in the new world. Little did they know what a beautiful rose would spring forth from their soil.

Rose was the fourth of thirteen children. She was incredibly beautiful, even as a baby, and when she was an infant, a rose appeared in front of her face (some accounts say her face itself changed into a rose). It was clear that her name should be Rose. She steadily grew in beauty and sanctity amid many thorns and leaves. She would encounter much opposition from her family and vain attraction from admirers but also saintly friends like St. Catherine of Siena and St. Martin de Porres. Finally, she bloomed in the Heart of God, answering the call of Jesus Himself: *Rosa de mi corazón se mi esposa!* "Rose of my heart, be my spouse!" Jesus loved His Rose, and Rose loved her Lord. Her entire life was dedicated to being a rose of Jesus that grew in the garden of His heart.

One of Rose's trademark qualities was her beauty. From her birth until her death, Rose displayed a beauty that even today would be considered admirable. Many a songbird was attracted to her. Repeatedly she had to battle with attention that she did not want. As her spiritual mother Catherine did, Rose cut off her long hair to dissuade men. It is important to note that Rose did not hate her beauty. Some can assume that her asceticism was an attempt to punish herself or mar her beauty. On the contrary, she knew her beauty was a gift, but she also desired to be beautiful in the eyes of the Lord above all. For many saints, especially Mary, the more an inner beauty and joy fills them, the more it shines outwardly for all the world to see. Such was the case of Moses on the mountain when he had seen the backside of God and his face became radiant (see Ex 34:29). Mother Teresa was said to have shone a wondrous light from her face as well. Rose possessed her physical beauty as a gift from God, but it was even more captivating because it was a manifestation of her inner beauty and purity and formed part of the great harmony among her soul, body, actions, and life that was summed up by her name: Rose.

Rose planted herself in a garden, both literally and figuratively. She loved to garden and grow flowers and be immersed in nature, so she built a hut in her garden to be alone with her God. She also loved to cultivate devotion for God in the soil of her heart. As it was in a garden that man's twisting of the truth occurred, it was in a garden that Rose stood in stark contrast to that event. Jesus Himself appeared to Mary Magdalene as a gardener after the Resurrection (Jn 20:15), showing that the image of a garden was not only man's place of falling but also the place of restoration. A garden is a place of natural growth with the addition of a gardener's skill and labor. In a similar way, within the 'spiritual garden' there is the natural growth of gifts, desires, hopes, and dreams along with the labor and skill of virtue and discernment, assisted by God's grace. The growth of a garden is silent and hidden, which was Rose's great desire. Gardens need work and pruning; Rose performed penance to do this in her own heart. Gardens are also places where things of earth are nourished by rain from heaven. Rose, despite her constant involvement in the trials of this life, had roots planted in the firm soil of God's promises, the sacraments, and hours of silent prayer.

Very early in her life, Rose would be given her own guide and companion from the heavenly realm: St. Catherine of Siena. As a little girl, Rose was said to have been taught to read by Jesus Himself and the first book she read was the life of St. Catherine; she not only was inspired by Catherine's example but found her to be an intimate friend who inspired her and walked with her. Their interaction and closeness were so dear and nurturing that Catherine became a spiritual mother to Rose; Catherine shared the gifts and traits of her own life, just as a mother does to her daughter. Their companionship was so real and Catherine's care and sharing of her own gift was so tangible that Rose's life reflected Catherine's in a new and fresh way. In fact, people later called Rose the "Catherine of the West." St. Catherine inspired Rose to take on intense penances, such as fasting from all food except the Eucharist, and to stand against the evils of her time prayerfully and courageously. Rose received a share of the love in Catherine's heart to do works of charity and ultimately imitated Catherine in receiving an engagement ring from Jesus Himself. They both were great mystics, who had powerful and intimate times of prayer with Jesus. At times He would appear as a child resting in their arms, as real as any mother holding her own child. Jesus was their great bridegroom, but they both had an incredibly familiar relationship with Him, always seeing Him mystically, but also in all things and in every person they met. Their deep prayer life and spiritual depth not only connected them to each other but allowed them to give a similar beauty to the world.

As this little rose continued to grow and flourish, she attracted the admiration of many people. Men and women of the day were attracted to this beautiful little girl with a crown of flowers and thought she would make a suitable wife one day. This attention was the last thing Rose desired, since she knew she was admired by the greatest spouse in the Lord and her heart would find rest only in His love.

Her days were filled with work for her family, the poor, and the nobles. She was a gardener, seamstress, almsgiver, and caretaker. During her daily work she found small ways to meditate, like saying the name of God or composing songs to sing to Him. She practiced the art of mental prayer and encountered the child Jesus who made His abode in her heart. Her mother forbade her from entering the religious life and called her to help with the many tasks of their home. Rose's mother, seeing her beauty, also had intentions to marry Rose off. Since she could not go off to the monastery to find Jesus there, she let Him find her in the depths of her heart, in the middle of her life. Especially in her garden, where she loved to work, she found the wonders of her lover so close to her. One of her great miracles is that her garden was always in bloom; it was never without flowers. This was one external sign of the interior life she had with the Lord.

Rose is the patron saint of seamstresses and needle workers. This was the occupation that took up most of her time as she tried to raise money for her family. To make clothes one must take several small, humble, fragmentary pieces of bland cloth and form it into an outer garment to clothe the body of a person. Rose saw that as she worked, she could tailor spiritual "garments" for the Lord. Her writings reflect how she was constantly fashioning spiritual garments: sewing together various prayers, meditations, small offerings, fasts, and penances that she could take from the small, humble actions of each day and to make "clothing" for the Blessed Mother and Jesus. As she counted and added the stiches she used in various garments, she made this a basis for numbering and organizing her prayers and penances. Garments made for colder weather were longer and had more material, those for working were of a stronger, more durable type. So too, she would meditate on the cold Jesus experienced in Bethlehem as a baby and offer certain prayers and penances to accompany Him or she would meditate on the trials He endured in this life and offer another set of prayers for Him then. Her prayer and penance contained great power and effect because it had such a connection to Jesus.

Like a rose has thorns underneath, so this beautiful saint hid penance under her serene appearance. She had a true heroic and generous life of penance, freely and willingly accepted. She did not believe that suffering was good in and of itself, or that she had to merit the love of God. God's love is unconditional—it is not based on our merits. Rather, because Jesus suffered greatly and willingly accepted it, and because she loved Jesus and wanted to imitate Him and unite herself as much as she could with the one she loved, she desired to take on suffering. She could become closest to Jesus in suffering. Jesus took on not just a single human body but the entire human nature. The divinity of the Son assumed the entirety of the human person and now was able to suffer. Sin brings suffering because it does indeed wound the human person. Now united to the life of God, human nature is forever changed; divinity has touched every aspect of the human life and since suffering was how Jesus saved us, giving us grace, grace now comes to us in suffering. We will not be free of suffering until heaven, but through Jesus we can find heaven through our suffering if we offer it up. How beautiful that God took on something so common to the human condition to save us. In something as horrible and pointless as suffering, God is not only seen but He is identified, as we hear from Pope Benedict XVI: "Jesus can now be recognized by His wounds and not His face. Thomas holds that the signs that confirm the Lord's identity are now above all His wounds, in which He reveals to us how much

He loves us." [66] Now, every man who suffers finds that it is not meaningless, it is not pointless. It can be a means of grace for them and an offering and an encounter with the one who suffered out of love for us.

As Rose grew and matured in her penance, she found that her beautiful appearance was a way to hide her fasting. Jesus teaches in the Gospel to "wash your face so that people may not know you are fasting" (Mt 6:17), so she daily placed on her head her signature crown of roses (lined on the inside with small nails as a discipline) and faced the world with a smile as she internally sacrificed and prayed to the Lord in the secret of her heart. She indeed went into her inner room, or in her case, her inner garden and prayed to the Lord in secret. She was able to build a small hermitage in her garden to find time to pray and contemplate at night, only giving herself two hours to sleep. In her nightly vigils and meditation in the garden she delved deep into contemplation and mysticism. Though she never left her garden, she went everywhere, from the heights of heaven to the pits of hells. She even mentioned to close friends that, when she was not able to physically go to mass, she was somehow transported to a location to attend mass!

Much like her spiritual mother St. Catherine who not only was blessed with mystical experiences but expressed that love in charitable work, so too Rose expressed her love for God in action. In this new land of mission territory and of new promise, poverty was present in not only her family but the city. In her own house she welcomed the most pitiable of the poor and sick and cared for them. She gave them roses and rosemary to cover the smell but also to be a small gift to them. She worked as a doctor on some of the most foul and

---

66. Pope Benedict XVI, "Jesus, the Apostles and the Early Church," (Our Sunday Visitor 2007), 103.

disgusting poor out there without giving the slightest show of disgust or reluctance: a true sacrifice of love.

Rose's life was anything but, well, a bed of roses. Firstly, Rose herself experienced many health issues, everything from arthritis to ultimately dying of tuberculosis. The area of Lima provided terrible heat and humidity throughout the time and, outside of the fasting she regularly performed, she had to be denied essentials such as water because of scarcity.

One of the greatest crosses Rose carried was her family's great resistance to and even persecution of her desire for sanctity. Her mother normally paraded her around at parties to try and win over a suitor (not knowing that Rose had made a private vow of virginity). Her mother was determined to marry her daughter and get her into a prosperous life. As Rose grew in holiness and desired to spend more time in prayer, her family interpreted this as presumption, that Rose considered herself better than her family and wanted to separate herself. As Rose also began to increase in holiness and miracles such as multiplying food, causing roses to grow in wintertime, and being taught by Jesus how to read began to take place, rather than considering her a saint, her family saw her as a witch. At this time the Inquisition was highly active. Rose's acts drew unwanted attention from the Inquisitors as well as gave a bad name to their family. Hence, they tried to quench her flame and draw her into various tedious tasks and labors. However, try as they might, on account of the various miraculous events that transpired during her service of the poor and during her prayer time, she drew upon herself an Inquisition.

During this examination and scrutiny, Rose, out of charity barely mentioned the persecutions she experienced, but focused mostly on the spiritual tribulations she found herself in. Spiritual dryness or being in a rut does not come close to what she went through. For long hours she stayed, almost physically paralyzed, as in prayer she felt the abandonment from God, the weight of judgment and condemnation, and even saw hell itself. As physiology was just beginning to be seen as a real, credible science, most of her family and even priests wanted to diagnose this reclusive, anxious, socially avoidant girl in her mid-twenties as depressed or what they called melancholic. Even her confessors and spiritual directors considered her crazy, depressed, or a disobedient rebel. At this time, the full study and understanding of the dark night of the soul and the various mystical theologies had not yet been fully developed, so her misdiagnosis was easy to occur. It was not until her inquisition, which hosted not only several priests but a medical doctor who was studied in the theology of the time, that Rose was found to be experiencing some of the heights of spiritual growth and prayer.

As Rose herself said, "without the burden of tribulation, it is impossible to reach the heights of grace, the gift of grace increases as the struggle increases." All the trials she experienced strengthened and opened her to the great treasures God would give her. One of these would be the various mystical experiences she would have; experiences that beautifully paralleled and mirrored two saints that lived thousands of miles away in Spain: Teresa of Avila and John of the Cross. St. Rose wrote of the fifteen or so *mercedes,* [67] or spiritual riches, that she received over several experiences of prayer. Such riches included having her heart almost physically burned by God's love, the piercing of her heart with a dart of heavenly light, and having Jesus mystically rest in her heart. Rose explained these riches and experiences to her confessor by drawings she made,[68] which mirror these saintly Spaniards. She uses the image of a heart being pierced

67. There is no good English translation of this word. The significance would be something like "favor," "grace," or "mercy." For the sake of being respectful of other languages, I will simply refer to this word in the original language.
68. Referenced by Rosa Ligarda in a beautiful book, *Santa Rosa de Lima Escritos de la santa Limeña,* (Facultad de Teologia Pontificia y Civil de Lima, Lima Peru, 2016). All quotes of St. Rose are from this book in the original Spanish.

by darts of love and burning with love. These *mercedes* are almost identical to the experiences that St. Teresa of Avila had in her great *transverberation*, in which the angel of God appeared and stabbed her heart with a flaming arrow of love that pulled out her selfishness and ignited her heart with love.[69] Rose's writings also mirrored John of the Cross's: she drew a ladder leading up to heaven with the word "humility" written on it. This image is unmistakably similar to John's *Ascent of Mount Carmel* by the middle road of nothing. The resemblance and shared experiences she had with these two other mystics shows the communion the saints were already beginning to experience and reflect in their prayer and writings.

More than just mystical friendship and spiritual communion, God also gave Rose beautiful saintly companions already on earth to walk with her. Among the first was a saint already at work tending the garden of the Lord: St. Turibius, who was the second bishop of Lima. Called to be a bishop before he was even a priest, Turibius jumped into this mission at the age of thirty-nine. He served in Lima and the surrounding area as bishop for thirty years and had three saints pass under his care. The growth of saints such as Rose and Martin were the fruit of his sanctity and prayers for the people under his care.

Turibius traveled over 40,000 km throughout his dioceses (most of this being done either on foot or horseback), wearing himself out to be as close to all the people as he could. He was a vigilant and wise overseer, as well as a courageous and charismatic missionary in a massive and uncharted new land.[70] He was a man of action, but he needed one who was the soul, the life force, to pump spiritual grace through his

---

69. Upon her death, the autopsy revealed actual perforations in St. Teresa's heart!

70. Biographical information for St. Turibius taken from Benito, Jose Antonio "Tercer Concilio Limense" *Obispos participantes en el III Limense. Semblanzas: Santo Toribio Alfonso de Morgrovejo.* Facultad de Teologia Pontificia y Civil de Lima/Universidad Pontificia de La Santa Croce. Lima, 2017 , 99–100.

ministry. Rose, as recounted by biographers, was the hidden, spiritual power behind his ministry, offering her prayers and penances for his work that saved countless souls and brought the Gospel to so many souls wandering in the dark. Rose not only physically drew near to this bishop as the leader of the Church but she spiritually supported his work through her prayers and penance. Eventually, Turibius' life of labor took its toll and he died years before Rose. From then on, she remembered this holy man, and he remembered her, praying for her from his place in heaven.

However, a story of St. Rose, her life, and her companionship with other saints would be incomplete without talking about one of the most important friends she had, in earth or in heaven: St. Martin de Porres. Martin was a mulatto, born of a Spanish father and a Negro mother. He was considered an outcast of the society at that time, with black skin and poor demeanor. Martin, born in 1579, was about seven years older than Rose, but lived twenty-two years longer than her on this earth. Martin was born and grew up only a few blocks away from the Flores family. He probably heard the joyful news of them welcoming their fourth child and stories of her remarkable beauty, and maybe even saw it for himself. He experienced some of the terrible racism that existed during that period, even to the point of not being able to profess religious vows in the Church (this injustice was imposed by the state rather than the Church). Rose and Martin's lives intertwined as they both sought more and more the face of the Lord, but also as Rose took on the task of caring for the altar of Our Lady of the Rosary and Martin went forward to join the Dominicans.

Rose's love had learned to embrace all peoples: nobles, poor, slaves, freemen, Spaniards, Incas. Most of all, her understanding of her own beauty and the Lord's attention to her heart, caused her to look beyond the cover of the book, to see into the soul. She befriended this black Dominican and they were an image of the true and perfect friendship that is the goal of Christian life. The Catechism declares that "chastity blossoms in friendship"[71] and in no more beautiful way has it blossomed than between the rose of Jesus' heart and the humble violet of the Lord's garden. Rose and Martin were two flowers that created a sweet, pungent honey, forged from hours of deep conversation about the Lord and His mercies, held in check by their various penances and acts of self-discipline and steeped in a deep respect and love for the other as one destined for heaven. The bee of the Holy Spirit took this sweet pollen from the two of them and formed a potent honey that speaks to the world of true unity and peace.

They would spend recreation time speaking about spiritual matters and discussing and encouraging one another in their own path. Even though Rose was living a holy life, sustained by God, no one is saved alone and even saints need saints to help them: someone who sees the common goal, lives a similar life, prayers with and for them, and offers the support of a friend. Their friendship on earth also points to the truth that saints want to draw near to one another. Their friendship is a living proof of the desire the saints possess to support us on our journey.

Martin was a humble friar who fulfilled many tasks such as janitor, barber, and almsgiver. He was very charitable, later called the Apostle of Charity because of his love for the poor. Because of his humility, he performed many amazing miracles for both man and beast. However, he was always obedient to his superiors and did what was asked of him. Through

---

70. CCC 2347: "The virtue of chastity blossoms in friendship. It shows the disciple how to follow and imitate him who has chosen us as his friends, who has given himself totally to us and allows us to participate in his divine estate. Chastity is a promise of immortality. Chastity is expressed notably in friendship with one's neighbor. Whether it develops between persons of the same or opposite sex, friendship represents a great good for all. It leads to spiritual communion."

the heavenly example of Catherine and the brotherhood of Martin, Rose too eventually joined the family of the Order of Preachers.

All of Rose's prayer and intercession would prepare her for one of the greatest trials to come to her country. America at that time was not only the new world but also a land of riches that were newly discovered. Spain was one of the first nations to bring some of the riches such as gold from this new world back to the homeland. However, some people saw an easier way to receive such riches. Piracy was a very common enterprise since the tracing of exports and policing the waters was very difficult and perilous. Many of the great stories we know of that deal with pirates and swashbucklers developed during these days. Truth is normally far more interesting than fiction.

The Dutch were masters of the sea and so were their pirates. In 1615 a ruthless Dutch pirate named Joseph Spillburg was wreaking havoc on the South American coasts with a large pirate fleet. Lima eventually became his target. The city began to brace itself; young men and old were all gathering strength and supplies to assist the Peruvian navy; women and children were bracing themselves at home; the churches were praying and invoking God to spare them. Rose doubled up on her prayer and penance. She placed herself before the Blessed Sacrament exposed on the altar and prayed harder than she had before. The pirates were coming; the strength of men was failing. Soon they were on the shore, and nothing would be considered too much for them to pillage, take, or destroy. Only God could help the people of Peru now. As people filled the Church with Rose, the fear and panic was palpable. But the young girl, who for years had wished to hide herself from the gaze of men in the heart of God, now discovered a new impetus. As she looked at Jesus in the Eucharist, she wept for how she was not able to be there to save Him the first time He was captured and crucified by blood thirsty men, but she could save Him this time. With a spiritual zeal found only in the martyrs Rose stood up from her hours of prayers on her knees, pulled out her large embroidery scissors from her pocket, cut off the dress she was wearing at the knees to give her more movement and marched to the doors of the church. "If they are going to come for the Eucharist, they will have to go through me" may have been her thought at that moment.

As Captain Spillburg peered through his telescope at the lavish city ripe for his picking, he felt a sudden stinging in his chest, then a gripping power over his body, and with a powerful thud, he hit the ground dead from a stroke.[72] The crew, fearing what this omen might mean and unable to continue without the guidance of their captain, had to retreat. Just like that, the pirate ships turned back, their masts disappearing into the pacific horizon. Rose had stood faithfully ready, but God proved himself more faithful. The prayers and courage of His dear rose had paid off; her city was spared.

No good deed goes unrewarded, and the power and devotion of this little rose's prayers could not remain planted in the earth for long. God soon plucked this rose from His garden to Himself in heaven and her power of prayer on earth became her joy and life in heaven. Rose predicted the day of her death. In her writings, Rose reflects on a deep love for her spiritual father and great apostle Bartholomew. That was not only the name of her spiritual director but also the disciple of the Lord who, at his first meeting with Jesus was told, "You shall see heaven opened and the angels of God ascending and descending upon the Son of man"[73] (Jn

72. This story is recounted in *Saint Rose of Lima, Patroness of the Americas* by Sister Mary Alphonsus O.ss.R. (Tan Books, 1982). Other more fantastic accounts exist as well.

1:50–51). As with so many of the apostles, Jesus promised him that he would see something greater, which is the vision of God face to face. Bartholomew carried this desire in his heart and Rose wished to follow him and see God's face.

She knew that she would die on the eve of St. Bartholomew, and it was the greatest struggle of her life yet, as she died not only from tuberculosis but also issues with her brain. It was a long and grueling struggle that left her bedridden, asking for water. But midnight on the eve of St. Bartholomew, she saw angels ascending and descending as she passed from this world on August 23, her heavenly birthday.

Despite a very testing and painful death, her body remained beautiful and gave off a wonderful odor. Her confessor said she seemed to almost be laughing when she died! Her body had to be buried in the church overnight because so many people were praying and touching her tomb. Between 12:30am when she died and 4pm the next day when they moved her body, there are several accounts of people having visions of Rose in heaven, rejoicing with her love, Jesus, and walking with the other great virgins as she received her palm of victory. A Dominican missionary named Fr. Vincent Bernedo, who had been out in the Sierra preaching to the Incas was mystically transported to Rose's sickroom the night of her death and saw the beautiful vision of her soul going up to heaven.[74] Rose almost immediately began to receive veneration and started her work.

In 1627, only ten years after Rose's death, a grieving mother took a piece of garment from Rose and place it on her daughter who had died the day before and instantly the young girl was brought to life! In 1631, a young man named

---

73. In this verse of Scripture, he is referred to not as Bartholomew but as Nathanael. They are traditionally believed to be the same person since "bar" means "son" and he would have been named after his father who was also Nathanael.
74. *Saints Who Raised the Dead*, Fr. Albert J. Hebert, (Rockford, IL: Tan Books and Publications, 2004), 143.

Anthony Bran had died of a fever and, after invoking Rose's intercession they placed a picture of Rose on his body and Anthony came back to life and, without being told who they had invoked, he began to give thanks to Rose.[75] Beside raising people from the dead, Rose was also attributed with interceding in several other miracles.

> Rose cured many after her death: she saved infants, helped women with difficult childbirth, cured lepers, healed a dying Negress who had been carried to Rose's tomb, and straightened Alphonse Diaz, a cripple who previously could only drag himself around.[76]

Reports such as these began to pour into the Pope's lap. Pope Clement X, the Pope at the time was going over all the reports about this beautiful rose and was awestruck with so many miracles taking place. It is said that he himself testified to one of her most famous miracles. One night, as he is reading over all the reports of miracles, he stopped and pondered: "Rose, a saint and a patron? Hmmm, I'd like to see some petals from her." Suddenly, a shower of rose petals fell upon his desk! Proof enough. Rose had one of the fastest canonization processes at that time, being canonized 1671, only about fifty years after her death. This marked her as the first saint of the new world. Moreover, Pope Clement X assigned her a very big task: the patroness of all the Americas,[77] Philippines, and Oceania! A big task, but for one who loves great, the gift of love increases as one loves more. It's no wonder that Rose's canonization process was so short! Coupled with the miracles from her intercession was

---

75. Fr. Hebert, 140–141.

76. Fr. Hebert, 140–141.

77. At this time, North and South America were together considered "The Americas." Hence, Rose can and should be considered the patroness of all those in North and South America.

the necessary *fama sanctitatis* as her devotion and imitation spread. Many missionaries who, engaging in the fierce work of missions and evangelization, invoked her intercession and called upon her patronage as they traveled throughout the Americas, establishing new missions. As she had done so much on earth to help Turibius and his work, so now as the patroness of the Americas she was more active in heaven. Many cities in North, Central, and South America were named 'Santa Rosa' as they looked to her heavenly intercession in the new missions, even if now that name is much separated from the saint who spread her fragrance all over the new world.

My Journey with St. Rose

It was the spring of 2019. I was finishing my canon law studies in Rome in June and then would be back in America for parish ministry for good! I wanted to go to Peru, not just because it was a great way to practice my Spanish before returning home, but also because this was my last chance to take a good bit of time off for a mission. I contacted a community of missionaries, and they were very excited to have a priest! The community's charism is to prepare areas that never have had a priest; finally getting a priest was a joy. My university offered us two weeks off for Easter break, which basically was Holy Week and then the Easter octave. I figured this was a great time for the people of these areas to have a priest visit and the sisters had already been planning on doing ministry there. So, I left the Thursday before Palm Sunday, going all the way from Rome down to Lima, Peru. I landed in the early morning and soon found myself consumed in a country of traffic jams, street vendors, car exhaust, crammed into a 4-wheel drive truck with four tiny sisters dressed in blue.

Lima was our first destination, but the mission location was a six-hour drive away from there. Upon arriving, the sisters gave me a day or so to rest. Early Saturday morning came, and I loaded all the essentials for my mission trip in a big, 4-wheel drive truck driven by a little sixty-year-old Peruvian sister who was so short she had to pull the seat all the way up to the steering wheel. The drive took all day, but on the way out of the city, the sister arranged a special visit.

We went into the center of the city of Lima, a place of both New World culture and Old Spanish architecture. We went to the capital building, the sanctuary of El Señor de Los Milagros, and then the Sanctuary of St. Rose of Lima. It was a very beautiful and peaceful garden, filled with roses, the original well from Rose's Garden, and the small hut she built with her hands. Here, Rose spent her time praying, attached to a gorgeous church that housed the last painting of her ever made. We then went a few blocks over to the church of Santo Domingo, the Dominican church that housed the remains of Sts. Rose, Martin, and John Massias. It was beautiful to see the number of people moving back and forth, praying in the church, the huge confession lines, the various people of all ages writing down intentions, and how much the images of these saints were kept alive in the beauty of these churches and in the hearts of the people. As we talked by the altar of St. Rose, one of the sisters asked me who my favorite saint was. I mentioned that I had a devotion to St. John Bosco and St. Philip Neri but not too much of a devotion to these saints.

At the end of the mission, the sisters were extremely grateful for my visit with them. As a gift they gave me a large, hand painted image of St. Rose of Lima. It was incredibly beautiful and was set in this unique wooden frame with roses carved into it. Then the thought came to me: how would I get this thing home? I was going to have to put this thing in my suitcase and get it from Lima to Rome as a first step. Luckily, since I had filled my suitcase with clothing, candy, medals, and such that I was leaving in Peru, my suitcase was empty. But gosh, the way they handled suitcases in Rome! It was a miracle the suitcase itself survived such treatment. Stepping out in faith, I loaded it up and came back to Rome. Amazingly, it made it back to Rome in perfect condition!

Then the big problem came: what would I do with it now? I had about three weeks left in Rome before I moved back to America, and I had to pack up everything that I already had from my room. Luckily, I had planned ahead, and I was basically able to fit everything into my suitcase, a carry on, and my backpack. But what about this painting? There was no way I could also fit that into my suitcase. I then remembered that we had a convent of the Dominican Sisters of Mary, Mother of the Eucharist residing in our house with us. Since Rose was a Dominican, and I didn't have a big devotion to her, and I didn't want to risk carrying it home, I decided I would give it to them. A way to practice detachment, right?

Well, a lot of things began to happen all at once. I was taking final exams. A lot of time was spent studying, as well as working on a final paper. In the middle of this my sister called me, frantic. Mom was in the ER. She was anemic and her kidneys had completely shut down. She had been losing blood and her heart rate was dropping. No one knew exactly what was happening to her, we just knew it was serious. I was floored. Nothing had happened like this to my mom before! She had fallen and broken her arm a few weeks before but that was it. Well, it turns out that she had been in kidney failure for a long time, and it was just reaching a critical level. Everyone was panicking and information was being thrown out incredibly fast. I felt lost and trapped. I was several thousand miles away and did not know what to do. Should I leave Rome now and go home? I'd have to come back at some point just to finish three exams. Should I try to stick it out and come home after exams? What if something happens to my mom? I began to pray a lot for guidance. I was finally able to talk to my mom and she told me to not worry, to do what God was asking of me and to finish up and then come home. So, I dedicated these last days and these exams for her.

On the vigil of Pentecost, I was in our chapel, praying about everything that had been happening, and I heard something very strong speak to me. It was very clear and I still remember what it said to me. The words were gentle yet stern: "You may be simple and detached with many things, you can give a lot of things away in your life, but you are not to give that painting away." I knew right away which painting it was referring to. Gosh I was going to feel bad about asking for it back from the sister. After that, then what should I do? I only have about two weeks left in this country!

The next day I went with the Dominican sisters to the Pantheon for the celebration of Pentecost when they drop the rose petals from the ceiling as an image of the tongues of fire. It was here that I told them about the situation with my mom and asked for their prayers for her. I also told them of my prayer encounter and how I had to ask for the painting back. Without skipping a beat, they agreed and said that since they had received it, they knew they were not supposed to keep it.

I went to their convent and picked the picture up from them. As I was leaving and walking back to where I stayed, I crossed another priest who stopped, looked at me very seriously and said, "Wow, she is going to keep you out of hell." A bit stunned, I looked at the painting and said to myself, "well, I've certainly gotten worse predictions." I placed her in my room and said, "Ok God, I did what you asked of me. Now, if it is your will, somehow I will get this home." I asked some guys how to ship stuff back to the US. Most of the guys said it takes several days to just begin the process! I only had a few days at this point, so I did what I could. I started to wrap the picture in bubble wrap and box it up. I emailed the shipping company as soon as I could to hopefully get the process started. Maybe I could get it started and before I could leave the painting with another guy to finish it. Hopefully the company will reply in a few days, before I leave at best. Surprisingly, the guy emailed me back the same day! If you know the Italian pace, this was like going warp speed! So, it was packed and sent within three days.

The time to leave Rome was soon approaching. I had finished most of my exams, packing was going well, and my mom seemed to be stabilizing (they had begun the first round of dialysis and it seemed well). I was having dinner with a buddy of mine and we were talking about going home and starting parish ministry. We had both been studying so much the past week, we were hoping we would be able to make a smooth transition back into parish life. It became a big question of mine: what was going to be most important for me as I move back from Italy to America? After two years of canon law study, what was the most important thing to help make contact and lead the people of America closer to God? I was feeling dwarfed by the giant of ministering again, I prayed to ask God what my weapon going into battle would be. He gave me a simple answer: the saints. In 2019, America had just experienced another of the big priest abuse scandals and people were losing faith in the Church. Sanctity, and the image of goodness lived in the lives of the saints, would help the word of God and the Christian mission to become real, to become incarnate again. I started to pray then and ask God: "Which saint?" "Which saint do I begin with and which saint will help me the most?" As clear as a bell I heard the answer: St. Rose of Lima! Well of course! I have this big painting of her from Lima, I should learn something about this saint! I looked up online "best book on St. Rose of Lima," just to see what would come up, and I was stunned by the title: "St Rose of Lima: Patroness of the Americas." It hit me that yes, she was the first saint of the new world but then that she was also the patroness! She was the perfect choice!

I soon said my goodbyes to Rome, visiting my favorite saints like St. Philip Neri and St. Catherine of Siena and then I departed the day after my last exam. The flight was peaceful and I was excited to see my mom at the airport waiting for me. She looked great and said that the dialysis had gone well and she was in good spirits with new strength.

The next morning, I woke up and was sitting around visiting with my parents. I had about a week before I had to pack up again and move into my new parish assignment. It was a nice, slow-paced week with my family. As we were sitting around talking, I walked into my mom's craft room. She had had this room for years and it was filled with rosaries, books, and so on. When I walked in, I looked at a small table in the middle of the room and there, sitting right on the top, was a big picture of St. Rose of Lima! I was floored; I asked my mom where this came from and she said it just came in the mail the other day and she didn't know what it was or who had sent it. I turned it over and the entire story and prayer on the back was in Spanish. Something was going on at this point, I knew it. I asked my mom if she would mind me taking the picture and of course she didn't.

I felt a strong urge to take this to prayer. I prayed, but in a special way I felt Rose was there with me. So, I began to talk to her. I felt not only a very strong love for her, but a strong love from her. I felt that she was coming into my life for a reason. I felt humbled, touched, and honored. What did I do to deserve this? I wasn't all that remarkable. But I knew she loved me and was going to be there for me. So, I ran with it. I felt an urge on my heart and I asked her with the meekness of a child: "Rose, would you please be my spiritual partner?" I instantly felt a rush of peace and joy and her affirming me in this desire. I asked her to please help me be a saint, to please help me to be holy, to please help me in all my ministry.

A few days later, it was my five-year priestly anniversary and it was off to a very rocky start: my computer crashed, my car battery died, and then, in an interview talking about my vocation, I misspoke about someone, hurt them and had them confront me about it. I was humiliated and beat down. I had just had a spiritual high and now I felt lower than ever. Would I ever become a saint? I felt overwhelmed, so I turned to prayer for guidance. I went to check on my computer that had died in the middle of finishing an assignment and was able to get it started up again. I went on the internet and just searched, "quotes of St. Rose of Lima." I was again floored by the first quote that popped up: "Without the burden of afflictions it is impossible to reach the heights of grace. The gift of grace increases as the struggle increases." That was Rose's response. It was not only consoling but challenging. I had asked for help to become holy and I got tribulations. I knew now that Rose was going to help me to see in all the tribulations of life that God's grace is ever more present and powerful.

The next day, I left for my new assignment. With everything in my vehicle, I went to the chancery office to drop some of my stuff off and sitting on my desk was the painting of St. Rose I had mailed! It arrived in perfect condition! So, I loaded it up and brought it with me to my new parish.

A few days later, I was downstairs, talking with the secretary and telling her a bit about my mission trip and finishing my studies and then coming home. As we were talking, I looked over at one of the shelves and I saw a small, white box with a clear lid. I bent over to see what it was and I saw that it was a reliquary. Curious of who it was I picked it up and saw the name "Santa Rosae, V. OP". It was St. Rose! As a plus, she was in there with St. Thérèse: the first rose of the new world, with the little flower, patron of missions. I told my secretary that this was amazing and a very strange coincidence and then she grabbed the relic, put it in my hand

and said, "I don't know what came over me, but you have to have that relic." I was shocked and didn't know if I could accept it, but she was adamant about me taking it. So now, I had a painting, a book, a Spanish prayer card, and a relic of this saint who seemed to be following me. The communion of saints was now being lived out for me in a new way. As a priest I could articulated the points of this belief, but I never fully knew how it took flesh. All that changed with St. Rose.

I soon began to reflect and saw how much Rose had been present in my life and I was not even aware. First, I grew up in a family that loved to garden. My mother had a nanny who was African American and she was a dear friend of my family, as Martin was to Rose. I experienced some hardships for my decision to be a priest since I entered seminary around 2006, when the first priest scandal broke out in America. During this time, there was much spiritual attack as well and I remember going through a time of scrupulosity preparing for seminary. Fasting and penance was something I saw that I had to do to be good enough for God's call. Reading the lives of various saints seemed to confirm that this was what I needed to do to get prepared for this jump. Without even being aware of it at the time, only with the grace of hindsight, I passed over the story of St. Rose and her journey with scrupulosity and penance, and I remember feeling not so lost when I read about a saint going down this path. Even then, Rose was a companion.

When I left for seminary, I attended the Pontifical College Josephinum in Columbus, Ohio. I arrived a few days earlier than needed and in the quiet, empty seminary I went to find a chapel that had the Blessed Sacrament in it. Since no students were there yet, they kept the Blessed Sacrament in a small chapel in the center of the seminary: St. Rose of Lima chapel. Throughout my four years at the Josephinum, this chapel was one of my favorites and one that always offered a quiet, simple opportunity to pray. I slowly began to learn about this saint who was a marvelous woman of prayer and a powerful penitent for the Lord. Also, during seminary I went on a mission trip down to South America to minister to some natives deep in the jungle. It was a truly formative experience in my priesthood, and an opportunity that I will forever cherish. When I left the location, they gave me a little boat from the village. I happened to go look at the boat when I was visiting my parent's house to remind myself what the name of that village was. Sure enough, inscribed in the boat was the name Santa Rosa, St. Rose.

In February of 2020, I went back to Peru to help the Missionaries of Jesus Word and Victim with conferences on Canon Law. It was a wonderful trip and I had shared with the sisters my experience with St. Rose. Needless to say, they were excited since they had a deep devotion to St. Rose. Talking with them, they loved the diminutive, calling me "*padrecito*" or "little father". So, I called them "*madrecitas*" for "little mothers" and I referred to my special saint as "*Santa Rosita*" or "Little St. Rose." Their founder, Frederick Kaiser, had called them to be *geneROSA, como un otraROSA,* "you must be generous as a new St. Rose"[78] After giving my retreat with them, I wanted to go back to where it had all started: St. Rose's sanctuary. It was a moving experience being back there since all this had happened. I saw all the places I had learned about and was able to read and hear about her spirit of prayer and penance where she lived it out. The days there were beautiful, sunny, and the flowers were all in bloom. I had carried with me a bunch of prayer intentions from people back home to pray for. I took them to Rose's well, where she had thrown the key to her penitential belt. Many people threw their prayer intention in there for St. Rose. I knelt by

78. This play on words does not make sense in English but basically the word generous contains the word *Rosa* and so he called them to be generous and live as another St. Rose.

the well in her beautiful garden and prayed and then threw my intentions in. After I did that, I looked over, and next to me was this precious little Peruvian girl praying with me. I asked her what her name was. She replied "Rosita" because she was born on St. Rose's feast day. It touched my heart and I knew it was another little wink from this saint.

Since then, St. Rose has followed me and my ministry in a very powerful way. She has offered me spiritual consolations, as well as challenged me many times. In several moments when I was faced with suffering, a challenging situation of life, or a need to submit in obedience, St. Rose was there telling me where to go and what to do. Also, on several occasions she convicted me of mistakes I was making, sins that I had grown accustomed to or that I had committed and forgotten about and offered me stern guidance. However, through all this, I felt love. I felt a great love from her, like I had never felt from a saint before.

During the 2020 Coronavirus outbreak, it was a very scary time for many people. No one was sure of what was going to happen or how to move forward. Hard decisions such as closing churches and shutting down the economy had to take place. It was hard, but amid the chaos, I could see fruit being born. In January, I had made some small prayer cards of St. Rose from the painting I had as well as from some of her writings. Since so much fear was coming from the spread of this virus, I wrote another prayer to St. Rose asking her intercession for us as she interceded for Lima to save it from pirates. If she could save Lima from pirates, she could save us from a virus!

A few other incidents stand out in my memories. The first was again during the time of the 2020 Covid pandemic. My mom was still going through dialysis, which was considered one of the more compromised conditions that was dangerous to catch the virus. On this account, I was being extra careful around her. I was being very cautious of keeping my distance and having all my precautions around her, especially since as a priest I had been around several people doing ministry. On one gathering, her blood pressure dropped and she was in danger of passing out. She laid out on the couch and begged for some water. Without thinking, I grabbed the nearest bottle of water and gave it to her. As she started to drink, I realized that it was the bottle I had been drinking from. Instantly my mind went into a panic: what if I had the virus? If my mom drank after me, she was going to get the virus and get sick and die! My mind was going through serious mental scruples and anxieties. I wish I had just grabbed a fresh bottle, why did I have to threaten my mom's life! So I did what I could: I prayed to St. Rose to protect her. I just continued to entrust my mom to her and pray for the best. The next morning at mass, I prayed for protection for my mom and began to get anxious again. I clearly heard a voice in my mind that I felt was St. Rose tell me: "Why are you worried? I will take care of your mom, just trust me!" I felt comforted, but I needed something more. I asked her: "St. Rose, please, just give me a sign my mom will be ok." When I got back to the office, I saw I had a letter and it was from *The Marian Sisters of Santa Rosa*! When I opened the letter, it was from a sister that I knew who said, "Father, I am so inspired to hear of your relationship with St. Rose. You need to heed her!" In those words, I had my confirmation.

Another moment took place when I was in my new parish in St. Joseph, Louisiana. After a particularly difficult day, I was feeling saddened about some challenging issues I was dealing with and some self-condemnation on my part. I just needed a little pick me up. I again turned to St. Rose and asked, "Rose, I know it's silly and I don't want to keep nagging, but I really would just love a small reminder that you are with me and you are still accompanying me. I would just like a little message from you." The next day I got a phone call. It was from a mom who was considering abortion but had decided to keep her child because of the generosity of some benefactors. It was so good to hear this mother being joyful and excited about having a child. "Yes, she is a sweet little girl", she said. "Her name is Milla Rose." "That's a beautiful name," I said, "Thank you for your little message." Thank you indeed for your reminder St. Rose.

Many times, I go into prayer and ask, why did she choose me? Why does she love me this much? I mean, I have so many faults and weaknesses. I'm not that extraordinary; I wear socks with sandals and like blizzards from Dairy Queen. The reason lay in the key virtue of saints: they love. Their greatest desire is for us to become saints as well and share in their joy. They share in the pure, agape love of God which is always looking for the good of the other and seeks union with the beloved. Rose really was the first time that I had encountered this kind of love from a saint, a very selfless and concerned love. I have failed so many times and found myself weak and unworthy of so great a gift. However, St. Rose loves not because of me earning it but just because that's what she is: a lover. She loves Jesus and those whom He died for, and the union of love she has with Jesus is so real that His love flows through her and all the saints. Someone loves not because the other person earns it, but rather because the lover has a surplus they wish to give.

Also, I read that right before she died, she mentioned to St. Martin de Porres that she had always wanted a priest as her brother. She had several brothers, but all wanted to be engaged in the world and married. She loved the Eucharist and wanted to have a close priest with whom she could share the joy of the Eucharist. Before St. Martin was able to find this seminarian, St. Rose died. In some ways, I feel I may have responded to her call: truly meeting her in seminary, coming from a large family, having experienced hardships in responding to a vocation, striving to overcome racial divisions, and meeting her in her country of Perú as a priest.

Regardless, I have taken her into my priesthood and I know that she has supported me greatly. Sometimes in prayer, I sense her kneeling next to me, other times I stop and ask her to share some of her virtues with me. I sense her with me very often and know that she is a dear and caring friend. Greater than any friend I've had before, Rose will never leave, she will not let distance or grudges put a wedge between us. It gives me great joy to know that there is someone at our home in heaven, waiting and excited to finally meet me face to face.

O glorious St. Rose of Lima, you who knew how to love Jesus with a kind and generous heart, teach us your virtues so that, following your example, we may enjoy your protection on earth and your companionship in heaven. Amen.

"St. Elizabeth Ann Seton"
Original Painting by Mary Frank

ST. ELIZABETH ANN SETON

As soon as my relationship with St. Rose began to grow and blossom into a real companionship, I realized I was not alone in this experience. As I shared the experience I was having with the communion of saints, I was met not with bafflement but belief. My former youth minister who had been a close friend of mine since high school, recounted a marvelous friendship and experience she had with St. Elizabeth Ann Seton. Indeed, the more I investigated this humble convert who was no more than five feet tall, the more I find a plenitude of virtues and graces to inspire as well as a magnanimous spirit in heaven.

Moreover, she is a simple reminder that holiness and union with God makes us more of who we really are, not less. Grace builds on nature and holiness on our personalities. We are called to the conformity of the one Christ, but the diversity of our lives manifests how God is all-present and his grace is all-embracing. Each saint's personality becomes in a sense the victim that is set on fire to be an offering to God. As they were on earth, so in a greater extent are they in heaven. Rather than being forsaken in heaven, our entire lives become absorbed in the offering of self which is the true life of heaven: love that brings forth life.

We can already share in this aspect of heaven through the giving birth to children: love that is shared and given between spouses is so real and full that it becomes another life. Motherhood is seen as a fruit of an overwhelming abundance of love and of self that it spills forth into self-gift—self-gift that is so real and life that is so generously shared that it becomes children. A fundamental principle is that goodness is a diffusion of itself, goodness grows as it is given. In the image of a mother this point is seen in a living icon. The life she receives within her is so loved and cared for that it burst forth as children without the mother losing any life of her own. The mother has an overabundance to share and even more is given to her by means of the sharing!

This reality is seen not only in the biological life, but even more in the spiritual. A biological mother is limited to the biological life shared and formed with her husband and the children born of their flesh. However, when the same principle of love and self-gift is focused on the spiritual life, and the spiritual mother becomes a vessel of forming and nurturing the spiritual life, then her children are not limited to biological births or relations but are all those for whom she has a care and concern and wishes to pour herself out for. Mother Seton is the quintessential mother in that she lived as a mother fully for her children and desired their material and spiritual well-being. Moreover, her great possession of goodness and love flowed over onto the poor children she wished to educate and sanctify. Her spiritual family and spiritual motherhood grew as her love and concern for more children grew. She cared for the children of America and began to spread the gospel to all these spiritual children of hers.

Mother Seton also shares something with St. Rose: she is the first native-born citizen of North America to be canonized. Fresh from the horrible war of the American Revolution, the land of America needed a mother's care. She was born only two years before the Declaration of Independence was signed and grew up during some of the worst battles of the Revolution. In this time of America's emancipation God saw the need to regrow faith in a new land. Separated from the Old World, God used the love of a mother and the zeal of a saint to firmly plant the faith in this new world that, as many of us know very well, is in much need of new foundations upon God and His teaching. The will of God also provided for Mother Seton to plant a religious order that could continue the work of education and catechism, long after she passed and America grew.

Not necessarily one for extraordinary signs or wonders, Mother Seton did however live out what would become the best of the American spirit. She lived a very down to earth, real life, practical application of the Lord's will. She had a deep love for Jesus in the Eucharist, but she did not need visions or locutions to grow in holiness. She showed how the gifts of God's mystical experiences are distinct from the act of becoming holy which only needs us to say "yes" to what God wishes to do in us. She became a saint in and through the life God gave to her. She showed the endurance and spirit of adventure that marked the first pioneers in the new world of the Americas and showed a resourcefulness that made great things from even the little that she had.

Mother Seton's decision to convert to Catholicism required the fiercest courage. In today's time this decision may seem mild, but we must remember the climate of America during her era. The New America was not only a wild and strange land, but it was hostile. It has been said that one of the great reasons for the French and Indian War in America was the fact that French Catholics were given equal rights. Many of the people who came to settle in America were Puritan protestants who were very opposed to the Catholic Church. Elizabeth's family was a staunch group of Huguenots. The presence of Catholics in America was small and unwelcome. Becoming Catholic almost automatically brought about separation from her family and friends and even made her lose much of the work that she was currently performing in schools. Parents did not want to send their kids to a school taught by a Catholic, and she was put on the fringe of society. She did not care. Elizabeth had come to know Jesus' love in the Eucharist and desired it more than anything. It was this heroic act of courage that won her the grace to stay firm in all the difficulties to come later.

Mother Seton reminds us that even living in the common, everyday life of a mother and house worker, we are called not only to contemplation, but to magnanimity. Contemplation is the way we consider, at every moment and in every place, the presence of God. Sometimes, those who live active lives and work, can have a beautiful gift of contemplating in that they are immersed in the creative world and the creative act and can see through them to the Creator.

Magnanimity is the virtue of great spirit. It always means that, we hope and aspire for greatness and to be and do the greatest we can. It is not limited to the actions we perform, but it is the spirit we place in everything. When one sees their tasks and duties as a great and awesome service to the Lord, not because it seems appealing but purely because it is His will for us, that is magnanimity. Elizabeth Ann Seton certainly encapsulated this virtue as she journeyed from task to task, motivation to motivation. She responded to her loss with devotion to the Lord, and He is never outdone in generosity.

It was not by sword or brute strength but by her love and motherhood that Elizabeth triumphed over this world. Even as a saint, she is still called Mother Seton. She was not looking for an extraordinary life; she simply followed the path the Lord had set before her. She accepted the hardships and sufferings, she accepted the joys and the opportunities of love. She let no thing or moment become an obstacle to her seeking the Lord. Every little moment and every emotion of hers became absorbed into the offering of herself to the Lord.

Biography of St. Elizabeth Ann Seton

by Jeanette Adams

It is often easy to breeze through the biography of any saint in which their most challenging moments may be condensed into one or two brief paragraphs. When I first discovered St. Elizabeth Ann Seton's story several years ago, I found myself drawn to know the details of her struggle, how she felt, how she responded. In other words, did this saint have moments of fear and doubt just like I do?

Elizabeth Ann Bayley was born on August 28, 1774 to parents who were part of high society New York. Her mother passed away when Elizabeth was only three years old. Mr. Bayley prioritized his daughter's education. She was brought up as a proper young lady in the Episcopal Church and married into a prominent family at the age of nineteen. Along with her husband, William Seton, and their five children, Elizabeth lived on Wall Street in the late 1700's. Great hardship fell upon their family business with the loss of the Seton fleet and then the grave illness of her husband. The once successful Seton family business faced bankruptcy. In an effort to treat William's deteriorating health, doctors advised that Mr. Seton travel to Italy and stay with friends there where the air quality would be more optimal.

This is the moment where I envision young Elizabeth at the New York port, boarding a ship with her ill husband and oldest daughter, who was only eight years old at the time. She left behind her four younger children. I can only imagine how heavy her heart must have felt, how uncertain of what was to come, yet her diaries depict a woman of great faith. She is recounted to have led prayer meetings and to have been an encouragement to other travelers. One biography describes her jumping rope with her daughter to keep warm on cold nights.

She accompanied her dying husband on a long journey

across the Atlantic, only to be by his side when he passed away while in Italian quarantine. After William's death, Elizabeth and her daughter spent time with their Italian family friends, the wealthy Filicchi family. Adorned in a widow's cap and traditional black attire, she experienced Catholicism for the first time there in Italy. The Filicchi family had a private chapel on their property. Elizabeth was drawn to the faith and devotion of those who prayed there and eventually came to know the true presence of Christ in the Eucharist.

Upon returning to America, she began a small school and thus earned income to support her family. As her faith continued to grow, Elizabeth made the life-changing decision to convert to Catholicism. Due to a social climate which looked down on Catholics, her students withdrew from her school, her family rejected her, and her hardships grew. Nonetheless, on March 25, 1805 she and her children received their First Communion. Soon God's providence would make itself known.

Antonito Filicchi arranged with the local Bishop to have Elizabeth's sons enrolled at Georgetown, a fine school. This connection furthermore led to the Bishop's request that she establish a new order of sisters using the Daughters of Charity as a model. The Bishop envisioned a means of educating young Catholics. Mother Seton agreed under the conditions that she could continue to care for her own children and that a free education would be offered to those who couldn't otherwise afford it.

She traveled three days with her children and the first Sisters of Charity to their new home in Emmitsburg, Maryland. There the group would persevere through harsh winters and meek provisions before gaining the respect and support of the local community. Eventually, they were able to build more suitable housing complete with a schoolhouse and chapel. The young order soon began to flourish as they gained more sisters and pupils.

Despite this progress, Mother Seton would face deep heartache through the loss of two daughters to consumption (tuberculosis), the same illness which had taken her husband. She faced the reality that her children had also traded their lavish lifestyle for the hardships she too faced. She continued to trust in what she coined "the will," referring to the will of God. She placed the utmost trust in God's will and providence. One reward of her deep faith was the conversion of her son William to a deep faith in God. He returned to her as an adult to proclaim that he too had developed a great faith inspired by hers.

The influence of the Sisters of Charity continued to spread as their congregation was asked to teach in numerous cities throughout the growing United States. Mother Seton endowed her sisters with the principles to "discipline with love" and to view "education as an inheritance." She taught young and old Catholics alike to live as "Children of the Church."

In September 1975 she was canonized a saint in the Catholic Church with the many ministries of the Sisters of Charity being counted as the fourth and final necessary miracle.[79] It is through these ministries which continue to feed the poor, care for the elderly, and educate many that she continues her mission as Mother Seton to this day.

What are you facing? Has God asked something of you that you'd rather not accept? Does it seem that He has more faith in you than you have in yourself? Imagine yourself in the shoes of Mother Seton. She became foundress of the Sisters of Charity, began the parochial school system, and much much more. Reflecting on Seton's story, I'm reminded

---

79. Originally, the canonization process required several miracles through the Servant of God's intercession. The exact number was based on if they were a martyr or not, if they had witnesses to their life, if they died recently, and so on. This numeration was eventually removed to not create more barriers or confusion to the canonization process.

that we never know what He has in store for us on the other side of the challenges we face. Often, as seen in the life of Elizabeth Ann Seton, He is calling us to a deeper a holiness, to a "YES" so firmly rooted in Him that we will follow where He leads, trusting that He is holding us the palm of His hand, trusting that our sufferings are a part of a far greater plan. We must resolve as Mother Seton did that "In all circumstances there is the mysterious potential for grace."

Friends of St. Elizabeth Ann Seton

by Jeanette Adams

"Be but faithful to God with your whole heart, and never fear. He will support, direct, console, and finally crown your dearest Hope." – St Elizabeth Ann Seton

In the summer of 2013, my husband and I, along with our five young children, visited an order of religious sisters who are very dear friends of ours. We went with the intention of assisting in the renovation of several retreat houses on their property. While my husband's carpentry skills and my sons' enthusiasm to serve were very fruitful, I found myself struggling with the fact that I had traveled nearly twelve hours to do nearly the same daily routine as I would have done at home. I had gone with the intent to serve in an extraordinary way and yet found myself simply tending to the needs of my youngest children. At the time, I saw only superficial meaning in these ordinary tasks… until Seton intervened.

One afternoon, while the other members of my family worked at replacing rotten boards and painting door frames, I returned to settle my two youngest children for their afternoon naps. Near the rocking chair was a shelf filled with various spiritual writings. A small book entitled Seton caught my eye. As I read through its pages about the life of a privileged young woman who became the first American-born Catholic saint, I couldn't help but grow overwhelmingly intrigued by her story. This mother of five, who was widowed at an early age, went on to establish the Sisters of Charity, begin the parochial school system, and set the foundation for many orphanages and hospitals. I was fascinated by her perseverance, her passion, and her simplicity. Being educated as a social worker and, at the time, myself also a mother of five, I immediately related to many components of both her domestic and ministry work.

That evening I read for hours about the life and works of St. Elizabeth Ann Seton. Her story is beautifully narrated through her journal entries and correspondence with family members. It felt surreal to read her own words. I felt an instant connection with Elizabeth Bailey Seton. Her life exemplified trust in the Lord, in "the will" as she'd say. She was a remarkable example of a mother, who prioritized teaching the faith and holy virtue to her children, as well as a woman who pushed passed her own fears to serve God and His people. Mother Seton once said, "In all circumstance there is a mysterious potential for grace." Her life reflects this truth beautifully.

As a young mom, I wondered "How did she care for her children while also building such an impressive ministry? Did she have some secret to 'doing it all?'" As I continued to study her life, two things began to stand out to me in these regards. Frist, when asked to be the foundress of a new order, her first thought was her children. Before proceeding with the needs of the ministry, she had set in place means of proper education and care for her children. Her two sons, William and Richard, were secured spots at a prestigious boarding school, and she was assured that her daughters, Annina, Catherine, and Rebecca, would be able to live, work, and play alongside Mother Seton, thus joining in her mission. Also, her journals give evidence to the intimate friendships and support system which Elizabeth Seton not only valued but leaned on. The Filicchi family, who had been instrumental in her conversion to Catholicism, her sisters-in-law, and her longtime confessor each played significant roles in supporting Seton in her role as a biological mother, as well as a spiritual mother.

Before returning home from our visit to the convent, I told my husband that I'd like to get a medal with Mother Seton's image on it as a reminder of my new friend and what she had taught me. On our last day, Sr. Philip, unaware of my recent connection to Seton, handed me a small box. Inside was a medal with St. Elizabeth Anne Seton's profile imprinted on it. God is so good!

Several months later, I passed by a church on the outskirts of town. I had been inside it once before nearly two years prior, following an appointment which confirmed my fifth pregnancy. My fourth child had been born prematurely and had spent an extended time in the hospital and under the care of specialists. The news of another pregnancy was rout with feelings of concern and uncertainty, so I turned to prayer. I had decided that particular afternoon to take the long way home as I processed my feelings. I then came upon this church and decided to go in and pray. In the back pew I found a card with the unabridged serenity prayer written on it. The words I read then would bring me peace throughout the following nine months. "Trusting that He will make all things right if I surrender to His Will." I would eventually realize that I read this prayer of surrender to His will, "the will" that Seton so often spoke of, while taking solace that day in the parish of St. Elizabeth Ann Seton.

Have you ever met a friend at just the right moment in your life? A friend who seemed to understand your circumstance? A friend who encouraged you by their life to persevere in faith? Seton was just that friend for me. She continues to be an inspiration and motivation in my role as mother and in all the ways that I minister to others.

Prior to this experience, I viewed the saints as holy men and women who had reached their final reward and were resting at the feet of Jesus. Seton has taught me that these holy disciples are still very much at work gathering souls for the Kingdom of God. She also confirmed for me the importance of godly friendships and accepting the gifts of others as ways through which the Lord allows for His work to be accomplished in and through you. The ministry of Seton, a young widowed mother of five, trusted in the graces sent to her through others and in her personal relationship with God. Her strength didn't come on her own accord but rather from the community and faith in which she rooted herself and her family. The Sisters of Charity continue to produce beautiful fruit as a result of Seton's life. Hospitals, schools, and orphanages have been established throughout the United States, Canada, and Bermuda as a result of their mission. Mother Seton's last words to her Sisters, on January 4, 1861, sum up the heart of their ministry: "Be children of the Church."

"Perseverance is a great grace – to go on gaining and advancing every day, we must be resolute, and bear and suffer what our blessed forerunners did." – St. Elizabeth Ann Seton

Katherine Ocello

It all started back when I was in seventh grade and getting ready for my confirmation. We were instructed to choose a saint for our confirmation name, to be our patron. I began researching saints—paying more attention to the names I thought were pretty than their lives and experiences. I had heard of St. Elizabeth Ann Seton before, I liked her name, and I read she was a patron saint of homemakers (#goals), so I chose her. I liked that she was married and had a big family; I always felt that would be my vocation. Basically, I thought she was a cool enough lady to take on her name for my confirmation. There was a brief period where I thought of switching to St. Cecilia because I also loved her name and I really liked that she was the patron saint of music and singing. Looking back, this is hilarious to me because at the time (ripe old age of 12), I thought I was musical. It turns out I'm not musical at all. At the very last minute I settled on St. Elizabeth Ann Seton as my confirmation saint for no particular reason at all.

Fast forward to my junior year of high school. My parents and I had gone on several college tours in a very short amount of time, and I was exhausted. Seton Hall University was the very last college we were scheduled to tour. I told my parents I knew I wasn't going to go there anyway, so maybe we should skip this one. They said that was fine, we didn't need to go to Seton Hall. It was clear to me they were just as tired as I was of meandering through campuses with musty dorm rooms and classrooms that were empty for the summer. Oddly enough, at the last minute I told them I felt like we should go to see Seton Hall after all. I had a strong feeling that I should give it a fair shot. We toured the campus and everything seemed fine to me. We walked past similar musty dorm rooms, decently sized classrooms, an occupational therapy program I was interested in, and a nice library. The very last stop on our tour was the Chapel of the Immaculate Conception, the church on campus. Our tour guide asked if we'd like to go inside for a minute and we said yes. I walked through the large wooden door and into the chapel, which has been beautifully restored to depict the Book of Revelation. We knelt to pray, and as I did I felt an overwhelming sense that I needed to attend Seton Hall University. Something was telling me, this was where I was supposed to be. It's a little crazy to choose a college based solely on a feeling you had while in the school's chapel, but that's what I did. Luckily, God is in the details and Seton Hall also happened to be one of the only schools I applied to that had the degree in occupational therapy I would end up wanting to pursue.

It wasn't until another two years later when I began my freshmen year at Seton Hall, that I finally made the connection that Seton Hall University is named for St. Elizabeth Ann Seton. I know! How could I miss that? Frankly, I don't know how I never made the connection before, and I don't know how I missed the statue of her in the chapel, but I was blissfully ignorant that I was attending the college inspired by the patron saint that I had chosen all those years before. I didn't live on campus during college, so I didn't make friends as quickly as everyone else freshmen year. Instead, I was saving money and living with my grandparents and great uncle who coincidentally lived down the street from Seton Hall. I loved living with them, but it didn't exactly give me the "college experience" I saw everyone around me chasing. I figured I would use my time to study and to delve deeper into my faith until I made friends outside of the classroom. In those first few weeks of college St. Elizabeth Ann Seton was my closest friend. I went to the chapel each morning to pray and I would ask St. Elizabeth Ann Seton to intercede for me. I asked her to intercede for my relationship with a boy from high school that I thought could really be something, but that I was nervous about making work while at separate universities. I asked her to intercede for my education and future career, that I would be on the path God had planned for me. I asked her to intercede that I make friends, real ones, soon. I asked her to intercede for me to grow in my faith, trust in the Lord, and to show me why she brought me to this school.

It didn't take long before I felt more confident in my relationship, I was doing well in my classes, and I had joined Saint Paul's Outreach on campus. Through this community-based organization in campus ministry I made more Christ-centered friendships than I thought possible and developed a significantly closer relationship with the Lord. All this time, I had continued to ask St. Elizabeth Ann Seton to intercede for me. During the next few months and years of college, I learned of more connections between me and the patron saint that I had half-heartedly chose. St. Elizabeth Ann Seton was married, though her husband died of tuberculosis. She was a mother of 5, worked in education, and was the first American-born saint. If you know me, you know that last one really thrilled me most of all! As I learned more about her, I realized just how many connections we shared. I felt that she was my friend, my sister in Christ, who was rooting for me from Heaven and interceding for me all along.

Years later, I was praying in the chapel at Seton Hall University for the last time as a student, this time a graduate student in my final year of occupational therapy school. I wholeheartedly thanked St. Elizabeth for bringing me here. I thought of all that had happened since that first time I prayed here, and I began to cry tears of joy. I thought of the beautiful Christ-centered friendships that I developed here that I knew would be lifelong. I thought of Saint Paul's Outreach, which really did bring my faith to life during my college years—and showed me how to live in communion with the Lord and with others. I thought of the unique experience I had of living with my elderly grandparents and uncle who lived nearby, that I knew I would be eternally grateful for. I thought about how close I was to earning my degree and beginning my career as an occupational therapist. Lastly, I thought about that same high school boyfriend I prayed about years ago. He had proposed to me in that very chapel just days before, and was now my fiancé. Tears streamed down my face as I thanked the Lord for every single one of these blessings and for answering all of my prayers.

In that moment, I thanked St. Elizabeth Ann Seton for choosing me—for being so much more than a confirmation name, and for showing me exactly why she brought me here.

O God, who crowned with the gift of true faith
Saint Elizabeth Ann Seton's burning zeal to find you,
grant by her intercession and example
that we may always seek you with diligent love
and find you in daily service with sincere faith.
Amen.

"St. Philip Neri"
Original Painting by Mary Frank

ST. PHILIP NERI

In Stephen King's famous novel *Salem's Lot,* the story centers on a sleepy town in Maine that is plagued by vampires. A small band of resistance joins together and decides to fight back. They know that above all they need to enlist the help of the local Catholic priest, Fr. Donald Callahan. When first introduced to the proposed mission, Fr. Callaghan is hesitant; not out of fear of the enemy before him, but out of reverence for the Church behind him. As he notes, "The Church is more than a bundle of ideals. . . . The Church is a force, and one does not set a force in motion lightly." The quote from this fictional novel touched on something very powerful: The Church, the body of Christ, is not just the sum of various people's common beliefs. It is more than just the manifestation of people's hopes and desires, it is the continuation of the saving power of God in this world. One who truly believes the faith of the Church and puts themselves in communion with the Church, is caught up in the momentum that was set in play by Jesus and has been gaining force over centuries. The saints, who not only are formed by the Church but also help form the Church, recognized this great power, and surrendered to its movement. They were moved by the awesome power of Jesus still at work in the world through the Church, and then became agents of that saving force in the rest of the world. Having been moved by the force, they in turn moved the world not with their own energy, but that of Jesus.

Philip Neri was a true force of reform in the world he lived in. However, he was not a force in the sense of dominion and control, but a force fueled by love and guided by the view of heaven. Seeing the great decay falling on the world, Philip was motivated in the face of a very trying time in the history of the world. Such was the time of the 1500s. This was the period of the Renaissance, literally the "rebirth." It was an attempt to go back to the world of the Roman Empire when great achievements and ideas were being born. People were trying to reclaim a world they felt was lost. It was a time of great extremes. Italy was going through a flowering of great art and architecture, while the rest of the world was in chaos. France and England had just ended the Hundred Years' War (which actually was longer than one hundred years), an enormous slaughter that took place between England and the Eldest Daughter of the Church, i.e., France. It was a true massacre that left not only physical but mental and spiritual carnage across the north of Europe.

Further, in 1453, the same year as the end of the Hundred Years' War, Constantinople, the second Rome and the kingdom of Christendom in the East was taken over by the Muslims in the Ottoman Empire. This event was a terrible blow; it essentially meant an end of the Crusades; the Holy Land was lost, as well as the eastern half of the Christian world. Hence, all that was left now was Europe. It is no wonder that in 1492, attempts were made to go west to try and find the New World.

With the east cut off and the north in shambles, it seemed that it was up to the flowering of Italy to save the world. This is man's weakness: in the face of disaster, he wishes to place himself in the center, while going beyond himself and his limits. The physical and spiritual are not separated, so when there is much physical and visible disruption, it can weigh on the mind, heart, and soul of the Church. Progress and advancement had become principal in man's mind. He did not want to look at his wounds. Man had been hurt so many times that his own wounds and abuse of power had scarred the heart of the men of faith. All the people who were considered followers of Christ were now showing themselves to be nothing like their Savior. It was a time of huge swings and shifts in the world. Man was again and again trying to reclaim a kingdom on earth that had been seen in its golden age in the Roman Empire and gilded with the coming of Christianity. However, one thing kept getting in man's way: man himself. There was indeed need for change, but not where man was looking for it.

To top all this chaos, we have Martin Luther rising during this period. We can see how much of this climate would weigh on him as he sought a solution to the world's problems, as well as his own personal ones. In 1517, on a memorable Halloween night, Martin sent his 95 theses of rejection to the local bishop, as well as post it on the door of the Cathedral.

In the city of Florence, which was the heart of the Renaissance, a new birth was truly taking place. On July 22, the feast of St. Mary Magdalene, Philip was born to the Neri family. Florence was the center of the new Renaissance, and the new growth of ideas was constantly springing up. Not everything that springs up is good; weeds can also grow. Much licentiousness and sensuality were to be found, as people tried to bury themselves in the pleasures they could build up in this world.

One great voice began to cry out against the decay of the world: Girolamo Savonarola. He was a famous preacher who went throughout Italy and preached reform and conversion and spoke against the corruption of the times. He drew large crowds and was known for preaching boldly and publicly in the squares of towns or a full house. As popular as he was and even though he had much success, his grounding was in building an earthly kingdom of peace and he sided with many of the rulers of this world. Philip was in many ways not only inspired by Savonarola but compared to him. The great underlying difference was that Philip's root and goal was heaven. He did not want to reform this world in its own image but wanted to bring a greater preference for heaven in the hearts of all and turn their gazes back to God. This turning would naturally bring a greater reform in the world, but it also kept Philip plugged into the source of the greatest reform and the most unstoppable force ever: the resurrection of Jesus.

On May 23, 1493, Savonarola was hung in the square of the center of the city of Florence. Philip's parents would most probably have been there to lament and hope that the zeal that was in this preacher could come back. Martin Luther would erroneously hail him as a forerunner of the Reformation. Such was the world into which Philip was born, but also it was for such a world that he was born.

Philip was a good boy. He was nicknamed *Pippo Buono* or "good Philip" because of his kindness and good behavior, especially with his sisters. As a young boy, he enjoyed going to church, praying before the altar, and listening to the sermons. He particularly loved the Church of All Saints in Florence where he would go to listen to one of the Humiliati brothers, a religious congregation in Florence. His early life was humble, and he acquired a very simple heart in the midst of a world and society of Renaissance excess

At the age of eleven, he continued to darken the doors of the church, but something else caught the attention of the Florentines. While Philip was spending his time praying, imperial troops were marching on Rome. The enraged troops of Charles the fifth, the Holy Roman Emperor, did not receive payment for their services and saw the Papal States (which included Rome) as an easy target to pillage and receive their just deserts. These mutinied soldiers, allies of Charles the fifth were on their way to destroy Rome and overthrow the Pope. In addition, the new Protestant Reformation was growing in supporters, and many of the enemies of Rome were going not only for political gain, but specifically with an axe to grind against the Pope.

Young Philp saw much of the revolting and rebellion. He may have been in church praying and witnessed the holy pastor go and chide the soldiers to leave them at peace. Worst of all, Philip heard the news of the horrible events that took place in Rome: the Pope was placed under house arrest in Castel San Angelo, churches and shrines pillaged and destroyed, and the flourishing city, the center of the Catholic world, reduced to only ten thousand inhabitants after thousands were killed and injured in battle and many more fell victim to disease and plague. Young Philip's heart was pained.

In the year 1531, young Philip made one of the pivotal decisions of his life: to go to Rome. Philip's father intended for Philip to study and become a prosperous man, but God had other plans. Philip, already so close to God's heart, would become a force of revival in the broken world of Rome. Young Philip bid his homeland of Florence farewell and set off for Rome: from this point onward, he would never leave Rome.

The Rome he was entering was a very different Rome than had been seen in the past. It was morally corrupt, although it had seen its share of prophets, saints, and even apostles; it had just been beaten down as low as could be by the sacking of Rome, with its population decrease, its hospitals full, and its churches in ruin. People did not want a saint.

Philip spent most of his time in study and prayer. He studied the philosophy of the time that was formed by great thinkers such as Thomas Aquinas and Bonaventure and then at night he would spend long vigils in prayer. He traveled around the city, visiting the different churches and being exposed to the vile sins of the time. His heart hurt to see the sins of the people and he often had to turn away to keep himself pure. He lived in a small room and normally only ate one meal a day.

At the onset of his time in Rome, he had an experience that would soon mark the rest of his life in Rome. He was walking through the streets one day as he normally did, being a young, joyful adolescent about eighteen years old. He passed another group of boys of around the same age: rough, unkempt, but worst of all, untamed in their passions. The accounts do not say exactly what they were doing, but they were surely engaging in some sexually explicit conversation or lustful activity. Philip happened to be passing by and these boys, not content with their own sin, wanted to drag him into it. Philip tried to go by unnoticed, but they pursued him, caught up to him, and surrounded him. Like bullies on a playground, they wanted to show him who was boss. They started with the teasing invitation, then the rough assaults. Philip just wanted to move on and go on his way. Saving his soul from sin in that moment was what mattered most. But they wouldn't let him go, they were going to make him give in. It would satisfy their desire for power. Then it occurred to him: he would only be able to save his soul by also saving theirs. Instead of running and only preserving his soul, he could convert them and save many more. As one of the most accurate accounts mentions:

> But suddenly it occurred to him that the word of God, which is keener than a two-edged sword, has a great influence in softening the hearts of wicked men. He launched into them then, with a sermon about divine matters, and about the vileness of sin, and so enlightened their minds that the word of God had the effect of setting them free from all temptations of that sort, and quite put them off the sin they had planned, more than that, it turned them into reformed characters. [80]

80. Antonio Gallonio, *The Life of Saint Philip Neri*, trans. Jerome Bertram (San Francisco: Ignatius Press, 2005), 5.

Philip made lemonade out of lemons. He used the devil's opportunity against him. These men that had been put into his life to tempt him, he in turn stepped in to convert. Such is the marvelous power of God's grace that, if we cooperate, can transform these moments into grace. "Those who came to entrap him were themselves trapped,"[80] was indeed true. Not only had he saved his soul, but that of others. This then would spark an idea in his heart: rather than just going through this city, trying to dodge and avoid sin and temptation, he could convert this city, and remove temptation! That would be the greatest and most sure way to save his soul and the souls of others. This is what would make him the great apostle we know him as.

This young layman began a reform that many others had tried and failed. He fulfilled Christ's call to love as He loved, to be the sower of seed, to seek the lost sheep. Philp lived out what 500 years later the Vatican II council would call the "sanctification of the temporal order." This great mission, which belongs primarily to the laity, is to imbue the common affairs and activities of the world as leaven in the dough.

> The laity must take up the renewal of the temporal order as their own special obligation. Led by the light of the Gospel and the mind of the Church and motivated by Christian charity, they must act directly and in a definite way in the temporal sphere. As citizens they must cooperate with other citizens with their own particular skill and on their own responsibility. Everywhere and in all things they must seek the justice of God's kingdom.

---

81. Gallonio, 5.

> The temporal order must be renewed in such a way that, without detriment to its own proper laws, it may be brought into conformity with the higher principles of the Christian life and adapted to the shifting circumstances of time, place, and peoples. Preeminent among the works of this type of apostolate is that of Christian social action which the sacred synod desires to see extended to the whole temporal sphere, including culture. [82]

Philip saw this not as an obligation, but a passion. The force of love had been set in motion and the power of Christ's thirst for renewal in His broken members filled Philip's bones. He started off small but in the most important place: the heart of each man he encountered. He met people on the street with great joy and asked his famous question, "So, when shall we start doing good?" He encountered people right where they were and he had a power of leading every conversation, no matter how ordinary or mundane, back to God. He found it wasn't in running from the world, but in embracing it that he saved the world. His speech was always of a joyful, attractive demeanor. He was often making jokes and smiling but then always drawing it back to God. This was how he was able to sanctify the temporal order, by going amid his work and past time, imbuing it with a human element that is itself a reflection of God. He showed what true humanism is in that the human person is a masterpiece because it is in God's image and likeness. Philip used his humanity to draw man back to God. He accepted the challenge right where God placed him, in the heart of Rome.

---

82. *Apostolicam Actuositatem, Decree on the Apostolate of the Laity.* Vatican II, (Vatican City, 1965).

He spent entire nights in prayer, asking for the conversion of the city. He was small and nothing in the face of this Eternal City, but God was ever more powerful than both. It was God, more than the task at hand, that placed the greatest burden on him: the bürden of love. The love of heaven and the love of others.

One of the great gifts that Philip was able to take from Rome was the spiritual treasures of the churches that had been consecrated by years of prayer and the many saints who had passed through them. He spent long hours in these churches, praying and begging God for grace but also in great and humble admiration of the good God. His deep love and connection with the city of Rome and the great churches of the Catholic Faith, which were the consecrated meeting place of heaven and earth, kept Philip plugged into that great force of the Church that had pushed forth great saints for centuries in that city. The blood of martyrs had saturated the ground of Rome, the prayers of monks had filled the air, the writings of scholars had filled the libraries. Now Philip stood on top of that great mountain built by so many and took sanctuary in the walls of Rome's holy sanctuaries. Among these were the famous Basilicas of St. Peter on Vatican Hill, St. Paul, St. Sebastian the martyr, St. Lawrence outside the walls St. John Lateran, the Cathedral of Rome, the Church of *Santa Croce in Gerusalemme,* and finally Mary Major.

These seven sacred churches had for years been places of great pilgrimage and prayer, filled with indulgences to those who made this almost twenty-mile walk. However, in Philip's day, he made it alone. He visited these seven churches almost every day, spending time on these journeys praying and contemplating the great things God had done and would do in this city. The catacombs were a favorite place of his to pray. These old underground tombs of the Christians offered a place for meditating on the souls who had consecrated that location with their blood, as well as a place of silence, far from the center of the city. As much as he enjoyed being around people to love them and serve them, Philip cherished his alone time. In the silence he found his God.

Once however, while making the pilgrimage, Philip heard footsteps. Actually, it sounded like hooves. Not just one, but three persons. It didn't take long for Philip to know who it was. The ancient enemy of all Christians: the devil. He was with two other demons, seeming to block his way on the road. They began to taunt him, to scream at him, to tempt him. How could young Philip overcome such an ancient and powerful enemy? The answer was simple: don't let him in. The devil is a legalistic spirit and respects territory. He can only enter in where someone lets him. Padre Pio once said that the devil is a dog on a long chain, he can only attack if you get close. The only door the devil can use to enter us is our will, by our accepting some invitation, by some willful submission of ours. Hence, sin is the worst and gravest way to entangle ourselves with the devil because we have chosen to put ourselves in the doorway of the devil. However, if we don't, the devil can't come near us. So too, though these demons screamed and hollered at Philip, he was undisturbed and continued his way to the church to pray.

As the catacombs were one of his favorite places to pray, it was here that the Lord gave him one of the greatest graces of his or any saint's life. Philip was in the habit of praying every day to the Holy Spirit. He asked for the fire of the Spirit to fill him as he did the apostles and that he too may have the zeal of the apostles. Indeed, the Lord always answers a request like this! It was late in the evening, deep in the heart of the catacombs of St. Sebastian on the vigil of Pentecost in 1544. Philip was only 29 at this time and still felt he needed to do so much more for God. Suddenly, he looked up from kneeling and there, in the air above him was a large ball of fire! It suddenly rushed into his mouth and down into his chest and entered his heart. An immense force gripped

Philip from within. It was not only spiritual but physical. It was a burning, a great fire and heat that had entered his soul and his body. He was being filled with the love of God and the power of the Holy Spirit. Philip described it as "a violent onrushing of the divine Spirit" and said that "his nature was utterly unable to bear it."[83] It was a physically painful experience, yet not out of agony. Philip felt that if the Lord did not stop he would die of love! This event was not a simply emotional, sensual experience, but had a truly tangible and discernable effect:

> So that he might be preserved longer for the salvation of so many, the Lord in his kindness enlarged the space around his heart in a wonderful way, so that it could beat more freely; two of the ribs on his left side, specifically the fourth and fifth, were broken and expanded outwards to the width of a fist or slightly more. This break was in the front of his chest, where the rib joins onto the cartilage. From that moment on, for more than fifty years, his heart used to palpitate violently, to a greater or lesser extent as soon as he was mentally attentive of God, so that not only his whole body shook, but even the bench or whatever he was sitting on shook during his prayer as in an earthquake.[84]

God filled Philip with the fire of the Holy Spirit and spiritually enlarged his heart to love others. This event was so real and true that it had a physical manifestation in his body:

---

83. Gallonio, *Saint Philip Neri*, 17.
84. Gallonio, 17.

the enlarging of his heart to the point of it cracking his ribs and giving him a heart palpitation so great that vibrations were felt. The physical body of Philip truly exemplified what St. Paul says when he declared our bodies to be a temple of the Holy Spirit. Philip Neri exemplified this Christian reality to the most dramatic and vivacious degree possible.

After this event, Philip could hardly keep up with the zeal he had for winning over souls. No place was off-limits to him. He went into the marketplace, into the streets, into the schools and tried to win more and more people over to Jesus. Every person, be they poor or rich, needed to know God's love. Although he regularly performed penance, he quickly set them aside if they any way meant the scandalizing or offending of someone who could come to the faith.

Philip was also accustomed to visiting the hospitals. Because of the sacking of Rome, so much injury and disease was brought into the city. Hospitals had mostly become a housing shelter for the dying, nursing care was extremely poor, and care of the soul and spiritual needs were neglected. Philip would come in with a smile on his face and rally a spirit of courage within the sick. He used his humor and wit to break the ice and bring a spirit of joy into the room, then he pointed their hearts to heaven and told of the hope in store, that not even their suffering could take away the treasure prepared for them. He was able to win over many souls who thought their pain was simply meaningless.

During this ministry in the hospitals, a young man came under his tutelage who had a haunting past. He had lost his mother when he was young and so he and his father traveled as soldiers for most of his life. They loved to gamble and, on several occasions, had been kicked out of the service for the feuds they caused from gambling and losing. They became vagabonds and eventually, the father passed away. This young man had just spent the last few years of his life hopping from place to place, gambling, and losing everything. He finally heard that he may be able to clean up his life by coming and working as an assistant in the hospital. His name was Camillus. He was broken and lost, but the Lord had great things planned for him. He soon discovered a love and passion for service to the poor that surpassed anything he had done before. Philip saw that he had potential but needed guidance. Philip offered what he could and told this young man to stay planted at St. Jerome's hospital. Camillus found himself not wanting to be limited only there but desired to serve all the dying. This became his great passion and served as the foundation for what became the Red Cross and the Camillites.

Philip's zeal and energy continued to attract much attention from the other laborers in the vineyard who were striving to win over souls. He soon decided to form the Confraternity of the Holy Trinity, which was a group of lay men and women who regularly joined together in prayer, confession, and sermons and then offered an open house ministry to the poor, the sick, and the alien travelers. This was a powerful leadership role Philip took on to continue to draw people to the Lord and to show forth his power of prayer and preaching. Many people were attracted by the zeal of Philip's preaching but even more by the charity that he showed to others. Hundreds of people returned to the practice of the faith, dozens were confessing sins they had not confessed in years, indifferent people were being set on fire with zeal, and zealous people were striving to become saints. This soon led many people to join his companionship.

Philip understood that the call of holiness was not identical with a vocation to priesthood or religious life. All people are called to be holy; Jesus Himself told all to be holy as the Father was holy. To that end, Philip did not feel that it was necessary for him to be ordained a priest to be holy. His spiritual director had to almost command him in obedience to accept that he was called to be a priest. Philip felt he was unfit for the responsibility, but his spiritual director saw that the role Philip had in the lives of others would be an even more powerful force for conversion if Philip became a priest. Thus, at the age of thirty-six, Philip was ordained a priest of God.

As a priest, he took up residence at the Church of St. Jerome of Charity near the Via Gulia in Rome. This Church was very near the hospital of St. Jerome where Philip used to minister, and it was here that Philip resided and performed much of his ministry. Here, he welcomed many guests to give them spiritual guidance and direction. He offered his mass here, and it was such a powerful experience that on some occasions he would levitate off the ground when consecrating the Body and Blood of Our Lord. However, Philip knew he had to hold his attention as much as he could to continue with the mass, or else he became lost for hours saying mass. Thus, he had the strange custom of, rather than praying and recollecting before mass, cracking jokes, swinging, and playing with the church keys and engaging in conversations about normal things that were taking place.

He wedded the human and supernatural so well and tried to allow his very person to be a door to God. For this reason, Philip knew no strangers and always had an open door to welcome in guests at any hour. One saintly guest that he welcomed into his house, was one of the founders of the new, great religious order the Jesuits. This man, Ignatius by name, himself carried a divine fire in his heart, and a desire to save souls that matched Philip's. Ignatius had passed through troubling times in his own life, when he was not so close to God. His slight limp was a constant physical reminder for him of his journey to Christ. Ignatius was the founder of the Jesuits, an order of powerful missionaries that dedicated themselves and all their energies to the greater glory of God.

Christ commanded his disciples to preach to all nations, and as the world was beginning to open up, so did the destination of the Gospel. India, a new land in the far East was a terrifying land of paganism, wilderness, and martyrdom. India had long been home of the far east religions of Hinduism and pantheism, and stories of the sultans and their dealings with traders and even St. Francis had long been in the minds of Christians. Philip, knowing and hearing of all these great missions, felt that great fire and palpitation of heart that had first inspired him to give his life to God. He wanted to set out for India! However, the course of heaven had him going somewhere else. One day, as he was on the outskirts of Rome, St. John the Apostle appeared to him on the road. Stunned to meet an apostle, Philip stopped and greeted him, unsure of the reason for this encounter. St. John's meeting was very intentional and direct: "Philip, Rome will be your India." With that, Philip never left the city of Rome again.

Hence Philip dedicated himself with ever new vigor to the salvation of the souls that God had put in his midst. Some people may find themselves discouraged with seeing the same old, same old. Not for Philip; his fire grew all the greater.

> It happened thus that he was so racked with pity for wicked men that he could hardly contain himself from bursting into tears whenever he saw them, clear evidence of the profound love within him. There was nothing he wanted more than the salvation of his neighbor. He would hear the confessions of those who came to him at any time, and helped them marvelously, either by consoling them or advising them, or in practical ways, with the overriding intention that they should be rid of all anxiety and become aware that God and all his saints cared about them and their salvation, till they were determined

> at last to use every means to free themselves of sin. [85]

Of the priestly services he loved to render, confession held a dear place in his heart, as it does for many priests. Philip spent long hours every day in the confessional, guiding and sanctifying souls. The confessional is not only a seat of mercy and absolution but also the seat of governance the Church has over each of her individual members and the way in which they open their souls to God. The sacramental absolution works not by the merits or holiness of the priest, since the priest is only an instrument and has no power of his own to grant forgiveness; such power comes from God alone. However, the virtue of a priest in confession can assist the soul as it journeys to overcome sin and temptation. In this arena, Philip had great success and many gifts. One of the gifts he had was ability to read hearts. Sometimes, before someone would even say a word, he was able to know their sins. On a few occasions, it was said that Philip could smell sins! He could smell a certain odor that indicated the sin someone had committed.

He had no personal, relaxation time that he considered to be his own; everything was dedicated to others. Even in his prayer, he said, like many saints, that to leave prayer to go serve someone was simply to leave Jesus to serve Jesus. Love of others was the same love that the saints found in loving God, that out of love for Him they went to others!

He used everything he could to win souls over and allowed himself to become all things to all. Very often, he used humor to reach men's hearts. "The cheerful are much easier to guide in the spiritual life than the melancholy"[86] was one of his

85. Gallonio, 78.
86. *The Maxims and Sayings of St. Philip Neri. Daily Devotions,* (St. Athanasius Press).

famous saying by which joy drew people to God and God kept people in the path of holiness. On occasions, he shaved off half of his beard in order to look more ridiculous and disarm people so that they would be opened to hearing him. Other times, he even staged silly scenes to attract people's attention, such as wearing full winter coats and hats in the middle of the summer and running into other of his fellows who were dressed the same way and complain about how dreadfully cold it was.

Philip's joy and cheerfulness were able to strengthen even the most frightened hearts. England was still repairing from the Hundred Years' War and had seen the rise of Queen Mary known as "Bloody Mary" who persecuted Protestants, followed by Queen Elizabeth Tudor who carried out a long reign and tried to make the queen also the head of the Church instead of the Pope. When the Catholics refused to acknowledge this, they were viciously persecuted. Being a priest essentially meant being sentenced to death. In the Venerable English College in Rome, there are several paintings in the college depicting the land of England as a land of martyrdom and the north gate of Rome (which led to England) and the final farewell to those brave souls. When Philip encountered any of these English seminarians in the streets, he paused, holding back his tears as he cheerfully waved greetings to these "fair flowers of England," knowing of their destiny. Though Philip was not destined to be a martyr, he wanted to support these martyrs in the small way that he could, by reminding them of the beauty of their destiny and encouraging them on their way with his words.

Above all, his deep and powerful sermons and words he drew many souls to Jesus. Philip gathered so many people into his place of prayer for sermons, prayer, preaching, and the practice of virtue. The people that came were from across the board: priests and laymen, men and women, children and elderly. Philip led them in great devotions such as Eucharistic

Adoration, and the famous seven Church pilgrimage.

Philip soon founded the Oratorians, a community of priests and lay people that were to strive for holiness and set up retreats for others. The Oratorians would be one of Philip's most lasting gifts to the Church. Philip expected them only to abide by a few simple rules: prayer, humility, and charity. For Philip, above all, his members had to have an internal change of heart, founded in humility. When some of his members asked for a penance, he gave something that normally humiliated them. If they asked him to wear a hair shirt, which was a coarse vest of camel hair, he agreed, but told them they had to wear it on the outside. On one occasion, a priest gave a fabulous sermon. It was so amazing that people were moved to tears. Philip agreed that it was good, and it was so good that the priest must give the same sermon every day for the next forty days! However, greater joy and holiness can spring up when humility is present.

Philip was indeed a humble man in spirit, but God greatly filled his cup. Philip performed many amazing miracles, such as predicting the future on several occasions, bilocating (appearing in two places at once), driving the devil out of people, curing the sick, and even raising the dead! Philip never attributed any of this to himself and, as with many saints, did not marvel at these, since God is the author and the only one worthy of praise. Rather, he marveled more at the internal gifts and miracles the Lord was working in his own heart and soul, as well as the greatest miracle of saving sinners from hell.

Eventually, Philip and the Oratorians took up the work of restoring and caring for an old church known as "Santa Maria de Vallicella." It was a tiny, old church in the middle of the city that had fallen into disrepair and had been abandoned. However, it was a perfect location in the city to have a new oratory and to offer lessons for the faithful. Thus, from the very foundation, the church was completely renovated to form a "new church." Still to this day, in Rome, right along the 'Corso Victorio Emmanuele' only about a fifteen-minute walk from St. Peter's, stands the big, beautiful Chiesa Nuova or "New Church," which is still a center in Rome for prayer, pilgrimage, sacred music, and lessons.

Philip would laugh at the saying that only the good die young. At the age of 79, Philip was still going strong. He heard confessions daily, for hours at a time, said mass prayerfully and cheerfully, and performed his works of counsel and direction, as well as continued to work miracles and prophecy. What Padre Pio showed in patience, long suffering, and meekness, Philip shows in generosity, joy, and kindness. The caricature of older people as grumpy, crabby, burnt out, and set in their ways is a false image for those who know the saints. True, many saints died young, but for those saints who live longer lives, their joy increases as their love increases. "Cheerfulness strengthens the heart and makes us persevere in a good life; wherefore the servant of God ought always to be in good spirits." [87] For Philip, who found his true joy in God and allowed himself to be filled with joy, the life of prayer and charity was a joy. He possessed that true magnanimity which not only allowed him to do great things in this life but to love this life as long as he was living it. Philip is an example to us who grow tired of this life and want change; we want to move on to greener grasses rather than to see the mission God calls us to right where we are. It's not that Philip didn't want that rest in God, but in some way, he already possessed heaven on earth. This made him joyful, this made him persevere to the end. Those who have too much of a stoic understanding of life and holiness, neither possess the hope that comes from the Lord nor the humility to receive

87. *The Maxims and Sayings of St. Philip Neri*

the gifts around them. Philip understood that sadness at not getting what he wanted comes from pride. When man lives in humility, charity, and holiness like Philip did every day, every moment is a new opportunity to accept God's will.

Eventually, this great apostle of Rome encountered the foe that all men must face: death. This moment is many times considered the most important of a man's life since it is the time when one's true character and virtue is revealed. In this moment, as in all, Philip showed a joy and strength hard to find elsewhere.

> Now the closer he approached to death, the more clearly, he showed us that he had no fear of it. As if challenging death to a fight, he raised himself up into a sitting position from the bed he had been lying on, and as long as he continued to breathe he remained in the posture which he then assumed.[88]

As a Christian and thanks to the incarnation of Jesus, we can already possess in this world and in our flesh, a foretaste of what is to come. However, all the saints longed for that banquet to rest from their labors. Finally, on May 25, 1595, Philip Neri passed away, surrounded by his priest companions, and gazing up to heaven.

Philip's passing away was a point of sorrow for those who knew him, but for Philip, it gave him even greater ability to be present to the members of the pilgrim Church below. He was able to assist them even more now that he was going to heaven and not limited to a physical location. Moments after his death, at least three people had either a vision or a

88. Gallonio, *Saint Philip Neri*, 206.

dream in which Philip appeared to them, clothed in white, encouraging them to preserve in living a good life and letting them know that he was now on his way to receive the reward of his labors.

Immediately after his death, his body was examined for autopsy purposes. As they examined his upper chest cavity, they found that indeed his fourth and fifth rib had been broken and expanded and regrew. He bore this condition for fifty years so that when his heart began to palpitate rapidly in response to the divine love in him, his body could endure it. They also found that his pulmonary arteries, which take air from the lungs to the heart, were twice as large as normal in order to help cool his heart from the divine heat inside of it.[89] Philip's heart, which on earth had grown and beat so much for love of others, in heaven is permitted to grow even more as it perfectly unites to God's love and stretches to embrace all pilgrims on earth!

As is common, people did not leave the saint to rest. From the moment of his passing, people came to visit him and pray for his help. In accordance with Philip's good and generous character, he answered for the greater good of man and the glory of God. Now, however, miracles were not limited to where Philip physically laid. His intercession was sought all around. He healed diseases, brought a child back to life, cured sicknesses, restored injuries and more. His body was eventually given a beautiful place of honor in Chiesa Nuova, on the left-side altar.

In 1622, Philip Neri was canonized in a remarkable ceremony, along with Teresa of Avila, Ignatius of Loyola, Francis Xavier, and Isidore the Farmer. All these saints were contemporaries; Ignatius, Francis, and Philip were all friends;

---

89. Gallonio, 212.

and they were canonized only about thirty years after their death! In an almost humorous statement, Pope Gregory XV referenced Teresa, Ignatius, Francis, and Philip and was rumored to have said, "Today we canonize three Spaniards and a saint." This was not to underplay the other saints, but it was a tip of a hat to the people of Rome. Philip had become their apostle. They loved him dearly as a father.

Still to this day, Chiesa Nuova is a flourishing and beloved church of Rome. On Philip's feast day, the church is packed with hundreds of Italians with their entire families and young kids to lay flowers at his tomb and ask for his protection. Many religious organizations take Philip as a model of evangelization and joyful witness to the Gospel. He is a model of how to not only preach the gospel courageously, but how to make that message understandable and approachable to all. It takes some skill and a sharp mind, but it is not impossible. In fact, the Word is always able to enter again in the flesh of man as it did once in Jesus. We, the bearers of that word, must simply say, with Mary, "Let it be done to me." Also, joy must spill over from us. Our current world that is crushed by depression, loneliness, despair, and sadness, will only lie more and more to itself when it tries to fill itself with the pleasures of this world. We Christians must show that joy that Philip had and allow our hearts also to burn with love as Philip's heart did.

Friends of St. Philip Neri

My Story

St. Philip Neri became a great patron for me when I spent my six years in Rome for seminary and further studies. Chiesa Nuova was a beautiful church that was always open and welcomed people to come and pray. Our seminary at the North American College was near one of the famous trees under which Philip used to sit and give his lessons to children, and my school of Santa Croce had their library attached to St. Jerome's church and we could visit Philip's room and chapel.

I loved Philip's joy and energy and boldness in sharing the Gospel. Myself being an introvert, I asked very much for his intercession. I was also shocked to find out that he and I have the same birthday, July 22! A few of my priest friends and I, on Philip's feast day, used to go into the big piazza in front of Chiesa Nuova and we would juggle, ride unicycles, and do skits to encourage the tourists to go in and spend some time in prayer with this powerful saint.

As I prepared to be ordained and leave Rome, I asked Philip to give me some of the joy and energy he had to preach the Gospel in the land of America. I used his method of meeting people where they are and that "all roads lead to Rome" or that anything can be led back to God. His spirit of humor and humility became a model I tried to use to engage people and make the Gospel message tangible. When contentious situations would come up, I found a little dose of humor would not only defuse the situation but would make people more receptive to the Gospel message. I still see him as a powerful saint example, but I also have a wonderful story of his active presence in my life.

At my first parish of St. Rita in Alexandria, Louisiana, we used to have our Tuesday masses broadcast over the radio for people to listen in. One year, the feast of Philip Neri fell on a Tuesday, and I was super excited to get a chance to share the love of this wonderful saint. I felt so full of energy and excitement as I preached the homily and no one noticed that I had gone on for almost twenty minutes! I felt that I was entering into the mass with a new zeal and a new fire as I held the hosts for mass, and I knew it was Philip's intercession.

After mass, I went back into the sacristy where the assistants had been set up with their equipment to broadcast the mass on the radio. When I came in they said, "Father that was a great mass, but we were wondering, who was the priest concelebrating with you?" I was very confused. There was no other priest there with me. I asked them what they meant by that. "Well, we heard another priest's voice speaking the words of consecration with you and so we figured it was another priest concelebrating with you." I was very perplexed, and I wanted to tell them that they must be mistaken when I realized: it was Philip Neri. He was there with me in the mass. All the saints are present, but he was especially present in that mass, saying the words with me. I just smiled and moved on. I knew that Philip was giving me a little bit of encouragement and I thanked him for a share in that great grace.

Christina Brinson

In the summer of 2017, I was in a month-long training course to be a Regnum Christi missionary with fourteen other girls in Rhode Island. We received lots of formation in this month. One night a woman who made vows in this community told us that we would be watching a saint movie. Little did we know how much this movie about the life of St. Philip Neri would affect us. It's at least a four-hour movie and by the end, we were all in tears, completely inspired by the love St. Philip Neri had for God and others. I remember feeling a desire to give myself as he did. Throughout that summer we would sing *prefisco paradiso* constantly (a song taught by Phillip Neri in the movie).

For three days all of us served in New York doing various works. It was an opportunity for us to practice working together and serving different needs. On the second day, a businessman hosted us in his penthouse above and adjacent to St. Patrick's cathedral. One of my fellow missionary sisters was giving a presentation. After the meeting was over there was a lot of food leftover which they were happy for me to take. I was extremely excited about giving out food to busy New Yorkers. So, my missionary sister Danica and I took the food down in a garbage bag to the streets. Our focus was spreading joy to everyone we encountered. At that moment I felt fearless, able to approach anyone (no doubt the Holy Spirit gave me courage because I can be nervous approaching some people). I wanted to make sure to touch the lives of everyday people for at least a moment with generosity and joy. If my memory is correct the first person to accept our food was a taxi driver. Of course, people might ask us why we were giving out food. This gave us the opportunity to share our mission with them and our passionate love for God.

The person we talked to the longest was a trash man. We offered him some food and he was extremely excited, opening a clean trash bag to fill with our food for later. His name was Phillip. After speaking we shook hands, parted ways, and we crossed the street to continue. Then, my eye caught a homeless man lying in a dumpster. He was sleeping so I quietly asked him if he'd like some chips, he politely declined. I started to move on but realized I hadn't even asked his named, so I introduced myself and asked him for his name. He uttered, "Phillip." As his name reached my ears I was struck with awe in the realization that Philip Neri was watching over us and guiding us. He was praying for us in our joy-giving, spontaneous missions. I caught up with Danica and expressed gleefully this amazing discovery. We were both moved and our hearts continued to burn throughout the day. We both remember this day with sweet appreciation for the saints' intercession.

Months later when I was in Manila, Philippines I purchased a plant. I cared very much for the tropical plant and looking at it filled me with joy. I named it Philip, somehow not even thinking of Philip Neri though. The name had just come to me. A few months later, somehow, I connected back with Danica who was in Washington D.C. for her mission. I have no idea how we got to the subject but she mentioned she had a plant and named it Philip. Once again I was thrown by the saint's intercession in both our lives in such a parallel way. During my mission year, I shared St. Philip Neri's story with whoever I could.

Most recently I was in charge of a group of young EcyD missionary girls in Atlanta. These girls were from all over the world, specifically one from Italy. I really wanted to have a movie night with the girls and the idea of showing them the St. Phillip Neri movie came to me. I knew the consecrated had many holy/saint movies so I looked through their collection. Amazingly I found the movie! I could not believe I would get to share something so incredible with them. None of them knew of him so it would be completely new. However, a problem occurred when I put the DVD in. The subtitles were only in Spanish which meant that my girls who only spoke English would not be able to follow the movie. This was a major problem, and I was faced with the possibility that they wouldn't get to watch it at all. So I went back, desperate to find the version with English subtitles. I looked intensely through all the DVDs. Until victory! I found it! I was so grateful to God for this gift as my heart was so set on this movie. In the beginning, the girls were arguing with each other and I was fearful they wouldn't absorb what this movie had to give but in the end all their hearts were moved. I would frequently pause the movie to help explain to them what was going on. I enjoyed the moments they gasped at his miracles. Throughout the rest of their summer mission, they would see different signs of Philip Neri like a random "Prefisso Paradiso" written on a note on a mirror. They would gasp and be astonished. I told them to expect this, as saints can show us they are watching over us in different ways.

After they left to go home, one of the girls sent a picture of a design she had drawn with the words "I prefer heaven." I was shocked to see this. I didn't realize St. Neri's movie touched her that much. She is now in the process of making it into a sticker.

I continue to pray to Philip Neri and ask him to help me be charitable and patient. Philip's humility greatly inspired me throughout my mission year and still does today.

To this day I'm so grateful for the love I can see through Philip Neri when it is hard for me to see it from God. Of course, we don't see every miracle Jesus performed and sometimes it is hard for us to comprehend His love. But I always think "Wow Philip Neri's love is so great and still Jesus' has to be even greater."

O God, who never cease to bestow the glory of holiness on the faithful servants you raise up for yourself, graciously grant that the Holy Spirit may kindle in us that fire with which he wonderfully filled the heart of Saint Philip Neri. Amen

"Stigmata of St. Rita"
Original Drawing by Fr Patrick Setto

ST. RITA

As I was writing this book, I saw a program by a Chaldean rite priest on St. Rita. He gave such a deep and moving biography of her that I found out was inspired by a deep and personal encounter he had with her. He was also inspired to draw an image of her that he since has not been able to replicate. I reached out to him and asked if he would be willing to share his biography, testimony, and image with me for this book to which he graciously obliged.

Biography of St. Rita

by Fr. Patrick Setto

St. Rita was born Margherita Lotti in 1381 in Roccaporena near Cascia, Italy. Her parents were older when she came into their lives. Miracles took place throughout the life of Rita, beginning when she was an infant. One day as she slept in her cradle, her family noticed small bees flying in and out of Rita's mouth. They took it as a sign of the sweetness with which Rita would one day bring to the world. As a child Rita desired to dedicate her life to God as a nun but her parents had other plans for her. After resigning herself to the will of God, Rita was married at the age of twelve to Paolo Mancini. The marriage was an unhappy one. Paolo frequently abused Rita both physically and emotionally and she in turn endured the insults with patience and humility, constantly praying and hoping to bring Paolo back to God. Rita eventually gave birth to two sons and raised them to be good Christians.

Finally Rita's prayers were answered and her husband

converted, asking for her forgiveness. Their marriage was finally a happy one but not for long. Unfortunately, Paolo and his family were involved in a feud with another family of Cascia. When her husband did not return home one evening, Rita discovered the body of Paolo. He had been murdered. In her sorrow, Rita turned toward God but her sons sought revenge. When Rita learned of their plans, she prayed that their hearts would be changed and if not, that God would take them so they could not commit such a sinful crime. Rita's prayers were again answered when her sons died before they could avenge their father's death. With no family left, Rita sought entrance into the Augustinian Monastery of St. Mary Magdalene in Cascia. After speaking with the superior, she was denied entrance into the community because of the scandal surrounding her husband's murder. Rita persisted in her prayers, bringing reconciliation between the feuding families through the intercession of her three patron saints: John the Baptist, Augustine, and Nicholas of Tolentino. One night, Rita was escorted through the locked doors of the Monastery by her three patrons. When the nuns awoke the next morning and discovered Rita's miraculous entrance, she was finally admitted into the community.

Rita lived her vocation as a nun with deep humility and faith. One time, her superior decided to test her obedience. She handed Rita a dry stick, instructing her to plant it in the ground and water it daily until it bloomed. The superior hoped to humiliate Rita but she obeyed and watered the stick each day. Soon, it miraculously bloomed and grew into a beautiful grape vine that still exists today.

When Rita was sixty, she heard a sermon one Good Friday on the sufferings of Christ crucified. Rita wept with emotion as she contemplated her Lord and upon returning to the monastery threw herself at the feet of a crucifix. She begged Jesus for a small share in His Passion and He granted her request: a thorn from the crown of thorns shot from the crucifix into Rita's forehead. It caused a deep wound which never healed and caused Rita much suffering the rest of her life. She was isolated in her cell by her fellow sisters because of the wound.

During the Jubilee year of 1450, the thorn wound on Rita's forehead miraculously closed up so that she was able to join her sisters in Rome for the great celebration. Upon her return to the monastery, the wound reopened. As time went on and Rita grew old, she suffered from an illness that confined her to bed. Shortly before her death, Rita asked a visiting cousin to go to her former home and bring her a rose from the garden. Even though it was the middle of winter, the cousin obeyed and found a single rose in full bloom. She brought the rose to Rita who shared it with her sisters. Another time, Rita asked the cousin to bring her two figs from the garden and again she shared them with her community. Rita died on May 22, 1457. The people of Cascia crowded the Monastery to look upon the face of Rita one last time. So many people continued to come that she was never buried. In fact, the body of Rita remains completely incorrupt.

Rita was canonized a saint by Pope Leo XIII in 1900. Since her death, countless people have asked for her intercession and received an answer to their prayers. Saint Rita is fondly known as the patron saint of the impossible because of her life and powerful intercession.

St. Rita has been one of the most treasured and beloved saints by Italians for centuries. Before she was ever officially recognized by the Church as a saint, she has been surrounded with a great love and devotion by the people almost from the moment she died until the present. This was quite a long time, despite that it took St. Rita 453 years to get canonized. This devotion is shared not only by the local people, but even by some of the most unique friends of the animal kingdom. It was said that on the day of what was to be Rita's funeral, white bees came inside of the of Church where she was and began to nest and have remained there until today... five centuries! What's most strange is that these bees are unique to this monastery: they do not make a beehive, nor do they make honey, they are entirely white and they only come out between Holy Week and her feast day (May 22). Bees have followed her throughout her life: one instance when she was a baby and bees were found swarming her but not stinging, another when she was baptized and bees appeared and finally at her death the bees made a final and lasting return into the walls of the monastery. Is it just that bees were attracted to her? Some called Rita the 'Rose of Roccaporena" or the "Gem of Umbria" and for this reason say the bees were attracted to her. Also, bees are considered to be a pure, motherly animal that works for others and keeps a certain purity in its own life. The honeycomb they make is also a very pure and strong substance and the honey that is made is said to be one of the only foods that does not decay. Capped honey, that is, honey that is sealed in the honeycomb, has been discovered in the tombs of Egyptians and is still edible! Rita's life was thus marked with purity, dedication, and service that bore an eternal fruit in heaven!

Rita also has a unique and singular privilege that surrounds her death: she was never actually buried. This privilege was a result of two factors: first was the fame of Rita that had risen after her death. As is the custom today, after a person dies, their body is left in the Church for the time of visitation. People can come and visit, offering their prayers for the deceased. As with many who are revered as saints, this praying for became a praying to, as people take the opportunity to touch objects to them and ask for their prayers. After about eight days, the body is then moved to its place of burial. Those that are of great esteem, usually the local bishop or one who is revered as a saint, are buried on the north or Gospel side of the church. This practice is so that at the Resurrection (which was believed to come from the East), these people would already be at the right hand of Christ (Mt 25:33). However, St. Rita was so famous and so many people continued to gather around her, that they were unable to move the body to the final place of burial. She remained in the church where, still today, pilgrims come to pray for themselves and others. The mob never subsided; the move was never completed. Rita remains in a central place to welcome those who brought her intentions.

Another factor that complicated the transportation of her body was something quite miraculous. After her death, she was laid in a cypress wood casket and then placed in the church for veneration. After a few months, there was a terrible fire in the church that even burned her casket. Miraculously her body was almost completely untouched! The body was then taken and placed in another wooden sarcophagus made by a man named Cesco Barbari who was a carpenter from Cascia and was healed through St. Rita's intercession. Additionally, her body showed signs of remaining incorrupt. This term refers to the phenomenon where the body of the saint does not deteriorate as quickly as it naturally should. If you visit the body of St. Rita today, five hundred years later, you can see the skin still intact, the body still together, and even color in the body.

Such miracles surround the saints' deaths because for them death was a freeing, life-giving moment. The greatest miracle in the entire universe was the death and resurrection of Jesus. In his death, Jesus was able to swallow up all of sin and suffering and then bring the power of His life to what seemed like the darkest moment of our lives. Death becomes an actual birth, and the saints' lives were a continual dying. Jesus' resurrection has given man a doorway into new life, ironically through death. Just as God deemed at the beginning of creation that the darkness of night be ended by the light of the new day, so too, God has made it that the darkness of man's death will not have the last word: it will be ended by the light of the new day of resurrection!

It is this power of resurrection that exists in the bodies of the saints. Their souls already see, imperfectly, the face of God. However, the beatific vision is not complete until they are reunited with their bodies. So their bodies are already waiting for the resurrection and hold within their very flesh a promise of resurrection and a connection to the glory to come. This connection and belief in the bodily resurrection is why the physical bodies of the saints are held in honor but also why sometimes their physical bodies even bring about certain miracles such as healings and such.

Saint of the Impossible

"But Jesus looked at them and said to them, 'With men this is impossible, but with God all things are possible.'" – Matthew 19:26

The word "impossible" seems to be a very absolute word in the English language. Originally, impossible meant "not having the ability to do", that is, a certain impotence. It can refer to weakness, it can refer to deficiency, or it can refer to something moral. However, there was never anything that was absolute in the sphere of religion. After all, what is impossible for man by himself, is possible for God with man.

Impossible simply means "unable to be done." There can be various reasons that something is impossible. It is impossible to grow a vegetable garden in the desert because it lacks water, has oppressive heat, and sandy soil. It is impossible to see your ears because of where your eyes and ears are placed in reference to each other. It is impossible to be in two places at once due to our body being finite. Each of these actions are impossible, but that impossibility can be fixed: with a change in temperature and a rainstorm, a garden could grow in a desert; you can see your ears with a picture or a mirror; I can be in my house but also in my mind. Impossibility has a limit, especially with God. He has no limits and thus all is possible for Him. Possible can be defined two ways: first, it can mean "able to be done." This definition is how we would usually understand ability: I can do it or I cannot. This possibility is the 'horizontal' possibility of man and created things in this world we live in. It manifests our limitations and our finitude. In this dimension, possibility or impossibility is defined in how close or far away from a certain good or goal I can place myself; either I can achieve it or its out of my reach. However, with God there is also a 'vertical' dimension to possibility: all things that happen, all that is done, all that takes place is drawn into the greater power and ability of God. St. Paul says that "in everything God works for good with those who love Him," (Rom. 8: 28) meaning that all things can be a movement towards the greatest good of heaven. The very presence and reality of God takes away the strain of isolation in our tasks in knowing that God works with us, but further that all that happens can move us upwards to the final goal of heaven. All things that occur can be swept up into the movement towards God Himself. God who is "All-Powerful" can lead all things up towards Him, as He alone is the author and designer of all nature. His nature is not limited and thus His ability to draw all to Himself is not limited. It is with these two definitions that we can say for man things are impossible, but all things are possible with God, not only because He can do all, but that all things can be draw into Him and his power and imbued with a new perspective and purpose.

Faith is then what allows us to see that God is at the end of all things and that we are not simply doomed to the consequences of this world. Faith tells us not only that God is greater than this world, but that the limitations of the physical universe are only one part of the bigger picture. We also must understand ourselves as more than just bounded by this world. Here and now, we can accept grace. Grace, which is God's life within us, is what allows us to go beyond what our weaknesses, faults, and failures dictate. What we can do is expanded, in a sense, by the life of God within us. Further and most importantly, the life of God within us gives new orientation and thus guides us through all events to our final end. Grace thus not only gives man the strength to endure suffering that is placed there by his physical limitation, but also to see suffering itself as a means to drawing near to God who draws near to us. The natural cause and effect of this world can leave us very confined and trapped, feeling that we are destined to be the fruit of the actions of this world or the measure of our own weakness. But not with God. God's measuring rod always allows us to bypass what seems to be the inevitable.

St. Rita is the patron saint of the impossible not necessarily because she was able to do anything. Her life testifies to much struggle with weakness, difficulty, and limitations. Yes, through God's grace she faced and brought about wonderful miracles of conversion for her family and other events in her life. She is the saint of the impossible because of the great power of God and His goodness, which she allowed to enter the difficulties of her life. Rita had to surrender to divine providence, the guidance of God that maneuvers the course of history and events, ultimately according to God's will, to a greater good than we can achieve by our own plans. Rita, first, is a model of that surrender. During difficult and challenging times, she surrendered to the simple thing she was asked to do, and humbly performed the task before her. By so doing, she was led to find the power and strength of God at work and guiding the course of her life to fill her with peace, and to know that God's goodness transformed what was evil into an opportunity for resurrection.

Rita, like many of the saints, did not want attention drawn to her. She did not want to have great power or ability. Her surrender gave her peace in whatever event took place in her life. She would be at peace because she knew the Good God was in control. Things did not have to go her away or according to her ability. By being so detached, she had a freedom in Christ which allowed these great events to take place. By surrender and prayer, Rita overcame amazing odds.

She was never alone in her trials. She found greater friends in heaven than she did on earth. Of special closeness were St. Augustine and St. Nicholas. As we have seen with many of the other saints, they are accustomed to brushing elbows with the inhabitants of heaven. Even though hundreds of years separated their lives, the communion of heaven and God's love drew them together. She never felt alone amongst the trials of life. In fact, God always wants His grace to appear to us in very personal, real, and tangible ways. Many of the graces St. Rita experienced came through her companionship with the saints who consoled her, prayed with her, and helped her. It also foreshadowed how she would become one of these personal channels of grace for others.

With St. Rita, we find that truth and reality is far more interesting that fiction. The events of her life that unfolded gave birth to a more marvelous life and splendor than had been seen beforehand. God directs the world so that even the evilest of events can bring about a greater good. Every Easter, at the vigil mass during "The Exsultet" the Church sings, "O happy fault, O glorious sin of Adam! That won for us so great, so glorious a redeemer." We believe theologically that had we never sinned, Jesus would not have been born. The reason of His Incarnation was for saving us from sin. Sin, remaining an evil and something displeasing God, can give rise to mercy. So, because of our sin, we received a greater intimacy with God than we had before! Sin is not good, but drawn into the power and goodness of God, it can be destroyed in His mercy and lead to a greater potential than existed before! St. Rita's own life of hardship and trials also shows how God, in His goodness and power, is able to bring about an even greater gift: She was able to bring salvation to a man (her husband) possessed by hatred and anger, she was able to deliver two boys (her own sons) from the poison of vengeance to the peace of heaven, and she herself was able to experience one of the greatest unions we can have with Jesus on earth: suffering. She was given, as a sign of this union, a small mark of the thorn on her forehead. Because she had in her life endured everything that the Father had sent her, she had a special union with Jesus in that obedience of acceptance.

Many times in our lives, we do not need to go and look for great and amazing adventures; they come to us when we are faithful to God. Just our faithfulness to the everyday things that God puts before us and our acceptance of the small opportunities that God sends us become the road map of our lives. God's love for us always directs us toward our final destination, our sanctification, and the Good Lord always gives us the graces along the way to achieve and complete what He asks of us. He only asks in return our obedience to what has been placed before us. There is a saying, "first, do what's necessary, then do what is possible, and suddenly you are doing the impossible." In the humanistic circle, this saying is meant to imply a person's greater potential that is hidden in everyday life. However, in the divine providence of God, it can lead to amazing conclusions. St. Rita was indeed a saint who treated as necessary the salvation of her soul and the souls of those God placed in her life. She did everything that was possible with her own abilities: forgiving evils, having compassion in the place of hatred and prayer in the place of despair. We see the fruit it bore. Her life is an example of how the impossible can become not only possible, but life bearing. She teaches us in moments of struggle to hope and to know that with God nothing should ever be out of the sphere of possibility. In fact, the darker the times the more we should rejoice to know and trust that God will not only give us the grace to get through it, but to make something even greater come from it.

More than just an example, Rita is a companion. After her life on earth and experience of the power of God's grace, not only was she given rest from the struggles of this world, but God invited her to share in the workings of His grace in heaven. She was invited to become a patroness and intercessor to all those who find themselves in impossible situations. She has seen the work of God completed in her life, and now her vision is perfected in heaven as she beholds many trials of God's grace that have pulled people to a higher level of possibility. She journeys with us as our companion when we feel everything is out of our control. She gives hope that nothing is impossible for God. She intercedes for us that the graces we need may be fixed in our hearts.

Friends of St. Rita

Fr. Patrick Setto

2017 was the year that my life's purpose came to fruition. My vocation was realized and I was ordained a priest in July. My life was full of joy and excitement! However, unbeknownst to me, an extreme trial for my life loomed just around the corner. In October my mother was diagnosed with Stage 4 Lymphoma. This news devastated me. As a young, newly ordained priest, I was distraught and began to wonder how I would be able to cope with the demands of ministry and at the same time deal with my mother's illness and possible death. Immediately, I turned in desperation to St. Rita, whose intercession has always proved to be a source of strength and miraculous intervention. St. Rita has shown a special love for me and my family since I was a young boy.

Minutes after my mom was diagnosed, I looked at her and told her that we would entrust her to St. Rita's care. I told her with full confidence that St. Rita would heal her, and I promised her that afterward, we would make a trip to Cascia in thanksgiving for her intercession.

Throughout my mother's treatment, my family made countless offerings for St. Rita's intercession. In addition, years prior I was gifted a relic of St. Rita when I was a deacon, which I deeply cherished. I gave the relic to my mother to pray with during this difficult time and I instructed her to wear it every day. So, every day she would pin the pouch that the relic lay within to the inside of her clothing. One evening, my mother realized that the pouch with the relic inside was missing! In tears, she searched anxiously and prayed to St Rita saying, "Why did you leave me when I need you the most? Do you not want to heal me? Why would you leave me at the most important and difficult time of my life?!" Immediately she heard the words in her heart, "Don't worry, I am going to make a miracle out of this." The next morning after my mother hesitatingly told me that she lost the relic, I immediately got the feeling that supernatural works were at play. I knew that St. Rita would take the loss of the relic and the suffering we were all enduring and do something incredible, beyond what I could ever imagine. At that moment, I made a prayer to St Rita willingly giving up and offering up the relic in exchange for my mother's health. However, I also felt in my heart that if the relic was found, it would serve as a confirmation that my mother would be healed through St. Rita's miraculous intercession.

That same week, I had plans to drive to New York with some friends to pick up a statue of St. Rita for our home parish. On our way back home, we were listening to hymns dedicated to St. Rita. The sky was dark and gray and the songs were so beautiful. As I was listening and taking in the natural surroundings, I became so overwhelmed with emotion and sorrow for my mother that I cried a prayer out loud in desperation for her healing. Suddenly, while making this prayer and in the midst of my cry, the sun broke through the dark clouds and rays of light beamed on my face, blinding me. It was incredible considering the weather. We had not seen the sun the entire day, so my friends and I took this event as a clear and obvious sign that St. Rita was interceding for us and would grant her healing. When we returned, we placed the statue of St. Rita in my parent's living room to keep there for a few days before delivering her to our church.

The next morning, exactly one week after losing the relic, my mother was resting and praying on the couch in front of the statue. As she lay there, she gently rested her hand over her chest and felt the thick pouch with the relic, pinned underneath her shirt. What was so bizarre is that the shirt was very thin and so it would have been impossible for her not to notice it in the morning as she dressed. She was elated and shouted God's Glory along with us all! Although we had no medical assurance, we considered this to be a sure answer from St. Rita and confirmation that my mother would be healed. Despite lack of confidence from her doctors, and after only a couple of rounds of chemotherapy, my mother went into complete remission! The doctors were astounded by her scans. They were completely clear! This is an extremely rare occurrence for Stage 4 Lymphoma. Typically, there is always some cancer that remains. We knew that the power of St. Rita's intercession was the reason that God granted our prayers. My mom's healing was truly miraculous, and my family is and will always be eternally grateful.

As if St. Rita's intercession wasn't evident enough, one year later my family and I scheduled a pilgrimage to Italy that was being planned by another priest friend of mine. Our itinerary included Rome and so I had requested that we add Cascia to the trip. When I made the request, I did not remember the promise I made to my mother about traveling there with her. When I initially made the promise, I had always imagined that we would make the trip alone, so it wasn't on my mind. On our way to the airport, prior to departing from the U.S., I wondered to myself what day we would be arriving in Cascia. I quickly checked the itinerary and remembering my promise, I went back in the calendar and realized that the day we were going to arrive in Cascia was exactly one year to the day that my mom was diagnosed. St. Rita was confirming once again that her miraculous intercession was at play; she was even helping me to fulfill my promise. When we arrived in Cascia, my father who still had some doubts about her intercession, was overwhelmed by this amazing coincidence. He had an instantaneous conversion of heart upon our arrival there and he now wears a St. Rita medal every day in honor of her.

The most beautiful fruit to come from this trial is that it brought my entire family closer to God. St. Rita gifted my family with renewed faith in God's grace and helped to deepen our trust in His mercy. She strengthened my vocation and helped me to carry my cross during that year. She continually inspires me in my priesthood and I am forever grateful for the miracle of my mother's healing and the many gifts of God's love that were given to my family. St. Rita, pray for us.

Bestow on us, we pray, O Lord, the wisdom and strength of the Cross, with which you were pleased to endow Saint Rita, so that, suffering in every tribulation with Christ, we may participate ever more deeply in his Paschal Mystery. Amen

"St. Therese of Liseaux"
Original Painting by Caroline Pellegrin

ST. THÉRÈSE

"Now the whole history of the Church shows that one saint is enough to transform thousands of souls."[90] This quote by Cardinal Sarah is a perfect epitaph of a little saint who did not even make it to the age of twenty-five and did not do much beyond household chores. What's even more tremendous is that most of her work in the souls of others did not begin until after she died. Since Thérèse's death in 1897, this little saint has skyrocketed in activity. Her first miracles began to take place in 1899, only two years after her death, and miracles have not stopped since then. She was canonized on May 17, 1925, only about thirty years after she died. Not only has her heavenly intercession been a constant impact on the Church, with thousands of people invoking her for the famous rose novena, but her autobiography, *Story of a Soul*, became so popular, widespread, and impactful that in 1997 she was named a Doctor of the Church, a title given to only two other women and only about thirty men in reference to the importance and power of their writings on the faith of the Church.

To try to write a sufficient story of her sainthood is a staggering task. However, the trouble comes not because of the actual content of her life. She lived a very simple twenty-four years. Over half of her time on this earth was spent at home with her family. But this simplicity is the remarkably powerful thing about her life that can speak volumes to us:

---

90. Cardinal Robert Sarah and Nicholas Diat, "The Day is Long Spent," (San Francisco: Ignatius Press, 2019), 29–30.

it is not about the progress or achievements of her life. The number of miracles or events is not what saturates her story with spirituality, but how she viewed her own life from the eyes of God Himself makes it such a remarkable story to tell.

A detailed view of her life must include a view into her intimate life with her family. Partially because most of her short life was spent at home with her family, which provided a foundation for her sanctity. Moreover, Thérèse's holiness was rooted in the remarkable holiness that did exist within the Martin family. In 2015, during the Synod on the family, the parents of St. Thérèse, Louis and Zélie Martin, were together raised to the altar as saints. To properly account for their charism of holiness and mode of sanctifying, a new category of saint was created: not martyr, nor virgin, nor confessors, but spouses. A new title for an ancient path to holiness!

There can be a temptation to say that they were canonized because Thérèse was canonized, and that they were named saints as a way to greater reflect Thérèse's holiness. Rather, Thérèse became a saint because they were saint. Indeed, God has always built His grace upon nature and has used the natural as a channel for the supernatural. So too, God made the family, and the parents, as the natural origin of life, also to implant and inspire the supernatural life. Thérèse first came to know and encounter the unconditional, ever-present love of God, because it was lived out and enshrined in her parents. Indeed, not only had they been a natural source of birth, but their entire lives were such a real self-gift of each other, both naturally and supernaturally, that it brought forth life both naturally and supernaturally in their children. The life of a child truly has its reason for being in the self-gift of the spouses, their gift of self and union with each other being so real that it is a new life, a one flesh. Every child's identity can truly be said to be one of a beloved, that the basis for every human life is self-gift, is the fruit of love! Moreover, when the spiritual dimension is added to the gift, it also flows into the children, and the education and upbringing of the children, which is just a continuation of their birth, can be enlightened with a supernatural education. Indeed, not only did the children learn from their parents the natural lessons of their identity and compassion for others, but in the supernatural grace-filled lives of the parents do the children learn who they are as God's children and what God, who calls Himself "Father," looks like.

Louis and Zélie each had a magnificent journey of holiness in their lives. As Thérèse described, "The two stems who brought these flowers into existence are now reunited for all eternity in the heavenly Fatherland."[91]

Zélie herself was a kind of living martyr. Her time in the family was short yet very influential. Zélie had discerned religious life but due to illness was unable to enter. She became a lace maker, but never lost her love for prayer and contemplation. Even as a secular worker, she had a powerful mystic side. Her first decision to pursue Louis came from a mystical voice that resounded in her when she had crossed him on a bridge. She carried this contemplative side with her throughout her entire life, as a lace maker and a mother.

Having lost four children, she carried sorrow, but above all this pain gave her a greater longing for heaven. Her spirituality was very much shaped by being a mother and later grew into being a nurturer, a teacher, and a caretaker. She was not content with only the earthly duties of motherhood, but her role as a mother was also to help her children reach heaven.

> Little Thérèse asked me the other day if she would go to Heaven. I told her 'Yes' if she

---

91. St. Thérèse of Liseux, *Story of a Soul,* Study Edition Trans. John Clark O.C.D. (Washington D.C.: ICS Press, 2005), 17.

> were good. She answered: 'Yes, but if I'm not good, I'll go to hell. But I know what I will do. I will fly to you in Heaven, and what will God be able to do to take me away? You will be holding me so tightly in your arms!' I could see in her eyes that she was really convinced that God would do nothing to her if she were in her mother's arms.[92]

Zelie had loved Thérèse with a love that was undying. Not only had Zelie's love convinced Thérèse that their bond would not be broken when Zelie went to heaven, but her love also fortified the hope that Zelie would still look after Thérèse and not let anything bad happen. Her mother was a very influential figure in Thérèse's life and in pursuit of holiness. She was a woman of remarkable patience through all her suffering, from the grief of loss to the pain of her breast cancer. Her faith also gave her an awareness of her upcoming passing to go to be with her little children. The loss of her mother was a very powerful event in Thérèse's life that sent her into a deep solitude. She loved her mother dearly, but she knew from a long time ago that heaven was not only our final and most blessed home, but it was a way that we could be closest to those on earth. As much as Thérèse hated her mom dying, she was joyful at this event because it not only brought her mom to the happiness of heaven, but through that it would keep her mom closer. She had natural sadness at her mom's passing, but she knew that getting closer to Jesus, the King of Heaven, would keep her close to her mother. At Thérèse's first communion, she began to cry shortly after reception. Everyone was shaken and figured it must be because she missed her mother.

---

92. St. Thérèse of Liseux, *Story of a Soul*, 19.

> They did not understand that all the joy of Heaven having entered my heart, this exiled heart was unable to bear it without shedding tears. Oh! No, the absence of Mama didn't cause me any sorrow on the day of my First Communion. Wasn't Heaven itself in my soul, and hadn't Mama taken her place there a long time ago? Thus, in receiving Jesus' visit. I received also Mama's. [93]

Just as her mother's earthly life had been formative for Thérèse, so was her heavenly life. Again, heaven is not a place far off, but very close. For those with faith, heaven and the dwellers of heaven are close companions. Thérèse was already experiencing the fellowship with the saints through her own mother!

Thérèse also expressed how she came to know and see the love of God as ever present from her father on earth. She was the end of the line, the last of nine children, only five of which had survived to adulthood. They were a very close family (seven in the house at a time) and despite the grief of the death of four of the children it had given the entire family a sense of love and appreciation for each other as a gift.

Louis continued the presence of faith and love in the Martin house. What could have been austere and unbending in the father's personality was compensated for by the indulgent kindness he showed for his noisy brood who could have upset his love for silence and peace. He did not disdain enlivening the family evenings by reciting the poems of famous authors of the day, the romanticists, singing old fashioned tunes in his beautiful voice, and making miniature

94. St. Thérèse, 5.

toys, much to the admiration of his daughters. [94]

He was a very kind and gentle soul, giving his daughters not only their first image of God the Father, but one of the best images of God. He loved little Thérèse, calling her his "little queen" and showering her with gentle yet firm love. For many years he alone had to carry the Martin family, despite the ache he felt for the loss of his four children as well as his wife. Much like his late wife, Louis was a man both of work and family life, yet also deep prayer and contemplation. It was from him and his example that Thérèse learned the way of holiness more than from any book or teacher. On one occasion, she related how much his simple devotion impressed upon her.

> When the preacher spoke about St. Teresa, Papa leaned over and whispered: 'Listen carefully, little Queen, he's talking about your Patroness.' I did listen carefully, but I looked more frequently at Papa than at the preacher, for his handsome face said so much to me! His eyes, at times, were filled with tears which he tried in vain to stop; he seemed no longer held by earth, so much did his soul lose itself in the eternal truths. [95]

Louis made the truths of holiness and the love of God incarnate for his family. Not just his words, but simply his devotion made this love a tangible reality. Every word, action, and gesture spoke to his children! Such is true of all parents: they are the incarnate presence of God's love and every word, action, and sentiment will be impressed

95. St. Thérèse, 58.

upon their children. Louis took his family on various trips, including the memorable trip to Rome where they were able to visit the Colosseum and offer their honor to the martyrs, as they desired to follow in their footsteps. They also were able to meet the Holy Father, whom Thérèse boldly asked for a big wish. For years she had been dreaming of entering the Carmelite Monastery and giving her life totally to God in silence and prayer. The minimum age was sixteen but the little saint wanted to enter at the age of fifteen. The Holy Father calmly told her to wait for the instructions of the superiors.

Her father was also an instrument of the Lord in the life of Thérèse, even when he was being harsh and chastising. One of the most powerful and memorable moments of her life was on Christmas Eve, after midnight mass, when she was fourteen. She was excited to get her slippers filled with goodies, as was their normal tradition. As she was going up the stairs to her room, her father, thinking she was already in her room, groaned about Thérèse still being so childish. He remarked that this year was the last year to perform this ritual. Her sweet, tender, little heart took this fact as a crushing blow. However, Jesus mended her back together immediately.

> But Thérèse was no longer the same; Jesus had changed her heart! Forcing back my tears, I descended the stairs rapidly; controlling the pounding of my heart, I took my slippers and placed them in front of Papa, and withdrew all the objects joyfully. . . . Thérèse had discovered once again the strength of soul which she had lost at the age of four and a half and she was

---

96. St. Thérèse, 153.

to preserve it forever! [96]

This moment was a sacrifice of the attachment to the things of earth and gave her the grace to never refuse the Lord anything again. Her father never knew the effect that event had upon her, but had he not acted in that way, Thérèse may not have been able to win over those graces in her heart.

Louis was a martyr in his own right. Having such great love for his family, he ultimately lived through the loss of four young children, the death of wife, and the spiritual departure of all his daughters to the religious life. He generously gave them all. The last life he gave to the Lord was his own, in a way no less than Jesus did. He had a stroke which left him paralyzed. Due to mental trouble, this once strong and very intelligent man was soon reverted to almost a vegetable in the hospital. He died a slow and agonizing death with only one of his daughters, Céline, present. Thérèse was at Carmel by this time but forever felt the pain of that loss.

The love and devotion of Louis and Zélie spilt over not only onto Thérèse but onto all their children. Thérèse found herself surrounded by wonderful sisters on earth, and family in heaven. All of her living siblings eventually entered the religious life. After the death of her mother, Thérèse took Pauline, her older sister, as her second mother. This exchange was very providential because Pauline, later known as Mother Agnes, was the one to give Thérèse the command to write her *Story of a Soul.* All her siblings were very dear to Thérèse, but Céline, the youngest sister to survive before Thérèse, held a special place in her heart and they shared many wonderful memories together. The relationships Thérèse had in this life greatly influenced her relationship and walk with God, as a familiar and loving figure.

Thérèse chose to look at her life through the lens of what God had done for her rather than through the lens of what she had done or failed to do. Thérèse mused upon her life from the vantage point of how God had graced it. In consequence,

Thérèse was filled with gratitude. "It seems to me that if a little flower could speak, it would tell simply what God has done for it without trying to hide its blessings."[97]

It was her faith in God's goodness and how He was active in her life that makes her story so powerful. Again, it was not necessarily what she did or achieved but how God was active in those simple moments. Her incredible awareness and faith that seemed to know no limit and saw every single atom of existence as a work of God is what makes her story so powerful. Her story is a model of a saint's story because it is really just the story of God. This could be the reason why there was such a seamless transition between her life on earth and heaven and why even now she is such an active player in the Church: because God is ever active! Our God is a living God! He was at work in her while on earth, and now that she has joined Him in heaven, she shares that activity. The joy she had to welcome everything from God on earth has reached its fullness in heaven.

As Thérèse reflected on her life through this magnifying glass of God's goodness, it shaped her life. She was not only able to use it as a reflective power, but as a performative power in the present. She shared an image from her youth that summed up how this view ultimately shaped her life and opened her heart to the boundless works of God.

> One day, Lėonie, thinking she was too big to be playing any longer with dolls, came to us with a basket filled with dresses and pretty pieces for making others; her doll was resting top. 'Here my little sisters, choose; I'm giving you all this.' Cėline stretched out her hand

97.St. Thérèse, 37.

> and took a little ball of wool that pleased her. After a moment's reflection, I stretched out mine saying: 'I choose all!' and I took the basket without ceremony.[98]

As simplistic and mundane as this scene may seem, Thérèse had saturated it with supernatural significance.

> I understood, too, there were many degrees of perfection and each soul was free to re-spond to the advances of Our Lord, to do little or much for Him, in a word, to choose among the sacrifices He was asking. Then, as in the days of my childhood, I cried out: 'My God, I choose all!' I don't want to be a saint by halves, I'm not afraid to suffer for You, I fear only one think: to keep my own will; so take it, for 'I choose all' that You will![99]

She reflects on this simple scene from her childhood and the desire that children have to obtain some gift or present. Kids want a certain gift based on their own imagination, dreams, and ability to enjoy life. For a little boy, a simple stick is enough to become a sword, a gun, a walking staff, and so much more. For others with more limited imagination, they need more of a visible, tangible reality to help them. Thérèse wanted to be the soul that whatever she was given from God, whether simple or complex, she would joyfully accept it and use it with the creativity of the Spirit for God's glory!

St. Thérèse and her works are most known for how centered they are on the love of God and love of others. But that love

---

99. St. Thérèse, 30.

was based and had its supernatural origin first and foremost in her simple faith. Her belief that God was ever present and working made love in the simple moment possible. Her faith, which was not only a vision but a contact with the living God, allowed her to see how active and loving God was in the present moment, where He was, and how easy it was to love and be loved by Him.

> "It is the spirit of gratitude which draws upon us the overflow of God's grace," said Thérèse, "for no sooner have we thanked him for one blessing than he hastens to send us ten additional favours in return. Then, when we show our gratitude for these new gifts, He multiplies his benedictions to such a degree that there seems to be a constant stream of divine grace ever coming our way." The truth contained in Thérèse's words is not that God sends more blessings when we are grateful but rather that we become more aware of the abundant blessings that we have. [100]

Thérèse's faith was a supernatural anchor in God: it allowed her on earth to see "thy will be done, on earth as it is in heaven." Because it was so overwhelmingly focused on God and His interplay in our world, it influenced not only how she saw her own life, but everyone else's life since her focus was on God, the Father of all and the author of all life. These insights were seen no more beautifully than in the famous image of the garden that she used to open her *Story of a Soul* and which is the key to interpret the rest of the book.

---

100. St. Thérèse, 30.

I wondered for a long time why God has preferences, why all souls don't receive an equal amount of graces. . . . Jesus deigned to teach me this mystery. He set before me the book of nature; I understood how all the flowers He had created are beautiful, how the splendor of the rose and the whiteness of the Lily do not take away the perfume of the little violet or the delightful simplicity of the daisy. I understood that if all flowers wanted to be roses, nature would lose her springtime beauty, and the fields would no longer be decked out with little wild flowers. And so it is in the world of souls, Jesus' garden. He willed to create great souls comparable to Lilies and roses, but He has created smaller ones and these must be content to be daisies or violets destined to give joy to God's glances when He looks down at his feet. Perfection consists in doing His will, in being what He wills us to be. I understood, too, that Our Lord's love is revealed as perfectly in the simplest soul who resists His grace in nothing as in the most excellent soul. . . . When coming down in this way, God manifests His infinite grandeur. Just as the sun shines simultaneously on the tall cedars and on each little flower as though it were alone on the earth, so Our Lord is occupied particularly with each soul as though there were no others like it. And just as in nature all the seasons are arranged in such a way as to make the humblest daisy bloom on a set day, in the same way, everything works out for the good of each soul. [101]

101. St. Thérèse, 14–15.

The magnificent trust she had in God was one that was aware of the big picture; she saw God as the great author of all lives who can move the entire forest to grow, yet help the delicate daisy unroll its petals. It was this same faith that was in St. Rose of Lima to humbly accept the call she had to be the rose of Jesus' heart and why she drew so near to the dark, violet petals of St. Martin. Each of them lived a different yet unified walk of holiness. Their faith was the same because their God is the same. It is He who gives this faith because it is He who has done all things. This remarkable light and attention that Thérèse had on the Lord is the golden thread throughout her story. It allows us to see her whole life and how she can be attentive to her own life with great detail, because God, even in His great care for the immense diversity of souls, is not diminished in helping her soul along the way. God can give Himself fully to each soul, without diminishing what He can give to another soul. Therefore we can look and marvel at these great saints and only grow in greater hope for our lives. It was this hope that allowed Thérèse to see and trust how He, from the smallest moment of her life, was leading her on a special path of holiness. And it was this faith that also brought her through the darkest moments of human life.

In Thérèse's childhood, everything had a remarkable radiance of God's presence. However, before entering Carmel, she had two memories that were both very distressing yet, through the providence of God, very fruitful in her life and her vocation. The first was her terrible sickness and the miraculous cure from Our Lady. This event took place when Thérèse was ten years old, during what she called "the distressing years" when she was in boarding school, separated from her family circle, teased by students, but worst of all, had to say goodbye to Pauline who entered Carmel. Pauline was her second mother, and after all that little Thérèse had endured emotionally and mentally, this separation was too much. Thérèse became very sick and had to leave school. She was an extremely sensitive young girl, but she was not faking or being dramatic. The spiritual and emotional weight was also affecting her physically.

Thérèse's faith did not replace any of her aspects of human nature. No, sanctity does not remove or destroy anything in the human person, but rather allows it to be lifted above the order of nature. Many of the saints dealt with various physical, mental, and emotional anomalies. They weren't spared, but rather saw that the brokenness of human nature becomes a vessel for grace and God is able to raise us where our nature fails to reach. Thérèse's sickness was just of this sort. It was born from an emotional wound caused by the hardships present in this world. "Ah how can I express the anguish of my heart! In one instant, I understood what life was; until then, I had never seen it so sad; but it appeared to me in all its reality, and I saw it was nothing but continual suffering and separation."[102] This sickness was first off all a result of the poor human condition that we all face: the loss and brokenness of human relationships. Her gentle heart was not ready for the disorder and chaos that sin and this world brings and the distance from those we love that takes places. Thérèse saw through all this pain that for those in heaven and for those with faith, when we are united in the Lord, we are ever together, but in the world, we still bear much of the pain.

Her sickness began simply as a strong headache. After a walk with her uncle, she became very tired and needed to lie down. Suddenly, she was gripped with a terrible tremor in her body. It took on some form of the cold, filling her with chills, but did not seem to have any remedy by the normal means. These spells hit her time after time and the

102. St. Thérèse, 87.

doctors were baffled at what was causing them, especially to a child so young. She was gripped with intense suffering and had to remain in bed for several months on account of this tribulation. It was baffling to so many, but Thérèse saw it as a beginning of her acceptance of martyrdom.

Moreover, this sickness also had a more menacing source.

> The sickness which overtook me certainly came from the demon; infuriated by your entrance into Carmel, he wanted to take revenge on me for the wrong our family was to do him in the future. But he did not know that the sweet Queen of heaven was watching over her fragile little flower that she was smiling on her from her throne in heaven and was preparing to stop the storm the moment her flower was to break without any hope of recovery. [103]

At every step, the devil is there to try to resist man. Thérèse, did not fear the devil. As a child, she had seen two demons cowering from her because of her great faith; the devil is more afraid of us, yet he attacks to try to discourage us. Thérèse truly believed that the devil had a certain power over her body, since he could not touch her soul. The devil is a legalistic spirit and only can have jurisdiction where he is given and where he is allowed. With the emotional wounds of Thérèse, the devil was able to grab onto some of that brokenness. God, who does not will for us to suffer, is able to bring good out of all. As the devil tried to use the wounds and weakness of Thérèse's tender heart as a way into her, God

103. St. Thérèse, 90.

used this suffering to raise his little flower above this world, teaching her to look to heaven for healing but also for rest from all trials and separations. Every moment of weakness and every wound, even our sins, can be how God breaks through our shield of self-reliance and shows His power to touch our wounds.

All of this brokenness and feeling of loss and separation not only put her in the prime position to be spiritually raised because of detachment, but also to find a cure that was truly other worldly. The cure came from none other than the Blessed Mother herself. Finding no help on earth, poor little Thérèse had also turned toward the Mother of heaven, and prayed with all her heart that she take pity on her. During the novena to Our Lady of Victories that was being offered for her, her sisters were by her bedside praying during a particularly difficult episode. Suddenly, Mary smiled at Thérèse and give her healing.

> All of a sudden, the Blessed Virgin appeared beautiful to me, so beautiful that never had I seen anything so attractive; her face was suffused with an ineffable benevolence and tenderness, but what penetrated to the very depths of my soul was the 'ravishing smile of the Blessed Virgin. At that instant, all my pain disappeared, and two large tears glistened on my eyelashes and flowed down my cheeks, silently, but they were tears of unmixed joy. [104]

The famous image of Our Lady of the Smile became one of the most tangible and vivid displays of heaven on earth that little Thérèse saw in her life. She still suffered from a few of these ailments and still had a fragile spirit, but her

104. St. Thérèse, 96.

functionality returned to her. This powerful grace above all left her with a desire to live not for this world of pain and brokenness but for the kingdom of heaven with its never-failing joys. The power of this grace, as many gifts of the spiritual world, was crafted and destined for her. This event was a powerful steppingstone on her hidden path.

The other powerful moment in her life was Thérèse's intercession for Pranzini, the convicted murderer. The little flower is remarkable for her faith, but this faith also blossomed into charity. Faith that leads to charity is nothing more than seeing all things through the eyes of God and thus loving as He loved because of a greater understanding and knowledge of the object of that love.

Thérèse had so many moments in her life where she received love: her parents, her siblings, the saints, the Blessed Mother, our Lord Himself. However, as she approached her entrance into Carmel, she was given a great opportunity of love in the person of a convicted felon. In July of 1887, Henri Pranzini was put on trial and found guilty. He was seen in the eyes of the world as a guilty criminal; in the eyes of Christians, he was an unrepentant sinner. How was he seen in the eyes of God? He was loved unconditionally. Unconditional love means the love of God has no conditions; it is not caused or ended by anything we do. Man is loved by God because of who he is, not what he does. In God's eyes, our identity is not identical with our actions. Too many times, man equates what he does with who he is. We are told by our performative, utilitarian world that you are only as good as what you can do. There is a direct equation of man's identity and worth with his actions, successes, failures, and so on. Lines like, "I'm depressed" or "I'm gay" are so common in our society. We are identified with these activities to the point that to see and love a behavior is to see and love us. Why? Because it is calculatable. We can have a measure for the love others have for us in how they accept, approve, and enjoy our actions. It gives a tangible nature to love. At the root there exists an insecurity in man, an insecurity that he is not loved because of something he has done. Man is thus afraid that love can be lost. However, man is something greater than an orientation, a disorder, a sin, or a struggle. Jesus, through His death, has shown us that sin is not our identity and death and punishment is not our destiny. This is why he loved sinners so much and drew so near to them.

Thérèse had seen so much of her world from God the Father's eyes and she knew well of His plan, His love, and His gifts to men. Now, she was invited to see the world through the eyes of the Son, as he hung on the cross.

> The cry of Jesus on the Cross sounded continually in my heart: 'I thirst!' These words ignited within me an unknown and very living fire. I wanted to give my Beloved to drink and I felt myself consumed with a thirst for souls. As yet, it was not the souls of priests that attracted me, but those of great sinners; I burned with the desire to snatch them from the eternal flames. [105]

Her love was for sinners as she sought the greatest good for them, which, as all the saints show, was to find union with the Beloved. To desire union with Him for His sake and for the good of the sinner is the true fruit of charity. Thérèse came to hear the story of Pranzini and immediately was impelled to love him. She learned not only of his crime, but also that he seemed to have no sense of contrition about his sins. It was this state of sin and blindness that drove Thérèse to focus her prayer and intercession on him. "I wanted at all costs to prevent him from falling into hell. . . . I offered to

105. St. Thérèse, 155.

God all the infinite merits of Our Lord, the treasures of the Church."[106] She had a hunger, or as Jesus demonstrated, a thirst for his salvation. She learned the power of prayer, and the ability we must implore the graces and mercies of God to touch and move hearts. As she said, "I told God I was sure He would pardon the poor, unfortunate Pranzini; that I'd believe this even if he went to his death without any sign of repentance or without having gone to confession. I was absolutely confident in the mercy of Jesus."[107]

"Hope does not disappoint because God's love has been poured into our hearts through the Holy Spirit who was been given to us" (Rom 5:5), says St. Paul. These words are perfectly summed up in Thérèse's experience. The hope for God's mercy came to be fulfilled in the mercy of God being poured into her heart and then transmitted to her love for Pranzini.

One morning, she looked at the newspaper and read the story of Pranzini's execution and how, right before going to be killed, he turned to the priest and took hold of his crucifix and kissed it three times. The joy and love that rushed into Thérèse's soul in that moment must have been unbearable! She called Pranzini, her "first child,"[108] in that spiritual motherhood that goes beyond flesh and blood.

Finally, at the age of sixteen, Thérèse was able to enter Carmel and give her life to the Lord, hidden from the world to be seen by Our Father, who "sees everything in secret" (Mt 5). Right from the start, Thérèse showed her love for God in the way she was asked to suffer and make sacrifices in the community. However, she accepted everything and carried her cross silently. She had to face separation from her dear father as he reached the peak of his illness and ultimately death; she was ridiculed for her youth and for being so

---

106. St. Thérèse, 155.
107. St. Thérèse, 155.
107. St. Thérèse, 155.

inexperienced in work and the religious life. The Mother Prioress was excessively severe with her and was also very vocal about how Thérèse would fall short. In all these trials, both spiritual and exterior, she remained silent and made them an offering to God.

One of the first events of her new life that was emblematic of her entire life occurred on a day like any other. She was cleaning and found a small jug that had been broken previously. She tenderly placed it on the windowsill to clean the room. The Novice Mistress then came in and saw the broken jug and severely scolded Thérèse, since she assumed that Thérèse was responsible for breaking it. This assumption, as many times assumptions are, was wrong and very hurtful. For most of us, we would have instantly justified ourselves. After all, the truth is that she didn't do it, right? However, Thérèse took a different spin on it.

> Without a word, I kissed the floor, promising to be more careful in the future. Because of my lack of virtue these little practices cost me very much and I had to console myself with the thought that at the Last Judgment everything would be revealed. I noticed this when one performs her duty, never excusing herself, no one knows it, on the contrary, imperfections appear immediately. [109]

She was already reflecting on the eternal, even in such a simple and short incident. It was also a lesson about how to look at misfortunes in our lives: They are out of our control. This was precisely where little Thérèse found her strength: in God's love for her rather than the opinion of others. It wasn't what she could do that was why she was loved, but

109. St. Thérèse, 244.

who she was. Therefore, she could accept these trials because she knew she was loved totally by God.

Thérèse walked on stepping stones such as these for the rest of her life. As small and pointless as they may seem to those of us who dream of holiness as bold and great achievements, the power was that she never turned anything down. As the Little Flower had summed up earlier, everything could be seen as a gift of love from God, and thus she never refused anything, she accepted it all. She accepted all, but then she desired all. Thérèse strove to find what plans God had for her, where he was leading her by inspiring such a great hunger. Soon, she found her answer. She wrote it out in one of the greatest spiritual exposés that has ever been composed. I write it out here in its totality for the beauty of its composition:

> I understood that if the Church had a body composed of different members, the most nec-essary and most noble of all could not be lacking to it, and so I understood that the Church had a Heart and that this Heart was BURNING WITH LOVE. I understood it was Love alone that made the Church's member's act, that if Love ever became extinct, apostles would not preach the Gospel and martyrs would not shed their blood. I understood that LOVE COMPRISED ALL VOCATIONS. THAT LOVE WAS EVERYTHING, THAT IT EMBRACED ALL TIMES AND PLACES . . . IN A WORD, THAT IT WAS ETERNAL! Then in the excess of my delirious joy, I cried out: O Jesus my Love . . . my voca-tion, at last I have found it. . . . MY VOCATION IS LOVE! In the heart of the Church, my Mother, I shall be Love.[110]

The simple action of love that Thérèse could achieve became the most powerful force in the universe. Aristotle had said that it was love that caused the planets to move. Indeed, love was what moved every great and mighty action; love was what united the Church together; love was what gave the Church her strength and her identity because God is love. If Thérèse could live that, she could live all vocations and be in and with all. Love drew heaven down to earth, and earth up to heaven. It could escape the bounds of our limitation. This then becomes the true power of her little way: "Jesus does not demand great actions from us but simply surrender and gratitude. . . . He has no need of our works but only of our love."[111] She strove to do little things with great love, since in the end, all that was needed was love. Love is accessible to all people, always, in all things. No one could despair of not being capable of fulfilling God's will, for whatever comes in one's life can become a gift of love.

Hence, Thérèse thrust herself into love. We must remember that love is not a feeling, it is an act of the will. We will have various feelings and emotions. These are responses that largely are out of our control. We can't help it if someone is disagreeable or if frankly, we don't like someone. There is no sin or virtue in mere feelings. The question is if we can respond correctly. For Thérèse, love was so habitual that it was her very being.

> There is in the Community a Sister who has the faculty of displeasing me in everything, in her ways, her words, her character, everything seems very disagreeable to me. . . . I told myself that charity must not consist in feelings but in works; then I set myself to doing for this

110. St. Thérèse, 302.
111. St. Thérèse, 295.

> Sister what I would do for the person I loved the most...when I was tempted to answer her back in a disagreeable manner, I was content with giving her my most friendly smile.[112]

St Thérèse's little way inspired many other saints, including Mother Teresa of Calcutta. The little way represented a true way of walking every day and every moment. It was made of small, concentrated steps, but each would be powerful in moving because they were so filled with love. Mother Teresa loved every person in front of her. Despite the great wall of poverty and hunger she faced, she eventually overcame it by focusing on the individuals.

In April of 1896, Thérèse entered her great trial of faith; she went through a great darkness of faith, where it seemed the presence of God was taken away from her. At this same time, she began coughing up blood. This was a physical trial that she carried quietly and patiently until September 30, 1897. Tuberculosis, which had claimed the lives of so many other saints, is commonly called consumption because the experience and effect of it is like being consumed from the inside out. Thérèse bore both trials as sacrifices of love to her divine lover and offered it for the conversion of sinners and the souls of priests. During this time, she went on almost as normal with her work and life. She drew near to and worked with one of the sisters who was so disturbing that she was basically isolated from the rest of the sisters. Thérèse specifically sought this sister out and requested to go work with her. She endured much complaining and bickering, but Thérèse simply smiled back, complimented the sister on how well she was working, and remained faithful by her side. Sickness is always a time when we struggle to be patient. We get irritated with the slightest inconveniences and yet, this

112. St. Thérèse, 346.

little child showed more courage and patience than any of us could muster, even on the best of days.

July became incredibly difficult as Thérèse began to cough up blood more frequently. She was moved to the infirmary and remained there until she died. She grew steadily weaker, and intense pain shot all over her body. However, she retained an incredible sweetness and joy. Not only that, but she was also able to keep a powerful sense of humor!

During this suffering period, she made the famous prediction that sums up the saints of this book. Her sister Pauline, who was the superior over Thérèse, had asked her to finish writing her *Story of a Soul* book. Pauline recounted these famous words of the little flower:

> I feel that my mission is about to begin, mission of making others love God as I love Him, my mission of teaching my little way to souls. If God answers my requests, my heaven will be spent on earth up until the end of the world. Yes, I want to spend my heaven in doing good on earth. [113]

This is the great and final change that love has within us: God truly can be extended through us to all others. Heaven is the great place where we share completely not only in the life of God, but in the love of God. His love is always reaching out to others to draw all people into His loving embrace. All the saints in heaven wish for others to share in their great joy and love. This is what made them saints on earth, this is how they are saints in heaven: love. Love drew them up into heaven and love draws them down to earth. God's love becomes expressed in a personal and 'incarnate' way through them and their personalities. This is why they are so active in our lives!

---

113. St. Thérèse, 422.

Earlier, Thérèse made a great cry that she belonged in heaven. She prayed to the saints: "O Blessed inhabitants of heaven. I beg you to ADOPT ME AS YOUR CHILD."[114] This was not because she dreaded earth or this life. No, she was already able to live the life of heaven here on earth through her love. However, heaven is the place of complete union with God without the separations that the weakness of this world has. It's a greater and perfect sharing in God. It's the complete vision of God as He truly and fully is. Yet, that does not disconnect one from the life of others. Seeing Him means seeing His love for the world.

Eventually, Thérèse received the wish she asked for. On September 30, 1897, she died and was finally born in heaven. From that moment until the present, she has not failed to live out the prophecy she has made and to fulfill the wish she desired. This little nun, who never left her cloister, now has a universal patronage over the world. She who wanted to be the love at the heart of the Church which pumps blood to all the members to give power to their activity, is now the patron saint of missions and missionaries. She is a reminder again and again of where the mission work receives its strength and what the goal of all mission work is. Every year, leading up to her feast day on October 1, countless people make the famous rose novena to St. Thérèse, seeking a favor and, as a sign, she has promised a rose. An entire book could be filled with the story of these events! She truly has allowed a shower of roses to fall, she has continued to not only spend her heaven doing good on earth but showing the life of heaven that can be shared in, already on earth.

Thérèse was absorbed into this joy of heaven and showed that every little sacrifice, everything that she bore, every act of love she made, was never in vain. Nothing is ever wasted! Not only does it draw one into heaven, but then the love wishes to be spread, and as it spreads, it grows!

114. St. Thérèse, 304.

> She will gather up my flowers unpetalled through love and have them pass through Your own divine hands, O Jesus. And this Church in heaven, desirous of playing with her little child, will cast these flowers, which are nor infinitely valuable because of Your divine touch, upon the Church Suffering in order to extinguish its flames and upon the Church Militant in order to gain the victory for it! [115]

All the gifts of our lives, after giving them to Jesus, will not stay stagnant in the hands of the Lord, but because they have touched His hands, are now great gifts of infinite value! The finite actions of the saints of earth, take on an infinite power in heaven. They can be patrons and intercessors in a far greater and more powerful capacity in heaven, without the burden and weakness of the earthly life. Their companionship with us is great and powerful! Thérèse marches powerfully in this army, and her small acts, done with great love, now are gifts for us on earth.

Roses

Indeed, there are hundreds of wonderful and amazing stories of people who have received not only answers to their prayers but also signs of those answered prayers. Thérèse showed her care, concern, and response to prayers with roses. Many people have testified to anything from a small petal to large bouquets being found. They have accompanied specific petitions or just general care and concern that Thérèse would show. I wish to first share my personal rose story.

While in Rome, one of my favorite celebrations to attend

---

115. St. Thérèse, 305.

was the Pentecost mass at the Pantheon. It is always a packed church and draws people from all over for the mass. Of course, at the very top of the dome in the middle of the ceiling is the famous "eagle eye," the giant hole in the top of the dome which was a sign of communion with the divine in ancient Rome. At the end of the mass, thousands of rose petals are dropped from the eagle eye into the church onto the attendants below as a symbol of the tongues of fire that came down upon the apostles at Pentecost.

In 2018, I attended this mass and I was so in awe of the beauty of this celebration. The rose petals feel in such masses that the air seemed to shine with a red tint. As the petals fell, I managed to catch several before they hit the ground. I quickly placed them in the pages of my Bible to press them and dry them to better preserve them. I figured these petals would be a great reminder not only of the mass but of the fire of the Holy Spirit.

Since I had several of them left over, I figured that I would take some and make them into some holy cards for a few people who were very charismatic and in love with the Holy Spirit. Once I got back home for summer, I got to work on my little project. I cut a small piece of construction paper, wrote some scriptures on them, dated it, and then put the petals on the cards. They looked nice, but I knew they would look better and last longer if they were laminated. So, the next morning I grabbed my cards and I went to town to get them laminated. On the way, I thought I would pass by my former parish and pray for a bit in the adoration chapel. As I was pulling up, I saw the youth minister of the church walking out. He and I had been great friends and had done a lot of awesome work together with the youth group.

He waved me down, I got out, and we talked for a bit since this was the first time he had seen me since I got back. "You in a rush, man?" he asked me. "No, I'm just on my way to get some stuff laminated," was my simple reply. He asked if he could join me on the errand so we could catch up. I agreed but then I realized I had all the cards in my back seat. I was planning on giving him one as a surprise since he and I had worked so well together and he was very charismatic. I didn't want to ruin the surprise but I guessed this would be a good time.

As he got in my car and we were about to drive off, I looked at him with a grin. "You know, it's very providential that you are in here with me." "Why you say that?" he asked. "Because, I have this little gift for you," and I reached in the back and gave him one of the cards that I was going to laminate. He looked at it with a dropped jaw and then threw his head back and laughed. "What's up?" I asked. "Dude, me and some of the core team here have been doing the St. Thérèse novena for guidance in our ministry, and today is the last day!" he exclaimed. "What's even better, I told Thérèse I did not want a rose because I didn't want that to be my reason for doing the novena."

Sometimes the saints have a sense of humor.

Fr. Brian Seiler

The next testimony was submitted by a brother priest of mine, Fr. Brian Seiler. He and I attended seminary together and are now both priests for the diocese of Alexandria. Fr. Brian was ordained a priest one year after I was. He has always had a deep devotion to St. Thérèse, but as I was writing this book, I came to discover that he had several beautiful experiences with our little saint.

My sister, Kim Renee, was diagnosed with an inoperable brain tumor when she was fifteen years old. The doctors promised us that it was the size of a green pea and would not grow. It would alter her hormone production but would not threaten her life. When she was in dental school in 2008, it began to grow and reached the approximate size of a walnut. I was looking for a saint to ask for their intercession for my sister when I came across a holy card with a novena to St. Thérèse. I remembered that my mother and grandmother loved her, and they would talk of her "little way" and urge us to offer up our pains for the holy souls in purgatory, advice which they credited to her. I began to pray the novena prayer for my sister's brain tumor during my run each morning after praying the rosary.

After about two months of praying the novena, I received a surprising phone call from my sister. She asked me if she could "vent" to me about her day, and I agreed. Dental school students are required to do a certain amount of dental work to be able to graduate, and she had an interesting patient that morning. This woman said that she was a psychic and told Kim's assistant that someone in her family had recently passed but wanted her to know that they are okay. The assistant ran off crying, so Kim had to work on the patient alone. Kim said that everybody has lost someone, so it didn't prove anything. The woman then told Kim that she saw flowers all around her. My sister said that she didn't care about the flowers, she just wanted to fix her teeth. The woman asked her if her boyfriend had given her flowers recently, and she said, "No, he has never given me flowers, and neither has any other boyfriend." The woman asked if they had any important day like an anniversary coming where she might get flowers. Kim said that she had never gotten any flowers and just wanted to help her. So the lady allowed her to take care of her teeth.

Later that day, the woman returned and told Kim that she had figured it out. "They are roses, and they are from St. Thérèse." Kim said, "I don't know who that is." The woman said that roses were a sign that St. Thérèse had answered a prayer, and asked Kim if she was praying for anyone to St. St. Thérèse. She said, "I told you that I don't know who she is, and I have not been praying to her. If you need any more help for your teeth, then please give me a call." Then Kim asked me if that was the craziest thing that I had ever heard. I asked her if she was sitting down, and then told her that I had been praying to St. Thérèse for her brain tumor for two months. Her next doctor's appointment was on Tuesday, and they said that her tumor had somehow shrunk to the size of a split pea. I went and bought a dozen roses and brought them to the Minor Basilica of the Immaculate Conception where they had a relic of St. Thérèse, and from that point on I have sought her intercession very frequently.

Last week, after I had finished setting up for Spanish Mass, I began to do my holy hour. A non-Hispanic parishioner showed up an hour early for Mass to pray. She asked if she could turn out the lights, and I agreed. After finishing my evening prayer, I began some silent meditation on Cardinal Sarah's book The Power of Silence. Well, with the lights off, the air conditioner keeping it cool, and the pew being relatively comfortable, I began to go in and out of sleep. After Mass, the parishioner approached me and said that she had noticed my falling asleep in prayer. I told her about Fr. Benedict Groeschel falling asleep during a holy hour with us seminarians during a retreat and that St. Thérèse used to fall asleep during holy hours. She said that she knew that about St. Thérèse, and that she had seen her in her habit sitting next to me while I was dozing, praying for me as she looked on me with a smile.

Noah & Julia Hale

The next testimony comes from a beautiful married couple that has this little saint to thank in part for their relationship. I met them through a mutual friend who lived near the Servant of God Charlene Richard. Come to find out, my friend knew Charlene's great niece! After meeting her, she and her boyfriend at the time shared their testimony.

We don't realize how evident saints are in our lives and how much we can connect with them, how much we can depend on them to help us and intercede for us. I think we can vouch for that. St. Thérèse of Lisieux not only taught us this but wanted to make sure we knew that she loved us and wanted to be there for us. St. Thérèse is known for her simplicity and so from the beginning she was simple and clear in her presence in our lives.

One of the first times St. Thérèse made herself very evident in our lives was the night of an annual Christmas concert that our hometown high school puts on. Julia sang in the concert and so our friend group got together and went to support her. After the concert was over, it ended up just being me, Julia, and Elizabeth sitting at the depot, an old train station stop in the middle of town where the concert was held. Everyone had left and we were the only ones there. We found ourselves deep in conversation about our lives, childhood, and family members. Julia started telling us about her aunt Charlene and her personal connection with her as a child. Soon after she started talking about her, we were all so intrigued that we got into our vehicles and headed to where she is buried. As I walked up to the grave, I found myself saying a novena to St. Thérèse and I asked for a purple rose. Low and behold, she never fails. On the center of the grave was one purple rose. I immediately knew that something greater was at work here that I wasn't ready for.

As we all prayed kneeling down, the subtle sound of footsteps were coming from behind me so instinctively I turned around but I saw nothing. These footsteps kept getting louder and louder, so I decided to forget about it. Then, I could feel the presence of someone right next to us so I looked again and there she was, little St. Thérèse in all her beauty and timidness. I crouched down on the kneeler and she just stood there almost like she was waiting for someone, and she truly was. It was so crazy. She just giggled and sat down on the bench right behind me at the same time as Julia. She was just next to her, watching over her in a sense of joy but a peaceful joy, and as she was there, she looked at Julia then back at me and laughed. Afterwards we all kind of sat in silence. She had gotten up and left but the footsteps were so evident it's like she was still among us and walking with us.

Around a year and a half later, Julia and I had become very much in love, and our faith drew us closer to each other in every way. We attended Steubenville South in Alexandria together and we spoke to each other about how the talks we had heard touched our hearts, especially the ways we could be just like the saints we had always heard of. I remember the desire to see one another in the eyes of Christ. I was thinking about asking Julia to be my girlfriend but didn't know how. It was up to me to make the move and that's where one of my great friends, founder of 'God Made Self Driven', Dustin Bertrand intervened. Once again St. Thérèse was working in our lives. The whole day I just kept praying and asking the Lord, "If this is truly what you want, can you please just give me a clear answer." As I was going into the last day of Steubenville, the thought weighing on my mind, Dustin came up to me and we talked a while. I was going to ask him what he thought about me asking Julia to be my girlfriend but before I could say anything he says, "What you think about Julia, man? Y'all seem super close, y'all should get a little something started." He's laughing but my jaw felt like it was on the floor. I was in shock, and I told him about everything I had been thinking about and it just pieced itself together.

Julia was out of town for a week to go to a wedding in Maine. I had to hold in my excitement and eagerness to ask her to go out with me until she got back. So I started praying a novena to St. Thérèse and to her parents. After seven days of Julia being gone, the day she had got back, she sent me a picture of a huge stuffed rose like one for a little kid. I remember in my novena, the prayer at the end was saint "St. Thérèse of the Child Jesus, pray for us," so it was so fitting in every way. That weekend we went back to her Aunt Charlene's grave and that's where I told her everything about Steubenville, Dustin, and the novena. From that day, July 6, 2019 we became a couple formed by St. Thérèse and God. Exactly year later I asked Julia to marry me, and again St. Thérèse was with us and helped it all go smoothly. St. Thérèse's plan was finally coming together. I can't thank God enough for the graces He bestowed unto us through the intercession of St. Thérèse on this beautiful journey.

O God, who open your Kingdom to those who are humble and to little ones, lead us to follow trustingly in the little way of Saint Thérèse,so that through her intercession we may see your eternal glory revealed. Amen.

"St. Padre Pio"
Original Painting by Lilly Hidalgo

PADRE PIO

"I am a poor friar who prays," was the somewhat disappointing description given to an inquiring journalist. After all, the man whom the journalist sought out and who delivered this response had been hailed as a mystic, a stigmatist, a miracle worker, and a living saint. The man, or friar, in question was born as Francis, canonized as St. Pio of Pietrelcina, but known to the world simply as Padre Pio. This description may seem an understatement when one looks at all the powerful events that occurred in his life: stories of bilocation, reading of hearts, bearing the stigmata that bled during mass, seeing and speaking with saints, angels, and souls in purgatory, and even battling the devil. This incredible man seemed to have pierced the veil to the supernatural and journeyed between heaven and earth (and even hell and purgatory) like no man had before.

However, at the heart and source of all these miraculous events lies the core reality of who Padre Pio was: he was a poor friar who prayed. Prayer was the reason and the source of all his life's events as well as his truest and greatest treasure. It was not just a means to an end, but prayer, conversation with God Himself, was an end in itself, a good to be desired and sought after, and he sought it with all that he was. In seeking, he found; in knocking, the door was opened (Mt 7:7-8). Praying, as many saints have seen it, is simply being present to the one who is present to us, the one who is more present to us that we are even to ourselves. St Teresa of Avila describes prayer as nothing more than loving conversation with the one who loves us. Padre Pio identified fully with this definition of prayer. Prayer was not just a personal, individual experience but drew him into the great mystery of God Himself. When this friar prayed, which was constantly, it was beyond just an experience of words and repetition: it was a lived experience in and with the very presence of God. The door of prayer swings both ways, and the more Padre Pio opened the door into the supernatural life of God, the more the supernatural life of God entered him. In the very person of Padre Pio, heaven and earth intersected. Heaven and earth intermingled in the person of Padre Pio, to the point that He was physically drawn into the eternal sacrifice of Jesus by bearing the marks of His Cross.

Prayer thus is the core of who Padre Pio is. I use the present tense because Padre Pio's life of prayer has not stopped, and his presence in this life has not ceased. The communion he experienced with God in prayer has now become a permanent reality. In truth, heaven is the reality that prayer is a state of life more than an action. Having come so much into God's presence through prayer, one enters the sanctuary of heaven. The evidence of Padre Pio's powerful prayer life come from various vantage points. Countless skeptics, atheists, and secular doctors were all convinced by the very incarnation of the supernatural that existed in this man. This is the great gift we find in Padre Pio, this living example of the life of prayer as a Christian. His prayer was not just mere words or sentiments, but a stable powerful mode of being.

Padre Pio is not only an embodiment of prayer, he is also a witness against secularism. Secularism is the anchor placed on man by focusing on this world (*saecula* is the Latin word meaning "age") and the immediate gains offered. It teaches that what is most real is what is here and now. In so doing, God and the supernatural is laid to rest and devalued. It is the great enemy of Christianity because it flattens the plane of this world to simply the present and physical moment. There is nothing beyond or after, and there is nothing that can't be seen and touched. Secularism imprisons man and blinds him from seeing that there may be more than meets the eye. Beyond just the two dimensional, horizontally oriented direction of this material world, Padre Pio showed that a greater horizon, extending in infinite directions, exists. Secularism is like staring through a magnifying glass at a speck of dirt; Padre Pio through his prayer lifted his head from the limited eyepiece of this world and became aware of a greater world around him, waiting to be seen. He stands in stark contrast against the backdrop of a world that is considered to have become pagan again:

> Our times have been called a 'post-Christian era' or a 'neo-pagan era.' It is characterized as an age of religious skepticism and disbelief, resulting in a secularism that has pushed God out of the picture of daily life. Padre Pio stands as a great challenge to the secularism of this time! This is because, as one writer put it, the measure of a person's holiness and effectiveness with others is the measure in which God becomes real in his or her life. [117]

Padre Pio's holiness is reflected not just by his impact on the world, but by the impact of the supernatural on this world through him. His person was a vehicle, a bridge uniting two worlds. The greatest testimony to his own holiness were the countless children he helped bring into heaven. He made God real to the world because God was real to him. His life is thus a great witness that God is still real; He is not dead.

So that sums him up: he is a poor friar who prays. The greatest definition of Padre Pio ultimately came from his

---

117. Franciscan Friars of the Immaculate, P*adre Pio: The Wonder Worker*, (Newbedford, MA: Our Lady's Chapel, 2009), Preface by Fr. Andrew Apostoli CFR, x.

relationship to God.

On May 25, 1887 a young boy was born to the Forgione family in Pietrelcina, Italy and was given the name Francis. He was a very good and holy boy, growing up in a religious family and very accustomed to praying and living the life of virtue. Though they were poor, they were very rich in devotion. Mary was given the first place, but young Francis did indeed learn much about his beloved namesake, St. Francis of Assisi, which planted the seed in his heart to follow a radical road of poverty so as to be rich in the Lord.

Young Francis was also very familiar with the power and patronage that other saints have over this world. In his small village, there was a shrine to St. Pellegrino or St. Pilgrim who used to draw great crowds of people seeking his intercession. On one occasion, young Francis was praying in the front row of this shrine with a great crowd gathered. A woman was there who had brought her deformed baby into the church.

> At a certain point, seeing she was not getting anywhere, she picked up her poor child and threw him onto the Saint's altar, crying, 'If you don't want to cure him, take him! I don't want him!' As soon as the child landed on the altar, he got up on his feet standing quite erect, and cried, 'Mamma! Mamma!' A miracle! . . . He would never forget the miracle that happened before his eyes, which convinced him of the power of prayer and of the intercession of the Saints. [118]

From that moment, prayer was not just a personal experience for young Francis but was a palpable force in

118. *Padre Pio,* 11.

this world. The saints were also not just examples of a good life or an image to be honored anymore, but channels of the living God into this world. Young Francis would hold this reality deeply in his soul as he would become more and more convinced that there was more to this world than simply what can be seen.

Francis' world would soon be forever changed by the addition and alteration of the divine into his human life. He felt called to dedicate his life totally to the Lord, and he realized that the goals offered by this world were not only minimal in comparison but also dangerous. He resolved to follow the path St. Francis of Assisi walked to find that peace and happiness he had in this world. However, this path would have it struggles, as one story from his childhood relates:

> At the age of fourteen he heard a majestic man of rare beauty taking him by the hand saying, "Come with me for you must fight a tough and aggressive warrior." On one side of a great plain were many beautiful people standing by his guide, who was dressed in white, while on the opposite side there was a huge, black, hideous, evil looking man and in back of him were repulsive looking people. Francis' guide told him he would have to do battle with the powerful ugly man. Francis trembled, turned pale and stammered that he could not possibly prevail against such a formidable enemy. His guide reassured him. "You must fight this man. Take heart. Enter the combat with confidence. Go forth courageously, I shall be with you. In reward for your victory over him I will give you a shining crown to adorn your brow." [119]

119. *Padre Pio*, 12.

This vision lasted only a moment and then come to an end, but the promise it contained would be lived out every day of his life. To engage in the battle, he would have to put himself on the front line by taking on the journey of religious life and formation for the priesthood. Young Francis soon followed in the footsteps of St. Francis and in 1903 he took on a new life, a new habit, and a new name: Fra Pio. In 1904 he made his first professions in the community and family of St. Francis and began his journey to the priesthood.

As Fra Pio entered the religious life the supernatural flooded into his life and he began to have more mystical visions. These visions ranged in type and frequency. Sometimes, he saw Jesus, other times the devil. These visions were not simply mental illusions, but were often very physical, tangible realities. One of his first was a vision of a large, black dog with glowing eyes that appeared outside of his room. He knew right away this was no normal dog but was something otherworldly. He was very familiar with the guises the devil would take to seduce and frighten. As a child, not long after his baptism, the devil even appeared to him disguised as a priest and tried to stop him from going to pray.

Around this time, Fra Pio became very ill. He was so ill that he had to go back home for several years to rest in hopes that the fresh country air would do him some good. Indeed, Fra. Pio loved the country, he loved his family, and he graciously received this little gift of love from God. He had serious medical conditions that defied explanations. On certain occasions, his fever would be so great that he would break the thermometers. As distressing as this condition could be, for Fra Pio even sickness took on a supernatural meaning. Throughout his life, he would continue to struggle with his health as part of the suffering he would bear with and for Jesus.

Sickness was not the only way that Fra Pio imitated Christ. He also took on the image and likeness of Christ in one of the most unique ways bestowed on man. On August 10, 1910, Fra Pio became Padre Pio as he took on the greatest image of Jesus in the form of the priesthood. The ability to become a living presence of Christ in the world through the priesthood is truly a humbling gift. Through ordination to the priesthood, Jesus manifests His great love for us. Man can experience His presence not just in intellectual concepts or doctrines of faith, but also in a living, breathing person. The priest represents Jesus, not through figures and symbols, but by truly allowing Jesus to be present anew in their person. The priest is given the power to effect the presence of Christ in the Eucharist, to offer the sacrifice of eternal love in the mass, and to bring about the power of Jesus' mercy in confession.

Because Jesus suffered every priest is also meant to be a victim. Every priest says daily the words, "This is my body given up for you." Even though the priest says those words *in persona Christi* or "in the person of Jesus," the priest still speaks these words with his own voice. Every priest is meant to pour out his life out of love for others so that they might have life in imitation and representation of Jesus. Padre Pio would thus be the quintessential priest because he made himself not only the priest but also the victim for others. He wrote a short yet beautiful prayer that summarized his entire ministry and life: "Oh Jesus, my heart's desire and my life, as I raise you up in trembling hands in the mystery of love, may I be *with* you, the way, the truth and the life for the world, and for *you* a holy priest, a perfect victim." [120]

Though his sickness gave him the opportunity to live out his vocation as a victim for others, it also brought setbacks. His health prevented him from becoming a preacher, but

120. *Padre Pio,* 17.

he was given the faculties and blessing to hear confession. This faculty became one of the greatest gifts that he offered to the world. Padre Pio would make some of the greatest announcements of the Gospel from one of the most unrecognized pulpits in the world: the confessional.

Padre Pio's whole life was a dwelling of heaven on earth, and this reality was reflected in his very body, which was an incarnation of the mysteries of the spiritual world and the life of Christ. On September 20, 1910, he became a living sacrament of Jesus' suffering when he received the invisible stigmata. He had recovered from his sickness and was returning to priestly ministry when one day, while he was sitting under an elm tree, he experienced a sharp pain in his hands and feet. He felt it was the pain of the nails of the Cross, though at this time he could not see them. He bore these wounds invisibly for eight years. No one was able to see them, but he felt the pain and the agony. All this pain he bore, in imitation of Jesus, out of love for others.

Padre Pio was both a man of love and of combat. When World War I began in 1914, no more than four years after Padre Pio became a priest, he was drafted for military service. However, poor health would put him on leave for a year, sending him back to his hometown for some rest and prayer. He had a love and understanding for combat and war, and he also loved and had compassion for soldiers and their plight. Several powerful miracles took place through Padre Pio concerning the war. In 1916, an Italian general had suffered a humiliating defeat and lost the lives of many men. The general grabbed his pistol to end his life when suddenly there appeared in his room a friar who persuaded him to not take his life. There was another case of Padre Pio appearing in the middle of the battlefield and calling a solider to come and see him. When the solider began walking toward Padre Pio, a bomb suddenly fell where the soldier had originally been standing. Padre Pio was even said to have appeared in the air: pulling the parachute of one man and showing up in front of airplanes to dissuade them from dropping bombs on a certain area (try to explain that to air traffic).

Even though Padre Pio was discharged from the army and went home for bed rest, he was far from leaving the battlefield. As the Great War was passing through the countries of the earth, Padre Pio would be involved in a spiritual battle between heaven and earth. His great combat was against the devil and the prize was the souls of men. Padre Pio physically experienced the battle against the devil who everyday was battling in the hearts of men to rob them for hell. Padre Pio experienced the reality and ugliness of this war. Sometimes he heard chains, hisses, animal beast noises, sometimes he saw the images of black dogs, animals, hideous little monsters. These apparitions were far from simply images to scare the holy Franciscan. On several occasions, objects would be thrown at him, he would be physically beaten by the apparition, objects in his room such as metal bars would be twisted and turned. On occasions, friars from other cells would be awakened in the middle of the night from these attacks. Most fiendish of all, the devil would take on various forms to try to tempt and seduce the holy priest. On occasions Satan would appear as a young woman doing an impure dance; at other times he would "disguise himself as an angel of light" (1 Cor. 11:14) and took the form of Padre Pio's guardian angel, his spiritual director; he even took the form of St. Francis or Jesus Christ himself! All these apparitions attempted to gain the trust of Padre Pio, but he endured them with a saintly smile.

He recounts in a very powerful way the real inability the devil has of doing anything against us by comparing the devil to a dog on a chain: "Beyond the length of the chain he cannot seize anyone. But, if you approach within the radius of the chain, you let yourself be caught. Remember that the devil has only one door by which to enter—the will. There are no secret or hidden doors."[121] The devil and all the fallen angels are what we call legalistic. This term means that they respect and operate within jurisdictions. Where they don't have permission, they cannot be; where they do, they can. Eve was won over by the devil not by power but by dialogue; she entertained the devil, his lies and offers, and by so doing gave him permission. If we give that permission to the devil through accepting temptations, believing lies, doubts and fears, or willfully allowing him into some part of our life, the devil has full access.

Padre Pio was able to take on these attacks from the devil because he never let the devil into his will. Padre Pio believed in the devil and thus was able to keep an eye on the devil. He was able to keep the devil external and gave him no room internally. The devil also attacked Padre Pio out of vindication for the souls that Padre Pio was saving and had saved. Being a victim soul, Padre Pio many times took on the attack of the devil that was meant for other people. At times it pushed the poor friar to his physical limits. God allowed it for two main reasons: 1) to humiliate the devil and show that he could be defeated by such a simple and humble friar doing something as simple as praying; 2) it was part of Padre Pio's great work of suffering for others. He was able to die to himself to live for Jesus and to offer to God a great gift. Padre Pio found that the key to overcoming the devil was clinging to Jesus both by faith and in imitation. It would be Jesus, the suffering servant, that Padre Pio would imitate the most through these trials. He would accept the attacks meant for others as Jesus did.

Above all the riches bestowed on Padre Pio, his love for others was the greatest. This again may seem a bit of

---

121. *Padre Pio,* 76.

an understatement, considering all the amazing gifts he possessed: he could bilocate, he had a heavy, heavenly aroma that followed him even while on earth, he could read the hearts of people in confession, he could prophesy various events that were to pass (including predicting popes that were to be elected), he could heal illness, interpret languages he did not know, and so on. However, all of these were united, subjected to, and flowed from his charism of love for others. St. Paul tells us in 1 Corinthinans 13 that love is the greatest of all gifts, greater than miraculous faith and mighty deeds. So too, more important than the miracles he would work and the faith he possessed was the tremendous love Padre Pio held in his heart. Everything he did, from the most fantastic and extraordinary manifestations to the simple unseen hours of prayers, was aimed at leading souls back to God, especially those who were lost and separated. "He would spread everywhere a ray of light, of warmth, of charity, of kindness, all with the greatest naturalness and simplicity, at times using playful wit and at others a stern look." [122] Whatever it was that he did, it was always to love God more and to bring souls closer to God. He would be soft and gentle when needed, stern and hard when that was called for. He was hidden in prayer when that was the call and sitting for hours in the confessional when that was needed. All of it came from his almost supernatural ability to love his children.

His gift of fatherhood would ultimately be the bedrock for his incredible power and ability to pray constantly. Padre Pio was constantly absorbed in the supernatural, either in battle with the enemy or wrapped up in the heavenly. His central occupation while in prayer was praying on behalf of others.

---

122. *Padre Pio,* 28.

He was marked with what St. Paul would say that ability to "pray without ceasing." He had a constant communion with God and the supernatural which was manifested in vocal, mental, and intercessory prayer and reparation prayer. His prayer was also what made him a spiritual father since it united him with the Father of all. He was constantly, in big and in small ways, speaking with God on behalf of the world. He was famously known as being a warrior of the rosary since it was one of the prayers that he would say almost ceaselessly. His prayer life joined all his gifts together and ultimately linked his own life to heaven. Most especially, when he offered Mass, the great prayer that unites heaven and earth, he took over three hours in imitation of Jesus on the Cross.

In his desire that everyone should go to heaven, Padre Pio had a great devotion to the souls in purgatory who were being prepared and purified for heaven. We could almost say that these souls had a devotion to him, so frequent were their visits to him! Because Padre Pio lived so tied to the great spiritual dimension of the Church, he was also opened to those poor, suffering members of the Church. These souls in Purgatory still have something unfinished from earth that they must either be purified from or rectify before going to heaven. They are released to continue to heaven in only two ways: either by suffering and being purged sufficiently or by the prayers of those members still on earth.[123] Frequently, these souls would come and visit Padre Pio, not only because he had such an openness to the supernatural, but also because of the power of his prayers. He saw the souls of friars who had died, relatives, friends and others. He prayed for them as he offered his daily mass and would instantly know of their

123. Isaiah chapter 6 relates that a great altar of burning coals stands between that on earth and the throne of God in heaven. This altar and its fire was able to purify the prophets unclean lips and so too it can the sins of others. 2 Maccabees also relates that the prayers of us can hasten people on their way to heaven.

entry into heaven. Padre Pio was so wrapped in prayer that he was almost more familiar with the supernatural than with the physical world. There is record of a playful encounter he had with a few of his spiritual companions witnessed by the other monks.

> On another occasion while the friars were at supper one evening Padre Pio abruptly left the table and dashed to the doorway and began a lively conversation with some people whom none of the other friars could see. They remarked to one another that he was going crazy. When he returned they asked him to whom he was he talking. 'Oh don't worry,' he replied, 'I was talking to some souls who were on their way from Purgatory to Heaven. They stopped here to thank me because I remembered them in my Mass this morning.[124]

For Padre Pio, the inhabitants of the spiritual world, be they demons, souls in purgatory, or saints and angels, were as real and tangible as any of his fellow men on earth; not only because of the reality and vivid expression of their manifestations, but also because Padre Pio had plunged himself fully into the spiritual dimension. Heaven and the spiritual are not far off across an unpassable abyss; it is not a matter of location; it is a richer reality. It is called the "super" natural because it embraces all that is natural but also surpasses it. We have access to it always and everywhere: prayer is the key that opens the door. Padre Pio's prayer

---

124. *Padre Pio*, 172.

life gave him opened eyes to penetrate this depth, but also allowed the door to swing the other way back into his life. Padre Pio was like a door man who peered into the depths of the inner house of God while standing to welcome those who walked by aimlessly on the streets into the feast of the Lord (Mt 27:1–14).

As with any good father, this great spiritual care and fatherhood would lead the Padre to suffer for his children in their place. Although Padre Pio recognized his own sinfulness and faults, he also dared to take on as much as he could for the sake of others. Padre Pio was able to not only stand before other people praying for them but also to stand in their place in a certain "mystical substitution"[125] where he heroically accepted the temptations, pain, and reparation meant for others as Jesus did for us. As a priest, united to Jesus, offers his body as a living sacrifice (Rom 12:1–2), so Padre Pio would not only accept what came to him for the good of others, but would even choose to take it on. Only being united with Jesus, the true lamb who has the power to take away the sins of the world, was Padre Pio able to take on the burden of others' sins.

Padre Pio would not only endure spiritual trials internally for the sins of others, but also the various persecutions and attacks from others. He was accused of heresy and false apparitions; he was told he could not say mass publicly for long periods of time; he was forbidden from visiting with people or even writing letters. He was banished to the far-off convent of Giovanni Rotundo in the hopes that it would keep people from going to see him. He had to remain in confinement in his convent, denied access to his spiritual director and stripped of almost all his priestly faculties. All this he endured in simple obedience and would never speak badly against any of those in authority over him.

---

125. *Padre Pio,* 36.

The suffering Padre Pio endured increased as his union with Jesus deepened and his love for others burned hotter and brighter until it reached its climax on September 20, 1918. In preparation for the feast of the Archangel St. Michael, whose sanctuary was very near the convent and who had assisted Padre Pio much in his life, the holy friar offered thirty days of prayer. Then, early in the morning, as he was praying and giving thanks after mass, he had another of his visions.

> I saw a mysterious visitor before me . . . his hands, feet and side were dripping blood. The sight frightened me. I do not know how to express what I felt at that instant. I felt like I was dying, and I would have died if the Lord had not intervened to safeguard my heart, which I felt was bouncing out of my breast . . . then the vision of the visitor passed away and I saw that my hands, feet and side were pierced and dripping blood. You will imagine the pain I felt then and that I kept experiencing almost every day continually. [126]

This most famous event was the mystical experience known as the "stigmata", the bearing of the wounds of Jesus. It was the physical sharing of the five major wounds of Jesus: in both hands, both feet, and one in the side. This time they were visible and tangible not only to Padre Pio but to all people. They were real; the physical evidence and tangible presence of these wounds was so compelling that many people believed his hands had physically been stabbed by someone. The wounds in his hand and feet went all the way through and light could be seen through them! A thin membrane

126. *Padre Pio*, 25.

covered the wounds, and they would bleed at regular intervals most notably during mass when they would produce a sweet smell. They would also cause him great pain every Thursday evening through Saturday as he shared in the passion of Jesus. Medical doctors were baffled by these wounds. They did not show inflammation or redness as something self-inflicted, yet they were clearly fresh wounds that shed blood from the arteries. Although they were examined at different intervals, they never showed signs of having been repeated as would have been necessary to produce such freshness. They did not inhibit Padre Pio's ability to work or use his hands, but they were sensitive to the touch.

Padre Pio's stigmata was a living testimony to the intersection that heaven and earth had in his very person. He truly encapsulated the words of St. Paul: "Now I rejoice in my sufferings for your sake, and in my flesh, I complete what is lacking in Christ's afflictions for the sake of his body" (Col 1:24). For love of the Church and for love of Jesus and in union with Jesus, Padre Pio manifested these great wounds of love. As Padre Pio's love was undying, so too he was able to bear these wounds for fifty years! This long-suffering is such a lost virtue in today's times. As the saying goes, "only the good die young," and many people consider that being holy is a sentence for a short life. Not with Padre Pio, his life was the long-haul. He shows us that holiness can indeed be lived in, matured in, and grows sweeter day by day. In our own way, we are called to bear with the sufferings we have daily, be it physical, mental, emotional, or relational.

As with many fathers, his duty called him to help pick his kids up when they were down, to clean off their wounds, and help them walk again. Padre Pio's ministry in the confessional was almost unparalleled in the Church. Any priest who ministers in the confessional has the awesome ability to distribute the sacramental graces of Christ's mercy and forgiveness. No other power on earth, and no gift of a saint can match this gift which passes through the priest as an instrument, not coming from his own merits, but by that of Jesus' sacrifice which entitles us to receive this gift. The absolution that Padre Pio gave and the graces that flowed were the same as those that any priest distributes. But a few circumstances in Padre Pio's life made those graces more accessible to the people. First was the amount of time he would spend in the confessional. Padre Pio would spend about fifteen hours every day, hearing over a hundred confessions a day and some five million confessions throughout his life! His loving fatherly heart wanted so badly to make this gift accessible to people!

Next, was his personal desire to not just check off confession as if it were a vending machine; each confession was a unique and personal opportunity for God's mercy to touch that person. Padre Pio desired each confession to be a true moment of conversion for that person in their unique situation. Because of that, sometimes he was incredibly stern with those who were not serious about completely uprooting sin; for others he was sweet and gentle in directing them in the unique trials of their struggles. For this end, he was given the power of reading hearts so he could know what was passing in a person's heart and conscience, their honesty in confession, as well as the other circumstances of life that influenced their decision making. Finally, it was Padre Pio's desire to suffer for the conversion of man that made him so powerful in the confessional. He knew the weight of sins and the price that it cost Jesus to save man. As he stood in the confessional as the immediate distributer of that gift to the people, he was reminded what this person's soul cost Jesus. He was so united with Jesus in love that in the confessional he took into himself that suffering for others. He saw it as his duty to safeguard that treasure and to be prudent in preparing the hearts of men to receive it. As a victim for the sins of others, he was able to see in the confessional the tie between his suffering and the gift for others. Jesus ransomed our souls with His blood, and Padre Pio used that same offering to win the souls of those who confessed their sins to him.

Not only in the confessional but also outside of it, Padre Pio gathered a huge following of people who sought his fatherly care and guidance. He was transformed into a true spiritual father, giving birth to children in heaven, which is why even today he is honored as "Padre" Pio. As priests, we do not marry a wife or have biological children, but that does not mean we avoid God's command in Genesis to "be fruitful and multiply." As Padre Pio grew in fatherly love for others, this fire drew to him many who wished to become his spiritual children. He loved them dearly and would offer direction and advice when and where he could. He encouraged them to go no longer than ten days without confession; to build up prayer groups and to follow Jesus more firmly. As the groups grew, he was could not be present to them all but he would write to them. These children of his were to also go out and form associations that would pray together, support each other, and seek direction when and where they needed it in their lives. To this day, many of these prayer groups exist throughout the world and draw people to the fatherly guidance of Padre Pio.

Padre Pio's death, as can be imagined, was a joyful day since he felt himself going home to heaven. Heaven was the permanent state of what Padre Pio's prayer had been preparing him for: complete surrender to God. Some would see only that the world had lost an amazing spiritual father; people would be denied the great gifts he had to offer. This thought is far from the understanding of death, of the saints, and of heaven. Padre Pio knew for a long time that he would be of more assistance to the Church from heaven rather than from earth. "In Paradise I will work with both hands"[127] was his humorous outlook on his death. Considering all that he did on earth, it is a powerful realization that now in heaven he is an ever greater and more powerful servant of the Lord than He was on earth! He knew that death was passing into eternity, sharing the life and blessings of God, and thus he could be of more instrumental grace to the Church than ever before. His gifts and graces but also fatherly responsibility would be increased and more effective in heaven than on earth. Echoing the lesson learned from the parable of the talents, during life Padre Pio took the talents given him and made them fruitful and plentiful. Upon the Master's return (or his return to the Master), Christ gave him a greater stewardship and responsibility in heaven over the children on earth! He is now a father for more than he was before and can advocate on behalf of his children on earth. The saints don't blindly sit back and watch our suffering here below but work to bring a good solution. "I will make more noise when I am dead than when I am alive,"[128] is a motto for all the saints, as they share an ability to cry out to God ceaselessly and perfectly in praise and petition, as well as become more present than ever to those on earth. From heaven, his example will speak louder, his intercession will cry out more powerfully, and his companionship will be more widespread and palpable. They can be ever closer to the suffering members, and their sufferings on earth, as finite as they were, are multiplied for the sake of so many others.

The assistance he offered the Church was made very present to his spiritual children. He had boldly stated that, "I shall stand at the gates of Paradise and shall not enter unless first all my spiritual children have already entered."[129] As his love on earth grew with the number of children, so in heaven his love and care for them soared. He shared in the

127. *Padre Pio*, 45.
128. *Padre Pio*, 45..

rejoicing that the angel and saints would have over anyone who repented in preference to the company of those already in heaven (Lk 15:7). Padre Pio's whole life was united with Jesus' saving mission, and now in heaven he not only sees the fullness of the fruit of that life and future resurrections but also the desire to call more and more souls into this joy. His love was his greatest mark. Love is what makes us on earth transcend to heaven; it is love that then draws heaven down to earth. As Jesus stretched out His arms on the Cross, He united heaven and earth in His wounds of love. Padre Pio also bore those wounds. His wounds, as Jesus', were not truly made by any man or nail, but rather by his love. It was not Padre Pio's love, wounds, or suffering, but Jesus'. Jesus was allowed to live so much in him and had taken such possession of Padre Pio's life, that the friar physically reflected Jesus in his spiritual union with our Lord. Padre Pio's life shows the world that has put off Christ what happens when we open our lives to Him: He takes hold of us, He radiates through us, He moreover allows us to pass through this life with its sorrows and sufferings never alone but lived with and for someone greater. Christ becomes not just our goal, but our companion on our own walk up to Calvary. At Giovanni Rotundo, there has been erected a large representation of stations of the cross on the grounds. At the fifth station, Simon the Cyrenian helps Jesus carry His Cross, they etched Padre Pio in Simon's place to show Padre Pio's great sharing in the Cross and suffering of Jesus while here on earth, a fitting final legacy for this man who shared the wounds of the cross.

What is almost more miraculous than his stigmata wounds and their presence for so much of his life is not

---

129. *Padre Pio,* 193.

their permanence but the sudden disappearance of them. On September 23, 1968, Padre Pio passed away in the early morning. Within about ten minutes of his death, the wounds were completely closed: no scar tissue, no dried blood. They were completely healed! This event is a great reminder that as much as Christians are called to share in Christ's suffering, as much as we accept pain and even rejoice in the measure we share in Jesus' suffering, in the ability we have to offer suffering up for others, we remember that pain and suffering and wounds are simply a passing shadow on this earth. The great light of God's resurrection and new life is not only more powerful than suffering, but the promise of resurrection makes accepting pain possible! In heaven, there is no more suffering, God the loving Father can wipe away every tear and to give His children peace and rest. Padre Pio shared in suffering on earth, and now his body testifies to him being able to share in the rest of heaven.

In 2002, Padre Pio was canonized, not even forty years after his death. Even though he was named St. Pio of Pietrelcina he will always be Padre. The Lord truly sends and calls few people in the history of the Church as he did Padre Pio. However, we have not lost him; we have drawn ever closer to him! To this day, countless people pray to him, asking for his help, and receive powerful answers and signs that he is present. Many of these people smell the scent of pipe smoke as a sign that he is near to them! Padre Pio will be a story told and a figure known in the Church forever. He is now in heaven as he was on earth: the door man of the house of God, the poor friar who prays.

Friends of Padre Pio

Kristin Dilion

I had the opportunity to come across the next testimony as I was looking through social media and came across a post about Padre Pio. When I read the story, I asked if the author would be willing to submit her testimony.

I was raised in a Catholic household and went to Catholic schools, but in my late teens and into my early 30s, I wandered off the path and became more of a seeker of sorts. I always had faith in God, I would go to Mass inconsistently, and was fascinated by religion and beliefs, but I really wrestled with this idea of what a spiritual identity was. Did it matter? Can't we all just get along? Why does someone have to tell me what to think or believe or do? What else is out there? I loved a debate. I loved an argument. I loved questioning, pouring over books and conversations late into the night. My search was quite a wrestling match, and I know that it caused suffering beyond just me and my own walls. Mercy and kindness have given me the grace to view that seeking as part of me, but, at the time, it was like I was trying to use a sledgehammer to unlock a door.

In the late '90s and early '00s, a family friend went on a trip to Italy. Now this friend is not particularly religious, neither did she have involvement, concern, or anything of the sort when it came to how I was doing in my faith at that time. When she came back from the trip, she handed me a small, wrapped gift. It was very kind and thoughtful, but also strange because we were not the kind of friends who bought gifts for one another, and especially not when we travelled. So, I accepted this unwrapped oddness with a little bit of trepidation and confusion. You can imagine that only escalated, when I opened it to see that it was a tiny, bejeweled, framed portrait of a man with a white beard.

We chuckled, and she said something like, "I have no idea who this man is, but when I saw this in Italy, I felt compelled to buy it for you. I just knew I had to buy it for you. Sounds funny, but here. Maybe you can find out who that is someday."

I thanked her and was more than anything touched by the surreal kindness of it all. All the same, I had no urge to research who it was, let alone a clue how I would even start. (This was long before smartphones and Google!) I kept the image close to me for years, and when I'd move to a new house (which did maybe a half dozen times), I'd always take special notice of where I kept it, because I liked having it around and in eye's reach. Something about it brought me comfort. On the outside, it sounds quirky even, but there was this inexplicable draw that was undeniable.

After a series of personal events, I had a pretty dramatic reversion during Holy Week in 2007. Leading up to that, I had learned about Padre Pio and was astounded when I saw an image of him. This was the man in the portrait that had been with me all those years. How on earth could I ever explain such a thing?! But as I got back into my faith and learned even more about this marvelous saint, no explanation was necessary!

I love telling this story, especially because it is true: Nothing is impossible with God.

Padre Pio, pray for us!

Christina Branco

The next testimony was submitted to me after she heard of my project. She sent me an email and conveyed her story to me about Padre Pio and his work with her and her mother.

When I was a child I had some pretty bad OCD issues. (Excessive worry, hand washing, a fear of fires that had me checking baseboard heaters every night for anything flammable near them. I could not relax until I did it.)

My mom, Susan Allanson, liked to pick up holy cards from the back of our church. People often left things there when they were finished with them. There was a Padre Pio one there that she picked up and gave to me. She told me she thought it might help me. (I don't think my mom knew the extent of my issues; I kept a lot to myself)

Not knowing anything about Padre Pio besides the short bio on the card, I asked him for help. I eventually overcame my issues and worries and no longer deal with such extreme issues. (I thank Padre Pio for saving me from years of therapy!) One day it all clicked to just trust in God's mercy, and I started to unlearn my OCD tendencies. I continued to ask Padre Pio for prayers throughout my life. When my mom got sick with pancreatic cancer, she started to learn more about Padre Pio on her own and his "Pray, Hope, and don't worry" attitude became one she would often remind herself of while suffering so much. She was with us for two and a half years after her diagnosis, which is miraculous in itself for how advanced it was when they found it. Often people get only a few short months after diagnosis. I am thankful she got to meet two grand babies in that time.

About a year before she passed away, I was in mass at a Carmelite Monastery and looked up at the sisters behind the grail and for a brief moment I saw Padre Pio among them. "Oh . . . there's Padre Pio," was my first thought. And then I thought, "Wait-WHAT?!" But he was gone by the time I had registered what I saw. I was certainly not in a prayerful state at that time. I was simply trying to enjoy mass while keeping my toddler happy. It kind of bothered me for a while. I even questioned if I had really seen him. I told my mom about it and she thought it was wonderful. It sort of slipped my mind a bit in the whirlwind of a year that passed. My mom was getting sicker, which made me focus on spending time with her as much as I could.

I saw my mom go from dancing on the boardwalk during our July beach vacation, (she begged God to let her enjoy vacation and she did!) to suddenly sick upon her return. On August 25, she turned 50, and then she was sent to a rehab center because the cancer moved to her cervical spine, making it nearly impossible to walk. By September she was on her deathbed. Watching her decline so quickly was tough. Waiting and wondering when we'd have to say goodbye was pure torture.

Monday of the week she died, I looked at my calendar and saw that Friday was Padre Pio's feast day. I suddenly got this memory of the day I saw him at the Carmel come flooding back to me, and I knew in that moment my mom was going to die on Friday. It was a hard pill to swallow but comforting because Padre Pio said he would wait for all of his spiritual children at the gates of heaven. Friday came, and as I knew would happen, she passed away that afternoon.

Every time I get upset about her being gone, I remind myself that Padre Pio took care of her and she's better now.

Almighty ever-living God, who, by a singular grace, gave the Priest Saint Padre Pio a share in the Cross of your Son and, by means of his ministry, renewed the wonders of your mercy, grant that through his intercession we may be united constantly to the sufferings of Christ, and so brought happily to the glory of the resurrection. Amen

"St. Jude the Apostle"
by Norman Faucheux
digital copy provided by
Norman Faucheux: Sacred and Religious Art, LLC

ST. JUDE

To be honest, a great Catholic quiz would be to ask someone to name all twelve apostles; few would succeed. However, almost everyone knows the first and last name of at least one: Judas Iscariot. Judas was one of the twelve, the holder of the money bag, who eventually betrayed Jesus and handed him over to the high priest for pieces of silver. As grievous as this crime was, Judas' worse sin was that he refused to turn back to Jesus and come to His merciful gaze and seek forgiveness. Had he converted, it is certain that the Lord would have accepted him back, as He did with Peter. However, Judas' despair led him to commit suicide and die in his sin and rejection of God and His mercy.

Without making judgments on Judas' final state, it is safe to say that he was not in the running for the title "saint." As we said before, people know a saint when they see one, and the opposite is also true. Most faithful find little inspiration to turn to Judas for intercession.

Now each of the apostles was different and unique, and each brought to the Lord's service their own personalities and traits. Just as there were two with the name James, there actually were two with the name Judas. The betrayer is always known as Judas Iscariot, while St. Jude is known as Thaddeus or Judas Thaddeus. The listing of the apostles in Matthew's Gospel (10:2-4) calls him Thaddeus; The Gospel of Luke lists him as "Judas son of James" (6:16). It is Judas son of James that is considered the author of the New Testament Letter of Jude, where he is also connected to the other disciples Simon and James as the "brother of James" (Jude:1). The relation to these two Apostles, as well as Jesus is found in

Matthew 13:55 where he is considered a brother to Simon and James.[130] So, the apostle we focus on now is St. Jude Thaddeus, brother of James and Simon.

As with many names (Mary, Joseph, Simon, et alia), the best way to distinguish was by adding their family or their place of origin. By calling him Judas the brother of James, it connected him with a well-known figure of the time: James, who was bishop of Jerusalem in the beginning of the Church's history. Thaddeus was most probably a nickname. Although there was another Judas in the company, it was uncommon at the time to give him a different name. However, this does not mean that Judas the brother of James and Judas Thaddeus were two different people. As Benedict XVI stated:

> Then with regard to Jude Thaddaeus, this is what tradition has called him, combining two different names: in fact, whereas Matthew and Mark call him simply 'Thaddaeus' Luke calls him 'Judas the son of James' The nickname 'Thaddaeus' is of uncertain origin and is explained either as coming from the Aramaic taddà, which means 'breast' and therefore suggested 'magnanimous' or as an abbreviation of a Greek name such as 'Teodòro, Teòdo-ro.'[131]

Other sources say Thaddeus is a form of "Lebbæus" meaning "worshipper of heart." Regardless of the variety of considerations, it is held by tradition that Judas Thaddaeus was the brother of James, also an apostle and New Testament writer. Regardless of the ambiguity that exists about the

---

130. This point will be covered in more detail later.

131. Benedict XVI *The Apostles* 112.

direct connection of Jude the Apostle to the letter of Jude, the Church has taught, through her prayers and devotion, that the author of the letter is also the Apostle.

Another interesting point about Judas Thaddaeus that is worth mentioning: he was most probably a cousin of Jesus. Again, several sources say that Judas was "the brother of James" to denote what family he is a part of. However, we hear of a few other interesting sources that add breath and width to this family. First, let us start with a very famous scene: the Crucifixion. John 19:25 tell us that "standing by the cross of Jesus were his mother, and his mother's sister, Mary the wife of Clō'pas." We normally focus on the reality of Jesus' mother Mary being at the Cross as well as the beloved disciple, but we sometimes miss the other people present there. It is difficult from the text to deduce the exact relation but Mary, the wife of Clō'pas, was a relative of Mary. Compare this verse with Mark 15:40 which says that Mary the mother of James the younger[132] was present at the Cross. Connecting the dots, Mary the Mother of Jesus and Mary the Mother of James (the wife of Clō'pas) were related.[133] Her presence at the Cross tells of the strong bond she had with Jesus' mother. Since not even Jesus' dearest disciples (except John) were at the Cross, she overcame great odds to be present at the Cross and this point should not be undermined.

A final tie is given in Matthew 13:55 mentioned earlier when the crowd comments on the great works of Jesus yet remarks how such a common fellow could do these things. They say: "Is not his mother Mary? And are not his brethren James and Joseph and Simon and Judas?" Here, the mention of 'brethren' most likely was referring to the word "cousin"

132. This James is not James the son of Zebedee the brother of John but the one known as James the Lesser, another apostle. Tradition believes that he became bishop of Jerusalem and played a very important role in the growth of Christians in this area. Because of this importance and him being so well known in the nascent Church, it would have been an important note that his mother was present at the Cross.

133. This point brings up an interesting theory that I present to the reader. First of all, as in the case with Jesus' "brothers and sisters," the word for brother /sister in Hebrew was used for cousin due to certain Semitic or Jewish traditions. Also, knowing that at the Cross Jesus entrusted Mary to John would point to that fact that there were no other siblings of his due to the Mark 7:10–13 tradition. Hence, the basic rule could be applied with Mary and this sister of hers from John 19. Also, from some of the apocryphal writing (writings that existed at the time of the Scriptures but because they contain errors that the early Church identified from a knowledge of history and/or the guidance of the Holy Spirit, are not part of Scripture) says that Mary's parents were barren at the time they conceived her. However, an interesting theory comes from Blessed Anne Catherine Emmerich, who had several visions of the life of Jesus, Mary, and some of the saints. These visions are approved by the Church but are seen as private revelation, meaning they are revealed to a specific person and can be accepted and believed by others, but are not part of the mandatory revelation. In her visions, she saw that Mary's parents had a child when they were younger that they named Mary Heli whom they gave to the care of the grandmother and then they became barren for nineteen years. Mary Heli would then have had a daughter who was Mary the wife of Clō'pas. Again, this is private revelation, having no bearing on theology or history, but it can be an aid in the faith for those who wish, although it takes nothing away from those who do not wish to believe it.

---

in english since Jewish custom showed the closeness of relationship through the term 'brother'. So this verse is not meant to create confusion of Jesus having blood siblings but to further connect the known figures of James (the lesser), Simon, Judas Thaddaeus with Jesus.

So, we see St. Jude as a man of great heart and spirit, so much that he is nicknamed Thaddaeus. He was a close cousin of Jesus, possibly a brother to two other apostles, whose mother was present at the Cross when Jesus died. He also appears as a man of great humility. One of the only quotes from the Gospel we have of him is a question he asks Jesus. John 14:22 tells us: "Judas (not Iscariot) said to him, 'Lord how is it that you will manifest yourself to us, and not to the world?'" This question appears in the middle of Jesus' great Last Supper discourse with His apostles where He tells them that by loving Christ and following His commandments, they are loved by the Father as well. Jude appears very humbled by this statement and curious as to why they seem to have merited these special revelations and not others. It shows the way in which Jesus means the world, not speaking of all the people of the world, but the worldly minded who do not have the grace nor the desire to see the Father. Jude's concern for the world and his humility in receiving such an awesome gift played into his role as an apostle: the gift has been given by God not by our merit but by His love. Thus, those entrusted with the message have a duty to share it as much as they can, without discrimination.

As a close relative of Jesus, he was extremely familiar with the human side of Jesus and the tender love He had for all people. As a cousin, he knew Jesus from an early age, saw and grown up with Him and had some of the most unique opportunities of any human to have ever walked this earth. As far as saints go, Jude really takes the cake. Jude was able to witness the perfect, reconciled relationship of God and man in the person of his own cousin! Thus, his preaching was not about an abstract concept or a disembodied force, but rather about a God of such reckless love that He become one of us to love us. You could image the passion with which he would have shared his message when he preached!

Such is the tender, yet firm tone found in the letter of Jude of the New Testament. It is written as a general letter addressed to the believers known as "beloved." He speaks about the "common salvation" being that gift of salvation that is accessible to all but, as he says, we must "contend for the faith which was once for all delivered to the saints" (Judev.3). This wording echoes Jesus when he said those who are worldly will not hear it. This contentment, this turning from worldliness comes when you "build yourselves up on your most holy faith, pray in the Holy Spirit; keep yourselves in the love of God; wait for the mercy of our Lord Jesus Christ unto eternal life" (Judev,20,21).

Just as when he was a child walking with Jesus, just as when he was sitting next to Jesus at the Last Supper asking his question, so it is now too that Jesus, the central point of faith, was and is a person in the mind of St. Jude. This reality of the faith is why Jude will go on in the letter to warn of the deceivers who enter the faith and try to use it for their own gain. The faith is never about us making God into our image but about changing us into His image. The faith is real, alive, and personal, but it is not individualistic; it can't be what I want it to be or for what I want. Jude shows in his letter that it never really worked out for people in the Old Testament who tried to make religion about them and their wishes.

As with all the apostles, Jude's close and intimate time with Jesus was the foundation for a mission of going forth to proclaim the message of God's love made real in Jesus Christ. Jesus frequently took the apostles off alone by themselves with him. This was a time of formation for them to connect and set their foundation on God's love and reliance on His grace rather than anything else.

After the ascension of Jesus, legend has it that Jude went to Edessa, which is modern day Turkey. The king had long ago desired Jesus to come and heal him after he had heard of the great miracles that took place. Jesus had a grander plan than He Himself going and visiting. He placed a cloth on his face leaving an imprint and sent it to the king with the promise that a disciple would come and bring the message and person of Jesus to him. After the king received the veil, he and the entire city awaited this messenger. When Jude arrived, his face so much resembled that of Jesus' on the veil that the king knew this was the disciple! This is one of the reasons why Jude is traditionally depicted with a coin or image of Jesus.

From there, Jude was said to have gone into Mesopotamia and eventually with Simon, his other brother and fellow apostle, went into Persia. As the legend continues, Jude ran into trouble there with several pagan enchanters. Two enchanters had seduced the duke of this region who was preparing for a huge battle in India. The apostles predicted how the battle was to turn out: the enemy they were planning to face was going to ask for a peace treaty. The enchanters, disgruntled by the apostles' foreknowledge, tried their own hand at reading the future and promised a different outcome. Sure enough, the peace treaty was called for and the duke was won over to the apostles. Instead of killing the enchanters, the apostles asked to spare their lives for they came not to bring people to death, but to bring the dead to life.

Later, these enchanters became so enraged at the apostles that they threw serpents at them. As the legend goes, the apostles caught the serpents in their cloaks and threw them back at the enchanters. The snakes immediately came out and began to bite the enchanters and inject their venom into them. Although the duke wished for them to die, the apostles prayed not only to save the enchanters but for all the venom of the serpents to be taken out of them. This story shows the great work of all the apostles. which was to go and pull out the poison that the ancient serpent, the devil, had injected into the world. Another story says that the apostles tamed loose and wild tigers that had begun to attack the people. Similarly, at the true message of the Good News the wild passions inside of man are made tame and calm.

Another legend says that the duke's daughter had slept with a man, and she conceived and bore a child. When this news became public, they ask the girl what had happened. She defamed a holy deacon in the area, saying that it was he who had done this to her. The apostles were invited to come in and intervene to judge rightly about the truth in this case. It was said that they took the child, only one day old, and taught him to speak and to testify to the veracity of this statement! The child spoke clearly and plainly and testified that the deacon was innocent.

Jude eventually found his travels bringing him to a city where he encountered the familiar enchanters again. This time, they were not alone but had many more of their fellow believers. Jude found himself in a place of idolatry and began to again preach the true and living faith of Jesus as boldly as he had ever done. At this point the enchanters and worshipers knew the power this message contained and resisted it with force. Here, Jude was said to have been offered a choice: the angel of the Lord could either come to Jude's defense, save his life, and allow him to move on and preach, or Jude could be given the grace to die as a martyr. As with so many of the saints, Jude longed again and again to see the face of Jesus. He could have quoted St. Paul, who said that to live is a chance to work and preach for God, whereas death is the gaining of eternal life. Jude accepted either, but he knew the will of God and what it would cost to save the souls of these men. He accepted death; he died a martyr at the hands of these men to save their souls. The exact circumstances of his death are unknown, simply that it was at the hands of these unbelieving men but certain tradition say he was beheaded with an axe.

Finally, as with the other apostles, their witness to Jesus came to the point of facing death itself fearlessly. "The blood of the martyrs is the seedbed of the Church," is the ancient saying meaning that where there are those who have stood firm in the faith even to the point of dying, the Church has flourished. It is an amazing phenomenon that the more the believers were persecuted and even eradicated, the more the Church grew. This reality shows that the message had taken root so firmly in the hearts of believers that they were willing to suffer death for its sake.

Had the message just been a fantasy, a mere lie covered up, why would these men have born so much, even suffering horrible deaths? Also, how and why would the Church not only continue to exist but to constantly grow? There is proof just in this reality that something more real than just words had been planted in their hearts

The devotion of the people followed the legend; The relationship and devotion with the saints that the Church forms is always founded upon the story of their life and death. Example, intercession, and companionship are those three components of communion that build on each other and give life to one another. Traditionally when we see him depicted, he is holding a staff in his hand, showing that he was a pilgrim as he traveled over the earth and as he sought his true home in heaven. He is wearing a green tunic over his white underclothing. He is shown with a flame over his head as a representation of the tongues of fire that fell upon him and the other apostles who were gathered in the upper room at Pentecost. Finally, he is holding in his hand a golden coin or plate with the side profile of someone. This image is representing the image of Christ that the king had received, as well as Jude's resemblance to Jesus.

As the devotion to St. Jude began to spread a somewhat disappointing predicament occurred: people began to confuse this marvelous apostle with the betrayer, simply because of his name. In English we distinguish between the two by making one Jude and the other Judas, as the Latin form, but in the original language, they shared the same name: Judas. We have established that indeed Judas Iscariot, the betrayer, is not the same as the other apostle Judas, the brother of James and Simon, the cousin of Jesus who was traditionally called Thaddaeus. However, association is a common practice with people and the mindset is very hard to break. Just the name Judas strikes a chord of suspicion and bitterness in the hearts of believers. Even while the apostles were still alive and ministering, it is a wonder if Jude Thaddaeus did not receive some skeptical glances. After he died, most people, hearing the name St. Judas, thought that it was a hopeless cause to ask for the intercession of the betrayer of Our Lord.

It is also a lesson in humility. On several occasions it was not said "there is a betrayer in your midst" but rather, "one of you will betray me." This wording should be a stark reminder to us all that the sinful inclination is from within us. Jesus is forever merciful, but He is also not surprised by our sinfulness; and yet He still calls us. God knows all the sins we will commit and even the wounds it will cause Him, but He is still willing to call us. When we see members of the Church fall, from cardinals to laypeople, we should never take on a judgmental, condescending attitude. Each one of us has been chosen by God and He knows us intimately and knows how and when we will fall but He always gives a promise of mercy. God's mercy can raise us to where our virtue could not hold us. It is grace that converts, it is also grace that preserves. Judas is the reminder to us that only when we despair of God's mercy and refuse to turn to look Him in His merciful eyes and take on the burden of His mercy are we lost. We have to face our sins to receive His mercy.

Perhaps Judas Thaddaeus and Judas Iscariot are both present to show the two sides of the conversion story. Thaddaeus, as well as the other disciples, were absent from the Cross. They too had not been faithful, yet they faced Jesus on Easter morning to receive His forgiveness and they stood by His Cross through their own martyrdom. Jude, perhaps, can be an example of what could have happened with Judas had he repented.

As the apostles one by one gave their lives for Jesus, the stories and the power of their testimonies were passed onto the ever-growing Christian community. The stories of their lives and miracles and the love they shared for the people, were fruits of seeing the face of God in the face of man. The honor given to God by loving and serving Him in others became the root of the Church's growth. The apostles are considered those pillars, those foundation stones upon which the Church and the rest of the saints are built upon. Their lived experience became a gift that was passed down and relived through the rest of the Church. Jesus has kept a living unity with the Church from beginning to end.

Not only did the apostles receive the firsthand words of what Jesus did, they were also given the authority and the treasury of powers to build the Church. Jesus, the great source of all the saving graces and mercies for the Church, handed on these saving and sanctifying gifts to the apostles so that they may be given to all the future generations of people. These gifts, the sacraments, were entrusted to them to give out and thus build the Church. Since it is to the apostles that the gifts are given to build and sanctify the Church, they also have the authority to guide the Church in the direction of salvation and thus govern the Church. This unique mission of the apostles was handed onto successors, not tied just to their person, but to a stable office that united the Church throughout the ages and places.

Even in heaven, the figures of the apostles hold a special role in uniting the saints in heaven and earth, tying together the Church visible and invisible. Jesus promised to them first that His kingdom was not of this world. They heard for the first time the parables and their explanations of the glories of heaven. They were told to seek first the kingdom of God and the promises of the beatitudes. Finally, Jesus promised them their reward that was to come in heaven:

> Then Peter said in reply, "Lo, we have left everything and followed you. What then shall we have?" Jesus said to them, "Truly, I say to you in the new world, when the Son of man shall sit on his glorious throne, you who have followed me will also sit on twelve thrones, judging the twelve tribes of Israel. And every one who has left houses or brothers or sisters or father or mother or children or lands, for my name's sake, will receive a hundredfold,

> and inherit eternal life. But many that are first will be last and the last first" (Mt 19: 27–30).

The role and charism of the apostles for the Church did not end with their martyrdom. Rather, they continue to fulfill that role in heaven to pray for and in the Church. They share a special concern and stewardship over the work and expansion of the Church, have powerful intercession in the Church, and roles in judging and guiding the flock to heaven. As with Jesus, the good shepherd, so these shepherds have gone before the flock so that the sheep may follow confidently. They have been set up on earth but also in heaven as watchmen, as overseers of the Church. The true role of an episcopus, which means "overseer," is to be a watchman for the Church. As they are set up on high places they have watchful care of the Church below.

St. Peter was entrusted with the keys of the kingdom on earth, and passed that mission onto his successors, the popes. It is also believed that St. Peter stands at the gate of heaven to open to those who are judged worthy, whose names are written in the book of life, those who have offered to God the Father a worthy return for the gift of His Son, Jesus. The act of being entrusted with keys gave Peter a responsibility and mission of opening and closing. Peter did not write the names in the book of life, nor did he create the key and the door; he simply is entrusted with the task of administering in the name of the Lord.

St. John, the youngest apostle and known as "the beloved," has a special patronage over priests. It was St. John who leaned his head on Jesus' chest and heard His heartbeat; it was St. John who stayed present at the Cross and received Mary as his mother; it was St. John who went with Peter to the tomb early in the morning. He is a patron for priests as true lovers of Jesus and His mysteries and he teaches priests to stay close to the heart of Jesus as they minister in the Church.

St. James the greater was the first of the apostles to be martyred. It seemed that his career as an apostle was rather short lived with only minor success, but Jesus used him in a unique way to lead people to the kingdom. After his martyrdom, his body was placed in a tomb with several of his mourning disciples and the boat was cast off into the Mediterranean Sea with no sail, rudder, or keel. The disciples commended themselves to the will of God and the ship was mystically transported to the Galicia region in Spain, which is some 5,000 km away! When the boat arrived on shore, the disciples placed the body onto a rock and it sank into the rock as if it were melted butter, forming a tomb around his body. The queen of that area did not believe their message and tried by many attempts to discourage the disciples. She gave the disciples a chariot and said they could take the oxen from her field and wherever the oxen led the new formed tomb, they should make a church there. However, in her deception she gave them wild bulls to lead. Miraculously, the bulls became meek and, with no guidance at all, they led the tomb of St. James into the palace of the queen. She converted and gave the palace to be a church. Almost immediately, people mysteriously were led to this church on pilgrimage. A man in prison had prayed for freedom and St. James appeared to him, broke his chains, and told him to go to Galicia; several people who had died were brought to the tomb of St. James and were raised; St. James appeared to several people and promised miracles at his tomb. More and more pilgrims continued to come. Still to this day thousands of people every year from every nation and every walk of life, both believers and atheists, make the Camino of St. James, looking for guidance in their lives. St. James is thus a patron for pilgrims seeking direction in this life and a patron for those who have lost their way to heaven.

St. Jude also stands among these great saints. As an apostle, he was among the first to be honored by the early Church and to receive prayers asking for his help. Since some members of the Church already related him to hopeless causes because of his name, St. Jude willingly took up that challenge of being patron of hopeless causes! In the face of what seemed like a dishonor on account of another person's misdeeds, Thaddeus was given by our Lord a very important patronage: hopeless causes! Truly, those who were in a seemingly hopeless situation needed the powerful intercession of someone like an apostle, who knew the true hope of Jesus.

Throughout the ages, St. Jude has been the patron of all those who have felt they were lost, had no hope, or were despairing due to their situation in life. This class of persons certainly exists in our world and even in our Church. It is one of the devil's tactics to lead us to despair, to lead us to feel we are hopeless and that we cannot be helped. When we give ourselves that status, we become like Judas and no longer lift our eyes to the good Savior who wishes to come to our aid. St. Jude saw the face of Jesus after the resurrection; he saw the face of the one he had betrayed, his lifelong friend and relative that he had allowed to die on the Cross alone. When Jesus appeared in the upper room, He showed them His wounds; not to shame them, but so they might see that these wounds are fountains of mercy. St. Jude knew the true reality of hope: it does not ignore or imagine the wound is not there but knows that the resurrection is more powerful. St. Jude has thus been able to journey with people who feel the weight of darkness and sin in their life, and he lifts their eyes to a greater hope.

Not only on a moral level, but also on level of intensity, St. Jude has a special intercession for difficult tasks. As an apostle, he has a special seat in heaven; this means he has a special place to look upon the Church below but also a certain closeness to the Lord. The Lord can act in a special way when our faith is engaged. It is not superstition that praying to St. Jude when things seem hopeless will suddenly make things better, but rather it is the confident trust that even when there seems to be no other help, hope can always be placed in the Lord. St. Jude is a personal reminder that in the moments when hope seems to be lost, we are called to pray with and through the saints to our Lord. At all times the saints want to be those guideposts to point to the Lord, from whom all prayers are answered. Year after year, hundreds of people offer prayers to St. Jude and again and again the Lord works.

Friends of St. Jude

St. Jude's Miracle Hospital

The story begins in the late 1800s in a mountain village called Becheri in Lebanon. Two young Arabs, Margaret Simon and Shaheed Yakhoob each found a golden chance at a new life in America and made their way to Toledo, Ohio. It was here that they met each other for the first time, become lovers, and eventually married. They were Maronite Catholics—a sister rite to the Roman rite that we are used to—and lived a very holy, devout life as a young couple. They ended up having ten children, growing up on a poor farm in the early American Mid-West. Margaret was very poor and uneducated, not able to read or write, but she was a wonderful storyteller. She often told the children of the old country, of their family, and shared stories of their faith and the Church. With this, many stories of the saints were passed down to the young children.

In 1912, the family welcomed a young son whom they named Muzyad Yakhood. He grew up hearing tales of the old country, stories from the big cities, and tales of the faith. He was a good boy, but he was very ambitious. At the age of eleven he had already started a "business" selling candy and ice cream and eventually pursued his dream: show business.

His faith was very important to him; he attended Catholic school, learned of devotion from his family, and became close friends with the bishop of Toledo, Samuel Stritch, a native of Tennessee, who remained a lifelong friend and a spiritual guide.

He made his first big debut in show business in 1932 as Amos Jacobs Kairous, an anglicized version of his name, on the Radio show *The Happy Hour Club.* He had a gift for storytelling, which he had inherited from his family. This gift eventually led him to doing stand-up comedy, more radio shows, and eventually television. To hide the fact from his family that he was going into clubs, he took the name "Danny Thomas" after his two brothers and the rest became history.

However, his career wasn't an instant success; Danny had lost his way a few times, fell on a few occasions, and faced much opposition from his family and his wife. He also had a child on the way, which not only added a lot of emotional strain but financial strain as well. In these hard moments he felt like everything was against him and his dream looked like an impossible mountain to climb; he was just a poor immigrant living in America. But this was his dream, and something was driving him deep from within his heart. His young daughter was born but was sickly and needed extra care. As he had learned from a young age, it was his faith that he looked to for help. There was a church in Detroit that he went to for mass and one day, he was so moved during mass, that he gave his last seven dollars in the collection. Knowing God's generosity, he prayed for a way to pay off the hospital bills. The next day, he was offered an opportunity that gave him enough to pay off his debt. At this moment, Danny began to see the power that prayer had in his life. So, he made his famous prayer: he turned to St. Jude, the patron saint of hopeless causes, and he prayed, "Help me find my way in life and I will build you a shrine."

Around this time, a mysterious disease was spreading: acute lymphoblastic leukemia (ALL). It was a terrible disease, particularly affecting children, with only a 4% survival rate and no cure in sight. It was a very frightening time for all and left many families and small children in hopeless situations. There was no community to support those families that seemed so lost. In God's providence, the great patron of hopeless causes was already at work bringing a solution. Often, God uses various instruments for His plan. Many times, God calls unlikely people to work in His plan, so that it is overwhelmingly His grace that is seen to be at work and not man's. He also takes and leads all people from various places to draw all things into His glory.

So, the answer to this seemingly hopeless case soon came from this night club performer turned celebrity. Within a few years Danny's career had taken off, and now he and his family had moved to Chicago where life was good and his entertainment enterprise was flourishing. He became known for his radio show that later became a TV show called "The Danny Thomas Show," which was very successful. He also became a producer of various other television shows and had a prosperous career. One day, he went into a small church to pray and was struck with the reminder of the vow he had made to build the shrine. So, in the early 1950s, he began the make his vow a reality.

He collaborated very closely with several business-minded friends, as well as sought guidance from his friend Bishop Stritch. He set out, traveling America to raise funds and build awareness. After having seen the hope he was given as a child, knowing of the troubles his own children faced, and seeing the hopelessness that so many children in America faced, he made it his commitment that "no child should die at the dawn of life"; he integrated his vow with a vision of success for many children. With the help of a close doctor friend, Lemuel Digg, and an auto magnate from Miami named Anthony Abraham, Danny set to work on building St. Jude's research hospital. It was Bishop Stritch's idea to locate the hospital in Memphis, his native land, and thus the dream began to take shape.

It was here in Memphis that this dream became widely accepted by the local businesses and the vision more and more took shape to offer a research hospital to treat seemingly hopeless situations in the lives of children threatened by diseases and various sicknesses. It was not to discriminate on account of race, religion or finances. Not only a simple hospital, but an institution that would perform research and offer hope to children throughout the world.

Danny and his wife traveled all over the United States raising awareness and asking for funds for this new enterprise. Celebrities from all over came to Memphis to see and witness this wonderful vision becoming a reality. Danny also reached out to his own native Arabs living in America to seeking assistance. This move was a powerful way of helping to tie and unite all of America despite individual's background, culture, or race in this common vision of saving families and children from hopeless situations.

Finally in 1962, the vow was fulfilled and the dream was made a reality. St. Jude Children's Research Hospital was opened. From its beginning, the hospital saw amazing results and unheard-of cures. The child cancer survival rate went from 20% to 80%; and the survival rate for ALL went from 4% to 94%! From all fifty states, children have been sent to find not only a cure, but hope. They are welcomed by a loving community that helps them and their families feel accompaniment during these very dark and trying times. To this day, millions of people have found hope and encouragement in the fulfillment of that vow made so long ago. St. Jude's hospital is still known as a beacon of hope for many children. Standing watchfully at the door of this hospital is the ten-foot marble statue of St. Jude Thaddeus, apostle of Christ and patron saint of hopeless causes.

Bob Cash's story

I met Bob in September of 2020. It was a rocky time in my life. We were still juggling with Covid-19, Hurricane Laura had just hit Louisiana and took a toll on our state, I was still awaiting news about my mother's kidney transplant, and we were trying to minister as normal to the people of God.

On the September 8, the Blessed Mother's birthday, I craved a sandwich from FireHouse Subs to celebrate. An older gentleman was standing behind me in line. As I was ordering my sub (and piling on the extras), the gentleman leaned over. "Excuse me, are you a Catholic Priest?" he asked. "Yes, I am!" "Here, let me pay for your lunch." I was taken aback by his kindness, but I decided to accept his offer, as well as the extra peppers on my sub.

As we were waiting for our food, he and I had a casual conversation. His name was Bob Cash. He told me he was Catholic and had grown up not too far from where I had grown up. I told him I knew the new priest in his area and said that he hadn't met him yet because he had been "out" for the past few weeks. As we talked, he mentioned to me that he was a "covid survivor." He had contracted covid a few weeks before and had been down for a bit. I asked him what it was like having covid. He gave the usual physical symptoms of short breath, pneumonia, and so on. "Thanks to St. Jude, I'm safe now." My attention perked; was there a story behind that statement? Indeed, there was.

He explained that his mother had a great devotion to St. Jude and placed in him at an early age a love for this saint. During his time of sickness, Bob had entrusted himself to the prayers of St. Jude and truly felt his presence and care during the whole ordeal. Now he was on the road to full recovery. Bob was no spring chicken; he definitely was up in years and it seemed that this sickness could have crippled him. St. Jude had been present throughout his life and he had turned to him on several other occasions to help him out. He had no doubts that it was St. Jude who got him through those difficult times.

"I'll tell you about the first time I ever really prayed to St. Jude." In his younger days he was out working the yard, raking leaves, and doing yard work. It was a lot of manual work. When he looked at his hand, he realized that his wedding ring had slipped off. He had no clue when or where it had fallen off, but certainly it had not been recently. He searched low and high to no result. The ring was gone. He did not want to tell his wife that he had lost the ring, and he dreaded going to buy another one.

He remembered his mother's devotion to St. Jude, so he went to the local church, said his prayers asking St. Jude to help him out and then he went and put five dollars in the poor box. With that, he put his hope in this heavenly saint to solve his problem. Without much hope himself, he returned home, frustrated and upset. He grabbed the rake he had been using and angrily threw it down on the pile of leaves he had been raking. Suddenly, like a magic trick, his wedding ring jumped up out of the pile, flipped up about five feet high and then landed in his hand! At that moment, St. Jude won him over! He had been away from the Church for a while but this was certainly an occasion to come back. Bob became a devotee of St. Jude, supported the hospital built in his name, and encouraged others to turn to him in times of hardship and hopelessness.

I thanked him for the incredible story and remarked how these saint stories are hidden all over the place! We don't have to go and uncover them from hidden archives somewhere; we just have to open our eyes and see God at work all around us! From big to small, the saints look after us to bring light and support in any and every situation of our lives.

Emanuela's story

This next testimony was submitted by Emanuela. She is a Catholic living in Milan, Italy. She is part of a Catholic Movement known as "Communion and Liberation", which is a lay movement to help Catholic rediscover the faith. She heard about my work on this book and offered to submit a story, via email.

When I was young (probably five or six years old) my brother took interest in St. Jude and asked my family to go and visit a church in Bergamo that is devoted to him, because he wanted to fulfil a vow he made to St. Jude. To be honest, in Italy St. Jude is not very well known; we mostly associate the name Jude with the Iscariot. There aren't many churches devoted to him and it's very unusual to find one of his statues or images in a church. It's not even a name used for people, as it is in other countries. To this day I'm not sure how my brother came across this particular saint or what was the vow for. I just know that since then St. Jude became really important to my family, and he also reached me.

When I was twenty-four, I moved to Boston to study at BU for a semester. It was scary to be in a new country all by myself and it was the first time I had been far from home. Near my dormitory there was a small Catholic chapel inside a mall (the Prudential Center) and I started to go there to pray and attend mass.

The first weekend I was in Boston, without friends and without family, I went there and I remember feeling extremely alone and sad. I realized there was a statue of St. Jude and when I told my parents they told me that it was a sign that everything was going to be fine. I started praying to him and learned his novena prayers. Before that moment I knew that my brother was devoted to St. Jude, but I had never taken the time to know more about him and I didn't have a saint that I felt especially connected to.

After those months in Boston (that were truly a wonderful time for me and I grew in faith a lot) I got back to Italy and I went to visit the church in Bergamo again, taking home with me all the pamphlets and prayer cards I could find.

From there I started relying on him more and more and telling people about him. Whenever I am troubled or I need "extra help" I turn to him. I did the same when I was studying for my bar exam and he was a great help.

This year I moved to London to do an LLM (masters in law), after having a very bad year. I realized this coincided with me being a little bit lost spiritually and having too much pressure at work, which prompted me to take a year off to study and weigh my professional options. Without going into too much detail, I go into this spiral where my sins hold me down, but instead of taking this opportunity to pray more and realize how much I need him, I feel very ashamed and I tend to keep him distant.

To put it briefly, I needed to take a breather and regroup and work on all these things, but this past year it seemed like I almost forgot about St. Jude.

Here in London, near my university, there is a Catholic Church where I started to go to for weekday mass. One day while I was looking around I saw, again, a statue of St Jude and I was very moved that he came yet again to me to remind me of him and of all the help my family and I received through him. It was truly like seeing a friend who was just waiting for me to say hello.

I always go around with one of his prayer cards in my bag but still to this day I'm forgetful and I don't remember how saints are really our friends, helping to bring us closer to Christ. My friendship with St. Jude is showing me how he never abandons me and never forgets about me. I still need to take a step toward Christ and accept Him. I'm really grateful that He never gets tired of me and keeps sending me these reminders through St Jude.

Most holy apostle, St. Jude, faithful servant and friend of Jesus, the Church honors and invokes you universally, as the patron of hopeless cases, of things almost despaired of.

Pray for me, I am so helpless and alone. Make use I implore you, of that particular privilege accorded to you,to bring visible and speedy help where help is almost despaired of. Come to my assistance in this great need that I may receive the consolation and help of heaven in all my necessities, tribulations, and sufferings, particularly –(Here make your request)and that I may praise God with you and all the elect forever.

I promise, O blessed St. Jude, to be ever mindful of this great favor, to always honor you as my special and powerful patron, and to gratefully encourage devotion to you. Amen.

"St. Maria Goretti appearing to Alessandro"
Original Drawing by Elizabeth Michalski

ST. MARIA GORETTI

Children are notorious for short attention spans. Almost every time I have given a talk to younger kids, all it took was some small distraction: a cat, a squeaky door, another person talking, and their attention that I had fought for ten minutes to gain was gone. Frustrating for sure, but it should not lead us to underestimate children. In few words, with simple faith, children can reveal amazing depth. Case in point, let's turn to Maria Goretti, the youngest martyr in the Catholic Church. Not even fully twelve years old, she is a sign that we don't have to wait until we are older to get serious about our faith. Moreover, it's not so much her novel age that makes her a saint. True, her young age is part of the reason why she is the patron of youth. It wasn't the brevity of her life, but rather the life and love contained in that brevity that made her a saint.

Particularly, Maria was able to pack superhuman strength and love into three short words: "I forgive you." Her entire life, both on earth and in heaven, is a story of forgiveness. Forgiveness is what made her a saint not only because of her perfect and exemplary performance of it, but because she let the forgiveness of Jesus transform her whole life. The forgiveness of Jesus became a reality in her life. The mercy that she experienced from Him allowed her to live free from her own sins and its effects. Maria chose to live a life that drew its strength from that mercy. Having experienced freedom from her own sins, she embraced forgiveness and the choice to be free from the sins of others. Forgiving others allowed her to continue to live in that life free of sin, both her sins and others. By being so emptied of the weight of sin and its burdens and filled with the light and joy of mercy and forgiveness, she soared to the heights of heaven with ease. As the Good News itself is a story that wraps around the words of forgiveness uttered on the Cross, so is Maria Goretti's story centered on forgiveness. She imitated the Lord's forgiveness and discovered the Lord in forgiveness. It is important to see that forgiveness gives life, and that Maria's story and act of forgiveness is one that is completely wrapped up in the love of God, not dominated by the hatred of man. Her life on earth was given light and joy by God's eternal mercy, and her forgiveness allowed her to join herself to God's mercy and extend her life and joy into heaven. Her gift became a reality, a stable reality of life in God's love. Her short life was not focused on the evils of the world or of others, but on God's love and His constant care for her.

Maria was born on October 12, 1890, in a small town in central Italy. She was born into a small, hardworking family with five siblings, one who died before she ever met him. They grew grapes, wheat, and corn, providing them with a very poor life, in which they were able to hold onto the bare necessities. They were sharecroppers, so even with the little they had, they were forced to give half to the sharecrop owners. Money and possessions were thus held lightly in the Goretti family. The greatest treasure was the family unity they shared. As with many young girls, Maria took her name from the virgin Mary, much like her mother. To distinguish them, her mother commonly went by the name "Assunta" (her full name being *Maria Assunta,* "Mary Assumed"). The children, only educated by their parents at home, were taught the way of Christian virtue. Because they were poor, Maria had a greater ability to be detached from material things and so she was able to be attached to the people she loved.

The poverty and farming life also allowed them to uproot and move when they saw greater hope of opportunity. Faliano was where they moved to take up sharecropping. It was here that they became close with the Serenelli family, another tenant farming family. They were a rough family consisting of the alcoholic father Giovanni and his seventeen-year-old son Alessandro. The mother, who had been abusive as Alessandro grew up, was no longer in the picture. She was sent to a mental institution after she tried to drown Alessandro, and there she died. This was quite the contrast to the religious, loving, devoted family of the Goretti's. In addition to her family's devotions, Maria prayed to the different statues of Mary every day in some of the small churches that dotted the town on her way to and from various errands. Maria was very joyful, she loved life and loved those in her life, including the new friends that God had brought into her life.

Poverty forced both the Goretti and Serenelli families to leave and take up residence in a terrible, swampy region of Italy, Le Ferriere. Maria was taken away from many of the well-adorned churches she was familiar with and now lived in an area that was very dismal and isolated, with nothing except a few houses and farm homes. The two families were forced to live in the same residence, a small, rickety, abandoned factory. Maria's father had to work long, hard hours trying to drain the swamps, a place infested with mosquitoes that often-brought malaria and death. Eventually Luigi Goretti died and left his family with no father. Maria was only nine.

Both Maria and Assunta had to face this challenge not only with faith but with courage. They did not have the means to wait around and mourn. Assunta had to take on the hard work of the field and Maria was to work in the home. Maria learned the sacrifice of love very early: this world is filled with sufferings, burdens, and disappointments. Only in heaven can we truly be freed from suffering, and we must do all we can to preserve our souls for heaven. Her father's memory stayed with her, and she tried to make him proud by working for the family with housework and cooking.

Despite all her obligations, Maria had a strong spirit of

prayer. She often prayed the rosary while she worked and when she had to go to the city to buy or sell things, she stopped and prayed in front of the statue of Mary in the church in Nettuno. Maria insisted on receiving her first communion, even if that meant going on foot to the teacher's house on Sundays to attend lessons. In preparation for her first communion, Maria went and apologized to anyone she believed she had hurt so that she could live out the Gospel: "So if you are offering your gift at the altar, and there remember that your brother has something against you, leave your gift there before the altar and go first be reconciled to your brother, and then come and offer your gift" (Mt 5:23–24). Maria was already learning and practicing forgiveness daily. Her life was a continual journey, constantly loving, apologizing, and forgiving.

In 1901 Maria received her first communion. She was the youngest of the children to receive their first communion on that day. This was always a special occasion, also because at that time, giving frequent communion to children so young was rare. After the mass, the priest asked what each child wanted. Maria responded that she had never been happier in her life and would love to receive Him again. The priest was taken aback and gladly welcomed her again the following Sunday and then on July 1, the feast of the Precious Blood. Almost exactly one year later, Maria saw her own blood shed in imitation of the Lord who gave His Body to her.

Since her father's death and her mother began working in the field, Maria spent far more time in the house. They shared a house with the Serenelli family. Alessandro had started off having a very admirable relation with her, but that admiration, turned into attraction, attraction into desire. Alessandro had lived for years in isolation and anger toward his father and never fully learned to receive the tender love of a woman. Alessandro's mom was negligent and violent, so he twisted how he interpreted Maria's kindness. Very frequently,

Maria sewed some of his shirts for him and offered to help with other tasks. Despite her kindness and truly self-giving love, Alessandro's heart was drawn into the passions of a young adolescent. It must be understood, as we have seen with many of the other saints we have studied, that beautiful friendship between man and a woman is not sinful. In fact, chaste friendship can be a remedy for sin. Alessandro was not at the same level of virtue as Maria, neither from his upbringing, faith, or circumstances. He often told her bad jokes or tried to grope her. Each time, she earnestly resisted and did not entertain his ploy. On two occasions, Alessandro tried to make advances on her, and she fought him off (Maria was a young yet strong girl). [134]

The fateful day of July 5, 1902 came as any other day in the Italian summer. It was hot and oppressive and those out in the field, including Assunta and Alessandro, would have been worn down by the terrible heat. Maria was taking care of one of her sisters and doing some sewing outside of the house. Alessandro left the field and went upstairs into the house. Suddenly the door opened, and Alessandro dragged Maria into the kitchen area near the door. They were alone; no one was nearby to hear Maria's screams. This was Alessandro's opportunity; his passions had grown hot as a furnace.

Now was his chance, and he would make sure Maria either agreed or never had a chance to escape again. He pulled out a large file that was used to sharpen farm blades. Not the sharpest of weapons but, held menacingly in his hand, it got the point across to Maria. She knew that he was giving her an ultimatum: either give into his lustful desires or die. For Maria, there was only one choice: she could not give into

---

134. It is also important to understand that being a Christian, being a person of mercy and forgiveness, does not mean tolerating evil. Maria tried, through the circumstances of her life, to escape and get out of the situation with Alessandro. No person is obliged to remain in a place of abuse or burden. Ending or escaping a toxic relationship is not contrary to the virtue of forgiveness.

the sin, not only for herself, but for Alessandro too. To agree was to break her virginal chastity which was her great gift to Jesus. For Alessandro, it would mean mortal sin and Maria knew that hell is the punishment for those who commit it. One choice led to the horrible price of losing her virginity and seeing Alessandro fall into mortal sin; the other, also required a great price: offering her life.

With tears in her eyes and strength of conviction in her voice she began to scream, "No Alessandro, no! You can't! It is a sin! It is a sin! You will go to hell!" She yelled, pushed, and resisted as much as she could. As much as he tried to grip her arm and pull her, she planted her feet and pulled away. Maria was a strong girl, she held her own. He could not hold her down to rape her; she would probably escape.

The same pride that made him want to control and overpower Maria now brought about anger. He became enraged; His anger came from being deprived of his lustful desire. His adrenaline began to course through his body with an uncontrolled rage. Gripping the file in hand, he began to plunge the instrument into Maria's body. Again and again with greater intensity and speed. He ended up stabbing her eleven times in the abdomen. He used such force in stabbing her that seven of those eleven wounds pierced through Maria. The only reason why the other four did not go all the way through was that the file hit her spine. He hit her spine with such intensity that it bent the tip of the file.

Maria then collapsed and passed out from the trauma. All this happened in the kitchen area which stood at a halfway point between the Goretti and the Serenelli living areas. Leaving her lying on the floor there, Alessandro walked down the hall to his living quarters to take a nap. Maria was not dead though. The file, which was dull along its edges, had simply punctured her body, going straight through without really lacerating much on the way in or out. The wounds were like those made from stepping on a nail.

After some time, Maria regained consciousness. She very slowly crawled to the door to cry for help. She made it to the door and carefully began to undo the lock latch. Because it was an old and rusty latch, it not only was difficult to open, but also noisy. As she began to swing the creaky, metal latch, she unfortunately woke her assailant. Alessandro saw her there, trying to undo the latch while leaning her weight against the door. He then ran up to her, took out his file, and stabbed her three more times, directly in her back, making it a total of fourteen stabs. These were the three stab wounds that proved fatal, since they went directly into her upper chest cavity, piercing her heart, and collapsing her lung. Immediately, she passed out again, and Alessandro went back to his rest.

Maria laid in a state of imminent peril and was unable to call for help. However, her little sister had been outside on the steps with Maria before she was abducted. Since the child was left there on the steps alone for so long, she began to cry and woke up Giuseppe who had been sleeping below the steps. Seeing the child alone, he entered the house and found Maria lying on the ground in a pool of her own blood. Immediately he called for help; all who had been working in the field scrambled over in haste. A sword of pain stabbed Assunta when she heard the shrill cries of the people, and she prayed their report was not true. Maria was still alive but in critical condition. She had to be transferred by horse drawn carriage seven miles down a very bumpy and unpaved road to get to the hospital at Nettuno. It was here that her passion truly began.

Because of the numerous deep puncture wounds, her small body had lost a great quantity of blood. The doctors were baffled that, between the blood loss and trauma, she had not died already. They had to go into her body and sew up her puncture wounds to try and save her from hemorrhaging. However, because of the amount of blood she had already lost and how close she was to death, the doctors were not able to use any anesthesia since the effect they cause on the body is so traumatic that they push the body close to death. Maria, in full consciousness and with complete sensation of her body, had to endure a two-to-three-hour surgery, without any anesthesia or pain killer. The doctors had to cut most of her wounds open wider, go deeper into her body, and sew the wounds closed. The doctors attested that Maria never complained or said anything. This patience she showed was a crucial piece of information in her canonization process, showing that she kept full control of her mind and stayed lucid up until the moment of her death.

At the end of the surgery, after all of Maria's great ordeal, she begged for water. She simply wanted some water to help cool her during this terrible ordeal in the heated hospital. However, because of the multiple incisions and lacerated sections of her body, drinking water would prove fatal since it would leak through the wounds into her body and kill her. So even her small request was denied, and she had to suffer more. The priest who was there with her, held a crucifix to her face and told her, "Jesus was thirsty too on the Cross. Can you offer your sufferings up with him?" She replied, "Yes father."

As time slowly crept by and Assunta patiently sat there with her daughter, she wondered what more must be endured by her sweet girl. She had already lost one child; her husband had fallen to malaria. Now her dearly beloved Maria, who had so much to offer the world, who showed so much love for God, was being taken from her. Assunta could only sit by and watch helplessly. What daggers of sorrow must have been stabbing her heart! Any mother who has lost a child knows this pain, but how much worse to have to watch her child slowly suffer, without being able to offer a small glass of water! All because of one man's evil! What did Maria do to deserve this? The presence of evil and suffering is one of the great dramas the human person grapples with. It is the twisted result of original sin that affects not only the natural order, but also disorders the will of man. It is only in the all-good and all-powerful hands and providence of God that a greater good can be weaved from the meaninglessness of suffering.

Soon, it was apparent that Maria was not going to make it. The priest came and offered her last rites and prepared her for death. Her thirst was terrible at this point. Could they not let her have a little water before she died? Helplessly, they had to deny her wish. The priest again showed her the crucifix to focus on and now had to ask her the most challenging question yet. "Maria, Jesus on the Cross forgave the people who crucified him. Are you willing to forgive Alessandro?" For many of us in that situation, it would have been hard for us to even be patient with this kind priest, much less muster up the strength and love to do what he asked. But Maria, having lost everything, still had so much to give. Without a moment's hesitation, and with no sense of coercion or reluctance in her voice, she clearly spoke aloud to all in the room, "Yes, I choose to forgive Alessandro, and I want him in heaven with me."

Was she saying that what happened was not wrong? Where was the apology? Was Alessandro even sorry? He deserved to be punished! Is her forgiving him just giving up and letting him have the victory at her expense? Does forgiving him not say that he was in the right or give him power over her?

We all know what it means to be hurt; the experience is heightened when it comes from another person we know and trust. When this wounding is intentional, it can leave a deep scar. The anger, resentment, and bitterness that we hold onto from that event can not only be more painful but longer lasting in its duration. It seems a natural response to want to hold onto that anger, believing that by doing so we are honoring a good that was disrespected by another. We just want what is right. When we chose to stay angry or bitter, it in no way undoes the damage that was done, it does not correct the wrong doer, and it does not bring healing to the victim.

What happens, unfortunately, is that the victim becomes imprisoned. They remain controlled and obsessed by the actions of the other to the point that they are bound to the memories and emotions of the evil done. In effect, the attacker continues to have an impact on the victim. Years later, the victim finds themself unable to act freely: they avoid situations that remind them of the hurt or the attacker, they continually struggle with feelings and thoughts and are unable to be free. The weight of stress and anger can cause physical and psychological damage to the victim, resulting from the constant choice to hold onto the memory and emotion in hopes of retribution. Sadly, rarely does the attacker come back to give it. The drama of forgiveness versus unforgiveness is the entire drama of mankind that has stayed tied to the wounds and sins of man's past until the forgiveness of Jesus allowed man to be set free.

Mercy does not signify not demanding repayment or saying that what happened was wrong, but it means that you give the other a share in the peace that you have a right to. It is giving the other a gift they don't deserve. Mercy comes from a surplus, not a deficiency. The merciful person has more and thus can give, and by giving they doesn't diminish the love they have within. Like a flame is not diminished in sharing its fire, neither is the merciful person in sharing their forgiveness. But justice is never denied. Justice and mercy go together. Justice means acknowledging the wound caused and acting correctly in response. Mercy means giving the healing that is not deserved but is still freely given. The great image of these two is Jesus on the Cross.

> Jesus was the sacrificial Lamb offered to the Father for our sins. Jesus' crucifixion demonstrates the severity of the wound upon the heart of God, inflicted by Adam and Eve in their sin and perpetuated by our sin. Justice demanded death, but mercy promised a Savior, wounded for our transgressions because of love. Christ crucified is the picture of the justice and mercy of God. There can be no mercy apart from truth. If God were to take away our sin and its consequences, apart from revealing His sacrificial love, we would never know the very nature of God, which is love. [135]

Forgiveness in its truest meaning is at the heart of Jesus' saving work; not only in His forgiveness of our sins, but in empowering us also to forgive.

What is beautiful is that the victim does not have to remain a victim. Forgiveness, true forgiveness, is the ability to choose to give up that right to be angry and thus be free. The victim is the first one to benefit. But that space occupied by the anger must be filled; nature abhors a vacuum. What goes in its place? Love. Love that can replace anger gives to the forgiver a greater gift and strength than they had even before the attack. Forgiveness fills the victim with love and allows them to give their attacker a gift they don't deserve. This still doesn't mean saying what happened is right, but it is saying that what happened won't have the final word. The forgiveness process can be summed up this way:

---

135. Neal Lozano, Unbound: *A Practical Guide to Deliverance,* (Royal Oaks, MI: Chosen books, 2009), 75.

> [The process of] forgiving begins with pain and that we have a right to our feelings, . . . acknowledging that the offense was unfair and will always continue to be unfair. . . . We have a moral right to anger. . . . People do not have a right to hurt us. We have a right to respect. . . . Forgiveness requires giving up something to which we have a right—namely our anger or resentment. Forgiveness is an act of mercy toward an offender, someone who does not necessarily deserve our mercy . . . a gift to our offender for the purpose of changing the relationship between ourselves and those who have hurt us. . . . We are no longer controlled by angry feelings toward this person. . . . We are willing to treat him or her as a member of the human community.[136]

No one has encapsulated this definition better than Maria Goretti. She knew the pain both physically and emotionally, as well as the moral consequences of the act of forgiveness. She knew the gravity of Alessandro's actions and how undeserving she was of any of it. Maria could have been a prisoner of another man's sins and died with bitterness, never receiving an apology or the restoration of damage done. But with the freedom of her will, she took hold of the victory Jesus gave us over not only our sins but all sin in His resurrection and allowed her life to be freed and transfigured by an act of forgiveness that filled her with a love and compassion that could not be given or reached by any labor of man on this earth. She died, not alone as a victim of another man's evil,

---

136. Robert D. Enright, "Forgiveness is a Choice" (Washington D.C.: American Psychological Association, 2001), 25.

but freed from the weight of sin and this world; she died as a saint. She truly became one of those "who have come out of the great tribulation; they have washed their robes and made them white in the blood of the Lamb" (Rev 7:14).

At the moment of Maria's death, Alessandro was far from apologies. When Maria was discovered, Alessandro was immediately taken to court and tried for murder. He was found to have had no trace of mental illness to defer his crime on, and he was extremely indignant. He was found guilty and was given one of the highest sentences a juvenile could be given at that time: thirty years in prison. This also included several years of solitary confinement, partially on account of his demeanor and attitude, which made it necessary to separate him from others. This time of solitude was terrible but did not seem to wear on his soul. He screamed and cursed Maria and tried to place much of the blame on her. He almost bragged about his crime; at every turn, he passed the blame on Maria, saying that it was her fault and that she enticed him. Had she just given into his desires, none of this would have happened. He was facing thirty years in prison, barely missing a life sentence or the death penalty because he was still considered a juvenile. So again, he found himself alone and angry and unloved, as he had been for many years. It was at this time of darkness and despair that Maria stepped into his life again.

The year now was 1908 and it was six years into his prison sentence. Alessandro, still brooding over what had passed, had a long time to go. For the past ten years, since he first met Maria in 1898, she had been on his mind constantly. Now, she seemed to forever haunt him, cursed by his guilt, scorned by everyone he met. But Maria had Alessandro on her mind as well. God gives us not only grace to accomplish the mission He sets before us, but also, He puts people in our lives to be the instrumental players we need. Alessandro had wounds in his life that he never admitted. He had never learned or experienced unconditional love or true mercy. Since those earliest moments with his mother and then with his negligent father, all he had known was how unfair and cruel life can be and that what he deserved was at best his pitiable prison.

But Maria was not going to hold back the flood gates of love. In the goodness and power of God, the evil and malice of man never has the last word. God transformed Alessandro's act of hatred and violence into Maria's staircase to heaven. Evil was completely overcome by being transformed into the means of grace. God did not want this evil to have a moment to brag. Suffering and pain was transformed by Jesus and has been lived by every saint, not as a meaningless consequence of failure or malice, but as God's way of showing His power and goodness. Now the situation had to come full circle. As a true saint, Maria's love had only increased for Alessandro, who through his evil ironically brought her to heaven. Now it was her turn to bring him to heaven.

In the darkness of that prison cell, Alessandro saw a light. Where was it coming from? There were no windows in his cell, and he only got to see the sun about once a day during time when he was permitted to leave his cell. But the light was in his cell. It was coming from a mysterious garden. Grass and flowers appeared all over! He had not seen this type of greenery in six years!

There, in the middle of the garden, was Maria, standing before him clothed in a beautiful dress. He looked at her for the first time since he last saw her lying bloody on the ground. He felt no lust, no anger, no guilt, no fear. All he felt was peace. Maria looked at him and she loved him. She was really the first person who had truly loved him on earth, and this was the first time Alessandro saw and knew someone could love him in the face of his own sin. "For love is strong as death, jealousy is cruel as the grave. Its flashes are flames of fire, a most vehement flame. Many waters cannot quench love, neither can flood drown it" (Sg 8:6–7). No evil can escape the power and goodness of God! Sinner and saint are swept into the all-embracing power of His love. The assailant is now made a beloved, the victim a victory, the murder into a ransom, and the relationship into sanctity. Yes, for those who live in love, they are not victims to the cruelty of evil or the despair of chaos and hopelessness but are part of the ever more powerful and victorious force of God's mercy. The small sacrifice of love, which causes us to die to ourselves, makes us live with a power more grandiose than anything man can accomplish, either by his good will or his most horrendous actions. The victim and attacker are not set at odds with each other in God's kingdom, but rather: "The wolf shall dwell with the lamb, and the leopard shall lie with the kid, and the calf and the lion and the fatling together, and a little child shall lead them" (Is 11:6–7).

As Maria looked on him with love, she approached him. He still felt no fear at her gentle approach. She offered him a gift: lilies. She began to give them to him, one by one; fourteen of them in all. He knew right away what these were for. For each time he had stabbed her in rage, she had forgiven him with love. These lilies were her gift, the final sign of her forgiveness. As she finished giving him the lilies, she gave him one last gaze face to face before they saw each other after his death. She had finished what she said, "I forgive Alessandro..." and her last gaze was full of that true hope in her heart, "and I want him in heaven with me." With that, she vanished.

Even with the vision ended, there was still a light that shone, not in the cell, but in Alessandro's heart. He had been forgiven! The mercy he felt was palpable and the conversion it brought was almost tangible. Alessandro asked the bishop to visit. He made his confession and admitted that Maria was completely innocent; he had provoked the attack and Maria refused at every point to give into his desire. He consigned to the punishment that was his due. His demeanor changed completely. The aggressive, indignant young man had now become a kind, contrite, and reserved heart. His conversion was so evident and the change so apparent, that his sentence, for the first time in the Italian penal system, was lessened from thirty years to twenty-seven years because of good behavior.

Finally, in 1929 he was freed from prison, but he had felt freedom for several years at this point. He was quoted as saying "Maria's forgiveness saved me." Only one thing remained; he had an apology to make. He and Maria had made their peace, but he knew of one more person who was suffering: Assunta. When her husband had died, she had to take up the responsibility of working in the farm to raise the family. Maria had become her right hand. Assunta had to watch her daughter slowly and painfully die in front of her, unable to help even with the slightest glass of water. Moreover, after Maria had died, Assunta was not able to care for all her children. She eventually had to give her sons up for adoption. Sadly, Assunta was not even able to attend Maria's funeral because it was the last day she had with her children.

Then, on Christmas Eve of 1934, Assunta received a knock on her door. When she answered it, she saw a gentle man standing before her. It was a face she recognized immediately. How could she forget it? Alessandro looked at her and said "Assunta, do you know who I am?" "Yes, I know who you are Alessandro," she gently replied. "Could you ever forgive me for what I have done?" was Alessandro's shy, contrite request. Assunta had lost everything, husband, daughter, her other children as well. All on account of this man. How could he make up for all this? What good is forgiveness at this point? Her answer was incredibly powerful: "Alessandro, Maria has forgiven you; God has forgiven you. How can I not forgive you?"

Actions speak louder than words and Assunta's life soon became a pulpit of forgiveness. She not only spoke those words of pardon to Alessandro, but also adopted him as her own son! Again, the beauty of God's work: Assunta received a lost child, and Alessandro received the mother he never had. They had a deep spiritual union, and Alessandro eventually joined a Capuchin monastery. Very often he went to visit the grave of his old friend. Alessandro was not the only one to visit Maria, for by this time her grave received many visitors and many miracles occurred there. Paralytics left her tomb healed and others departed inspired and encouraged by her brave witness. Her fame and intercession continued to grow exponentially. So great was her popularity as well as the numerous miracles that came after her death, that within fifty years of her death, Maria was raised to sainthood!

Not only was the speed remarkable, but also two other unique facts surrounded her canonization in 1950: First, that there were so many people in attendance (500,000 more or less) that it was the first time a canonization had to take place outdoors, in the square of St. Peter's. Second, it was the first time that a mother of the saint, was present at her own child's canonization. St. Maria Goretti since then has become one of the patrons of youth, a message of forgiveness, and a model of purity.

Alessandro lived out the rest of his life with a great devotion to the little saint that, through his "happy fault," he helped bring to heaven. He offered penance constantly for the sins of his past life and lived as a quiet, contemplative hermit. When he finally died, it was found that he had a piece of paper with him that apologized for the sin he committed and warned the world to avoid temptation and falling into sin.

Even recently, Maria's life and activity has continued to inspire the world and her presence has been keenly recognized in the Church. In 2002, on the hundredth anniversary of her death, Pope St. John Paul II said that Maria heralded what is known as the "century of martyrs," a time of great Christian persecution. He said:

> The devotion to her has continued to spread on every continent, giving rise to admiration and a thirst for God everywhere. In Maria Goretti shines out the radical choice of the Gospel, unhindered, indeed strengthened by the inevitable sacrifice that faithful adherence to Christ demands...walking in the footsteps of the divine Teacher always means standing up for him and committing oneself to follow him wherever he goes (cf. Apoc 14,4). However, on this path, young people know that they are not alone. St Maria Goretti and the many adolescents who down through centuries paid the price of martyrdom for their allegiance to the Gospel, are beside them, to instill in their hearts the strength to remain firm in fidelity. Thus, they will be able to become watchmen of a radiant dawn, illumined by hope. [137]

Later, in 2015, during the Jubilee Year of Mercy proclaimed by Pope Francis, St. Maria Goretti and her story of forgiveness was exalted as an image of mercy for the Church. This small little girl, who in her poverty on earth had barely seen any large city, was, from the richness of the mercy of heaven, able to travel all over the world on a "pilgrimage of mercy" as her body was transported all over the United States and her

137. John Paul II, "Message of John Paul II to the bishop of Albano for the centenary of the death of St. Maria Goretti," (Vatican City State: 2002), par 5.

story presented to many, bringing healing to thousands. It is beautiful that this little girl who in this life was so small and hidden from the world became like the grain of wheat that is small yet full of life. A small grain remains a seed until it enters the earth in an act of self-gift. "But if it falls into the earth and dies, it bears much fruit" (Jn 12:24). In giving herself in mercy on earth, she exploded with life in heaven, first bearing fruit in her own murderer's life, who is now a Servant of God and on the path to sainthood, but also in so many other lives. As Maria's forgiveness on earth freed her from pain and anger, so now in heaven her act of virtue and forgiveness has an immensely communicable power to the rest of the Church. Through her example, story, intercession, and friendship she can release many more from the terrible pain of unforgiveness and hate.

Friends of St. Maria Goretti

Maria's Friend's Story

This first testimony was offered to me by an anonymous writer. They gave me their testimony but asked to keep all identities confidential so as the protect the good name of those involved. She simply asked to be referred to as "Maria's friend."

You don't pick the saint, they pick you. When I was getting confirmed and it was time to pick my confirmation saint, I wanted a saint that was pretty and interesting. As I scoured through multiple saint books, I came across St. Maria Goretti and thought she was a beautiful young girl and discovered she was also one of the quickest saints to be canonized. I don't know what exactly made me choose her over all the other amazing saints, but she was who I chose.

My sister had met her boyfriend when they were very young. He grew up in another country but was born here in America. Very early on in their relationship, they had gotten pregnant and then married shortly after and so he also entered into my life when I was very young. He had been abusing alcohol and also smoking marijuana, had no faith at all, and the rest of his life was very much out of order, to say the least.

It was then around the time of my confirmation that my brother-in-law began sexually abusing me. I didn't really understand that it was abuse at that time because, thankfully, things never got too far and as with most victims, I blamed myself for the situation. My sister and my brother-in-law had been having a lot of issues at this time as well and their marriage was falling apart. Without really being able to explain it, I felt that grace was already at work within me to forgive him, because I felt sorry for him, not angry.

A couple of years later the truth finally came out. I had mentioned it to my mother who initially didn't do anything about it but when the issues between them persisted, my mother informed my sister what I had told her. After school one day, my mom asked me to tell her the truth again, which I thought was odd. They had put the picture together of what he had been doing to me and what was really at play. They put the label on it that I was afraid to: sexual abuse. When the news came out of exactly what had happened and what it was, immediately I had an overwhelming peace that came over me to forgive again and again, which is weird because I can normally hold grudges!

My mother left the decision up to me if we wanted to press charges. I could not do that to him or my nieces and nephew. I cannot explain it except as something almost miraculous taking place. It was a powerful movement in my heart and a desire for his good and a strong feeling for no bad to fall upon him. I truly felt like I forgave him. I know it was a desire of forgiveness, and I know it was coming from something (or someone) other than just me. Looking back now, I can say it was definitely the intercession of Maria that helped me to make the act of forgiveness.

My family, rightfully so, was angry and my sister did separate from him. We did not press charges but a total separation did take place. He was out of our lives for a year and a half. As with many victims, I can see later in my life that there were several effects and wounds that were in me as a result of this, since the healing of forgiveness is a process. But in my own journey, and the grace of God's mercy in my life through confession, I was helped to close many of those wounds, and I was helped to break with my own struggles.

After several months my brother-in-law became sober from drugs and alcohol, became a US citizen, joined the military, and most importantly had a conversion to our Catholic faith. After a lot of hard work and penance, he is truly a changed man. I have never seen that type of turn around ever before.

And once he proved himself to my sister and family, my mom and sister felt that it was an appropriate time for me to see him face to face again. He asked me for forgiveness. I was able, again, with no anger or bitterness, to finally vocalize my forgiveness for him and to him. It was then that my family was also able to truly forgive him.

Since then, he has become an amazing friend and leader! He is the godfather for my children and has gone on to have a flourishing marriage with my sister and to be a father to many more children and a spiritual leader in their and my life. Were it not for the power of forgiveness that I was able to make, both his life and my life would be in much worse places. I truly believe that it was St. Maria Goretti's intercession that helped my brother-in-law become the godly man he is today and that helped me to be able to truly forgive, as with her situation with Alessandro. We all have a great relationship now. I didn't realize at the time how much I would have in common with St. Maria Goretti. Her story has inspired me more and more and her companionship keeps me strong. Still to this day, I see her as a special patroness in my life and the life of my family and a model of forgiveness.

Jessica Smith

This next story comes from a woman from one of my former parishes. She had a story with Maria Goretti that had started long before we met, but then it began to skyrocket in her relationship and became a real power in her life. She heard me give a homily at mass on Maria Goretti and forgiveness and reached out to me with her story.

I don't have much of a story that is filled with wonderment or awe, but I do believe that St. Maria Goretti and I "met" not by chance. I grew up learning and reading about the saints. I believe Maria Goretti was special to me when I was young because she was a young saint and she was so pure. My mother received my Maria Goretti relic for me when she was in Rome. I have had her with me since I was seventeen or eighteen. My mother got her for me for purity and protection. (I thought I got it when we went to St. Anne de Beaupre Basilica in Quebec, Canada but that was around the same time that she went to Rome.)

Not too much longer after that I met my first husband. I had never had a "real" boyfriend and he made sure to use that to his advantage. He led me away from God, my family, and my friends. He was abusive to me mentally and physically. He held me at gunpoint for multiple hours with a shotgun to my head, tried to kill us in his truck by driving over 100mph while swerving dangerously back and forth, and punched on multiple occasions in my head "so no one would see the bruises." He also turned into a drug/sex addict. He forced me or coerced me to do things that went against God. He committed adultery multiple times throughout our relationship/marriage. All of this happened from 2000-2006. It pretty much came to an end when I became pregnant with our son, and he said that I ruined his life by getting pregnant (even though we were married). I'm telling you all these things to explain that I had to have been shielded somehow by Maria and God.

It didn't dawn on me that she might have shielded me and wanted to help me. I have had tremendous issues because of all of this. I would get physically ill when discussing him or at the sound of his voice. I have gone to multiple therapists and have been put on multiple anxiety and depression medications to try to "fix" the problem. None of them did. This past summer I finally was able to see a therapist that helped me realize I had to forgive so I could let go to start healing—no medication would do that. It was so hard! I didn't want to forgive. I wanted him to hurt and pay for all the hurt he ever did to me (and our son). I had been in a virtual prison ever since all of that had taken place and had suffered other things that kept me in that mental prison.

[Side note: he tricked me into taking him back for about six months in 2016 - same person. During that time he met Jacob [our son] and Jacob met two of his three half siblings. I had just gone through a bad divorce from another man that had the same drug and abusive tendencies. My first ex-husband and two of his children lived with me and my three sons for four of those six months. The abuse and drug use quickly showed up again, and I told him he had to leave. (His children went to live with their mother.) His eyes turned black, and he told me that he would burn me and my children alive in my home. All of this just amplified the ability to not forgive him.]

He had randomly written to me on Facebook reminiscing in September 2020. By this time I was remarried to my current husband. I wrote him back explaining how I was sorry he was plagued with the "what ifs," if things would have been different. I had mentioned how every good and bad memory with him was so vivid. I constantly felt as though I was in a prison. I still didn't know that Maria was going to be able to help me until, I believe it was the next Sunday after writing the letter to him, you were sharing a homily about Maria. You used some of the exact same words in my letter. "SO VIVID." You talked about how she forgave her attacker. This was exactly what I needed to hear. She and God were talking through you in your homily about her, so that I could start to break out of my "prison" of hate and be able to forgive.

I know this story was all over the place, but it was a story that spans twenty years. I'm praying that Maria and God continue to help me forgive both of my ex-husbands for all the wrong they have done. I don't ask for vengeance anymore. I pray that they get help and get better. I have to deal with my second ex-husband because of our children, so I try to encourage him to watch mass with the boys and pray with them.

I do feel having her always with me in her relic shielded me from deadly harm and will continue to help me on the road to healing.

O God, author of innocence and lover of chastity, who bestowed the grace of martyrdom on your handmaid, the Virgin Saint Maria Goretti, in her youth, grant, we pray, through her intercession, that, as you gave her a crown for her steadfastness, so we, too, may be firm in obeying your commandments. Amen

"St. Dymphna"
Original Painting by Caroline Pellegrin

ST. DYMPHNA

In recent times, mental health has received a lot of new attention. More and more, we see how the health of the mind affects everything, and how everything affects the health of the mind. Primarily, society focuses on the various maladies that either seem to be on the rise or are just receiving more awareness: anxiety, depression, paranoia, panic attacks, mania, autism, schizophrenia, to name a few. There is a vast spectrum of mental conditions that are basically a mental prison that people live in, suffering a silent hell on earth unknown to anyone else. In the wake of the 2020 Coronavirus pandemic, there was a 50% increase in depression and a 30% increase in suicide compared to recent years. The struggles and pains of mental health are very real, but the negative realities are not the totality of mental health. Mental health refers to the function of the inner network that connects a person's thoughts, emotions, consciousness, and understanding.

The mind is more than just the brain. It is the intellectual aspect of man's being related with knowing, understanding, remembering, and willing. It forms a harmony with the rest of man's being, his body, emotions, and heart. Ultimately, it is one of the highest and most unique aspects of man. Man's appetites he shares with animals, his ability to grow he shares with plants, even his senses he shares with other animals. However, only man has the true power of intellect and reason. It has been argued that some apes can speak or perform certain levels of communication and problem solving, but abstract thinking is unheard of in the animal kingdom. A monkey may be able to distinguish and point out a square from a circle, but they can't break down or understand

WHAT a square is. Conceptual, universal thinking is beyond them. This rational capacity is the highest part of man; it is what makes him most unique. Rationality is linked with immateriality because it can go beyond just what is physical; it is able to make conclusions that are no apparent, deduce a general concept from particular clues, and generate artifacts that don't exist in the real world. Man's rationality forms a tie with his soul in that it is not just the product of or the sum total of the physical parts of man: it is something wholly other, that comes from the outside and informs his body. The mind and rationality of man is truly a power of the soul you could say. This immaterial soul is also why man does not die with the body. It is on the rational aspect of his soul that God has implanted His image and likeness.

Man's mind is a beautiful gift from God, despite much of the negative attention that mental health gets. Dr. Kheriaty beautifully explains our understanding of mind and the soul in theology:

> God endowed human nature with an emotional life – and it was good; indeed, it was very good. Among other things, our emotional life is essential for us to love and to be loved first by God and then by other rational persons whether angelic or human. . . . He created us for an authentic love, found in and through self-giving relationships. . . . Their [Men's] intellect, will, emotions, appetites, bodies, and relationships all operated in mutual harmony, because they were in harmony with God.[138]

138. Aaron Kheriaty, *The Catholic Guide to Depression*, (Sophia Institute Press, 2012), 41–42

All of man's senses draw their information into his mind, where it is sorted, organized, and categorized. Man's mind is truly what helps him to become a co-creator with God by aiding in making thoughts, desires and goal come to life. God made it that man does not just love, but knows what he loves and why it is good to love and is free to choose that he loves and even what it means to love. Our minds also unite all our various human experiences and emotions into a greater understanding. We are then led to a realization beyond what the senses and emotions tell us and to will a good that is known and understood. Our mind is not only how we know facts but know the power of love, the desire of another for our good.

Our mind, emotions, and senses can help us gain a greater understanding of the plan God has for us. As God's original design for us, this inner structure is a greater way for us to know Him and to reach Him in total freedom. However, man's fall created a break not only with God and man, but within man himself.

> This truth of faith reveals that depression, in the last analysis, is foreign to our original nature. It is no more a part of our fundamental human nature than cancer or dementia. . . . Christian revelation locates its origin in that fateful decision of our first parents to separate themselves from communion with God. . . . The human nature became deeply wounded as a result of original sin. The intellect was darkened, the will was worked to be inclined to evil and our emotions were no longer harmoniously integrated with our intellect, will, and bodily health. . . . The "lower parts" of the soul (emotions and appetites) rebel against the "higher parts" (intellect and will).

> The emotions throw off the wise and gentle guidance of reason that is suffused with divine love. [139]

The beautiful harmony that was man's being became wounded, and his mind became disordered. The beautiful tapestry which is man's inner self has become tangled. This original gift to man now can be a torture. Disorder is the perfect word not only for mental issues but for our entire experience now because it is out of the order that man was created in. The different anomalies, struggles, and conditions that plague man's mental health is a result of this deeper chaos that is taking place between man and God and is reflected inside man himself. Though various factors, such as cultural impact and pressures, can influence man's mind and how and why he responds in certain ways, there is a deeper wound and disorder of man's emotions, judgment, and understanding that must be acknowledged in the struggles man faces. [140]

The fall thus caused a huge rift in man and all his faculties, a disunity within him. The original design for all of man to work together, his mind, body, emotions, soul, and energy. The separation is a result of the fall and thus the remedy is found in a unity. Jesus becoming a man was not just to bring man to unity with God, but to bring man back together with man. Man still struggles with brokenness and disorder, yet Christ shows that we are not destined to the consequence of our disorders. He shows firstly that our human nature and emotions are good: Jesus used His human mind and emotions throughout His ministry and redemption to show that the mental reality of man has a part to play in our healed relationship with God and others. He loved, He felt

139. Kheriaty, 42–43.

140. The purpose of this book is not to go into, diagnose, or offer ways of coping with these realities. However, I recommend the book cited above, *The Catholic Guide to Depression*, for a more in-depth analysis of the interplay of psychology and spirituality.

anger, He felt sadness, He even felt loneliness and the sense of abandonment. He experienced these emotions in His human nature in their fullness. He also showed the strength we can have over these and how not every emotion, impulse, or desire should be followed but that many of the evils of the world come from within man (Mk 7:21–23). Jesus also shows and relates to the great pain that can be caused by mental anomalies. He shows this especially in His agony in the garden where he expressed great distress and stated that His "soul was sorrowful" (Mk 14:33–34). The great weight of stress that was so intense that he sweat blood[141] (Lk 22:44).

Even on the Cross, Jesus cried out with a sense of abandonment and forsakenness (Mk 15:34). Though Jesus truly was never separated from the Father, in His human nature He experienced this weight, to join Himself more to us. The experience of man's mental struggle has been touched by Jesus' saving sacrifice and everyone that endures torture is given a share in His Cross. Dr. Kheriatry beautifully expounds this belief:

> All of the world's sufferings are taken up into the death of Jesus and transformed in the revelation of his infinite and unconditional love for man. Sorrow and anguish, which used to indicate man's separation from God, is now paradoxically made into an expression of God's love for man and thus an indication of union with God. The Cross and Resurrection irrevocably and fundamentally alter sorrow and its meaning. Brought through the fires of the Paschal Mystery, neither man nor

141. There is an actual condition called hematohidrosis where the small blood vessels around the sweat glands will burst under extreme stress.

> his mental suffering are the same, because the individual who is united to Christ now finds himself in a previously unforeseeable communion with God: he is made a member of Christ's Mystical Body.[142]

Although sorrow fear, and anguish entered the world with man's sin, through man's reunion with God in Jesus these realities are transformed into something greater. They become part of a grander scheme. Though there is still sorrow and pain, and these conditions are a true trial for those who suffer from them, they do not automatically signify abandonment. God's love has embraced them and transformed them into an expression of God's desire for man.

Man's entire mental state has been assumed into the divine by Jesus. The inner life of man's mind, thoughts and emotions is powerfully drawn into a cooperation with the things of the spirit and of God. The condition of man's mind is now a key element in his proper function as a person but also in his relationship with God. However, even when there are the various disorders or imperfections that exist within man, this does not result in a great separation from God, but rather puts us in union with God who experienced the full gambit of mental and emotional realities. Our mind not only pursues God but can come into union with Him. We should not underestimate the importance of using our minds and balancing our mental health as we seek God.

The mind is now a place of union with God, but it is also a place to battle against the devil. The great author of all disorders wishes nothing more than to lead us away from God and deeper into the disordered chaos that he is

142. Kheriatry, 52.

the father of. We must see that Christ, though He united Himself with the suffering human condition, did not show that remaining with those disordered conditions or aimlessly following them was redemption. Jesus is our example; He is our means of salvation. Apart from Him, all our anguish and pursuits remain lifeless. Many people unfortunately look at disorders in their life and simply say, "I was born this way" or "this is me" and believe that is enough. Because of original sin and the disorder from that sin, man can be born with disorders that are very engrained in him. The struggle with various disorders and inclinations is that they feel natural and can many times be present from birth. The natural conclusion is then that they are something to just be accepted and approved. No condition of man, no matter how natural it may feel or seem, can define man. Just as man is born with original sin but must be baptized to remove it, so too man must work to root out the disordered effects of sin. Jesus said, "if your right hand causes you to sin, cut it off" (Mt 5:30), showing that natural faculties can still lead to sin and must be dealt with. Just like in a garden, there are natural elements such as weeds and grass that must be uprooted, so to in the human person. It is the Christian task to see that these disorders, weaknesses, and struggles do no define man and are something that we must strive to resist and cultivate Christ in our minds and hearts while not giving into discouragement or despair, fearing our dignity is lost. Our dignity is not defined or given simply by the sum of our faults and weakness, but only by God, and that can never be stolen from us.

Man's mental state is now, as it always has been, a battlefield. The saints also endured through much of the mental trials we experience. They are not saints because they lacked all mental struggles and were perfect, but rather because of how they bore them. The saints were never limited by their mental or physical conditions in becoming saints; they allowed their own brokenness to be offered up and redeemed by Jesus and it was their willingness to unite all to Jesus that sanctified them. Some saints had a disorder or struggle, but because they allowed it to lead them to God it was used for good; conversely, someone may lack all mental disorders and be mentally healthy and still choose to live a disordered life. "Man is responsible for the rectification through humility as for the deviation through pride, and this it is which gives its dramatic interest to the lives of the saints."[143] No matter what a man struggles with, he can always choose to either turn to God and the right path or to himself and his own designs. This decision is the heart of being a saint or sinner. Even when they do struggle with various mental illnesses or disorders, the saints are still able to bring it to that end of praising God. St. Benedict Joseph Labré was a poor beggar who had not the mental capacity to enter a religious order or become a priest, so he simply wandered the streets of Rome and prayed in the various churches. When he went to confession and spoke to priests, they said he performed a well-ordered and deep examination of conscience and had a clear recollection of his life, as simple as it was. It was said of him that he may have only had half a brain, but he gave it all to God. That is the mark of sanctity: saints allow God to fill up every aspect of their strengths or weaknesses. They were able to be sanctified, to be made whole through the struggle they endured, by uniting it to the Cross of Christ. Their condition still allowed them to feel care and concern for the things of God and of man.

Certain conditions are unfortunately associated with saints, such as being delusional, hysterical, overly sensitive, or anxious, depressed, even bipolar or schizophrenic. The

143. Joly, *The Psychology of the Saints*, 99.

sanctity or concern that the saints had for issues not of this world or the effects that prayer and mysticism had on them were not a result of these disorders. These disorders are chronic anomalies that are results of a disintegration and a lack of harmony in a person. A person struggling with one of these conditions "is no longer able, or, at best, only very imperfectly able to reduce his recollection to order or place them in their proper relations with his actual life. . .. His will no longer acts in connection with reasoned ideas."[144] Someone who struggles with one of these conditions finds their field of view and freedom of actions narrowed and the exact source of their thoughts and decisions is unclear and uncontrolled. Rather, the saints had a great deal of control and they exerted the same integrity of personality and desire in whatever stage of life they were in. Recollection is not only easy for them, but they could indulge in it for a long time; their desires were centered and clear.

Patron saint of mental illness

Those that journey under the cross of mental illness are invited to walk with a young maiden named Dymphna, who came to know the very complex and even tragic reality of mental illness. We call St. Dymphna the patron saint of mental illnesses which, as we have seen and as we experience in our world, is quite a big undertaking. Dymphna shows that the entire mental state of man must be approached with love. She sees how to direct, correct, and endure as well as embrace and console the various conditions of man's mental journey and the mark that original sin left on it. The story of

144. Joly, 105

Dymphna, from her life on earth to her ministry in heaven, is a powerful aid to all of us on our journey to God.

It was the late 1200s in the country of Belgium. At that time, the country was beginning to flourish in arts and science in many of its main cities like Leuven and Gent. However, much of the countryside was still being discovered and was revealing many hidden treasures. In 1238 Bishop Guy was assigned to the diocese of Cambrai, the second largest diocese in the country, which extended from the southern boundary with France up to the city of Antwerp and even touched some of the estuaries from the North Sea. From that small corner of his diocese, he received many interesting reports: a huge cult to an unknown saint. Hordes of ill people, including those with mental illnesses and demonic possessions, were brought to a small church in Gheel, Belgium. Great miracles were taking place through this young mysterious saint who had a strange patronage over some of the most misunderstood difficulties: from insanity to sleep walking, demoniacs to schizophrenics. Many pilgrims were flocking to two white marble sarcophagi in the corner of the church in Gheel. The visitors had to kneel, even crawl, to reach the white tomb with the inscription "MA DIPNA".

This Dymphna was a saint that Bishop Guy was not familiar with, and none of the current lists of the saints had any information on her. Even the famous *Golden Legend*, which compiled ancient saint stories from the apostles to the Middle Ages, lacks all mention of her. However, the reports were undeniable: pilgrims from all over flocked to this shrine to seek relief. The numbers were so great that many of these travelers had to wait for several days or even weeks. Because of this another beautiful influence of the saint appeared: the common townsfolk began to welcome the pilgrims, assist the mentally ill, and offer their own homes and families to serve these lost and abandoned people. Despite the increase in lunatics and demoniacs, the townspeople showed a remarkable charity that blossomed in response to the little saint's heavenly influence and heroic example. These families not only cared for the mentally ill's needs but also incorporated them into the various activities of daily life and helped them to regain a sense of personhood. It was here that the modern-day institution of group homes was developed: literally from homes of the townsfolk. For many of those suffering with mental illness this prescription was just what they needed: love and care and the assurance they were not alone. To this day, there is a wonderful system of care offered to those distressed with mental illnesses in Gheel. There is currently an actual institution for psychiatric help, but the townsfolk still offer their homes and their hearts to these less fortunate brethren. This effect on the people, this growth not only in devotion to the saint but this wonderful spirit of charity, and the presence of these *xenodochium*[145] or "houses for strangers" in addition to the miraculous healings, inspired the good bishop to look more deeply into this martyr.

Bishop Guy entrusted the case to a Canon Regular of St. Authertus named Peter, who was charged with investigating and writing about the history of miracles and the life of Dymphna. Peter quickly got to work on the investigation of this very famous as of yet unofficially recognized saint. However, there was not much writing at the time on this girl and the archives of the town did not contain well-preserved documents. However, he found something very interesting: the townsfolk themselves held onto a living memory of her. For the four hundred years since her death (from the time she was alleged to have arrived in Gheel to the moment Peter started his work), a very powerful oral testimony witnessed to the clear and cohesive facts of her life. So, Peter began to sit

145. These were very common in the Medieval times, acting as hostels or primitive hospitals.

with the people and hear them tell their stories of this young girl that had been passed down to them from generation to generation.

The stories related to Canon Peter were very interesting and detailed. These stories he received were supported by the presence of her tomb that confirmed her fame by the number of visitors it received. Peter soon made a startling discovery: Dymphna was not alone. In the church, her tomb was near the tomb of a priest named Gerebernus.[146] The town celebrated her feast on May 30. Peter was soon able to conclude that these two had been honored and recognized since about the year 600 A.D.! He also discovered that Dymphna and Gerebernus were not from Gheel or even Belgium but had journeyed there from far away. As Peter began to listen to the stories, more and more of a legend began to form.

Dymphna and Gerebernus were from Ireland, potentially near Dublin. Back in the 600's Ireland was primarily Christian thanks to the work of St. Patrick who had evangelized in the 400's or so. However, Ireland was still a country of the Druids and some paganism still endured. Dymphna's father was a pagan and a king. However, Dymphna's mother was a Christian. Though her father had married a Christian, he never converted and was not too favorable to the faith. Dymphna's mother must have been close to the priest Gerebernus, who probably gave her the sacraments.

Peter discovered that Dymphna's mother died sometime before Dymphna was fourteen, but she made sure that Dymphna was baptized secretly by the priest Gerebernus because of her husband's displeasure for the faith. Gerebernus became a sort of spiritual father for Dymphna. Because her mother passed away when she was young, Dymphna's faith

146. His body has been moved since this time to Germany.

life was something she herself desired and worked at.

The point of her mother's death was a tragic and pivotal moment in the family's life. Dymphna had not only lost her dear mother, but she lost the closest Christian support she had. On a human level, this event must have been awful. When anyone loses a parent, it is a turning point in their life; it is when they truly must take up the care of their own lives and come to face a world that does not love them in the same way. (My own mother use to say, "No one else in the world will ever love you like your mother does, and you won't know how much she means to you until she's gone.") Truly, mothers are the first figures to show their kids what unconditional love is: children are not loved because of their grades or performance but just because they are their child. This love becomes an image for the love God has for us, His children. I like to take the more common belief that Dymphna was older when her mother died since it explains the closeness they had and the reason why Dymphna was baptized in secret. Though the details do not specify, it is beautiful to imagine that Dymphna's mother was able to witness her get baptized in secret as a dying wish; she could have for a moment shared that wonderful joy with Dymphna while loving her, holding her, and admonishing her to hold fast to the faith. Much like Zelie comforted St. Thérèse, she could have comforted her daughter with the belief that in the Lord they would stay united, reminding Dymphna to hold close to Jesus as much as she could and that one day they would see each other again in heaven forever. This admonishment may have been one of the catalysts for Dymphna to make a vow of virginity to the Lord. However, whatever the case, Dymphna's mother certainly warned of the terrible consequence that would take place if her father found out.

For Dymphna, her faith was not only a connection with her mother, but it was a support in the grief and separation she naturally experienced. Sorrow, especially at the loss of a loved one, is normal and healthy. It is clear that Dymphna mourned her mother's loss, but her faith gave her hope in this trial. Most psychologists agree that those who have some form of faith in a higher being and reality can cope with sorrow better and their level of stress is substantially less, primarily because they know their lives are not simply in their own powers.

Her father was not so well off. We know that her father was either a king or some government figure in their area and thus had a public image, a status, and a community to uphold. This caused him a great deal of stress and anxiety. We don't know much about the father and mother's relationship before her death, but he must have clearly loved her and she must have possessed remarkable characteristics for the king to overlook the fact that she was a Christian. He had a deep attachment to her and her loss was tragic for the king.

After the death of his wife, he began to seek for a replacement. The gaping emotional hole was not something that he intended to heal, but rather to simply fill. He sought to find someone who compared to his wife in her beauty. He began to search desperately, yet in vain. All this time, his grieving heart needed him to slow down and process; he did not have the capacity to cope with this pain. He was a man of unorganized passions and desires, and they began to get the best of him now as his passions and lusts overruled him. His grief became such a strong impulse that it blinded his reasoning ability and discretion of judgment. The king sent his servants on a campaign to find him a suitable match. Every candidate they brought forward failed in comparison to his wife. Who else could compare to his beloved? Who else was like her enough in personality and appearance? How could he replace the years of shared life and intimacy that was exchanged?

At this moment a sadistic idea entered his thoughts: what about Dymphna? His own daughter was eventually presented to the king as a replacement. After all, she was literally the fruit of the king and his late wife's love and intimacy. She also resembled his wife more than anyone else. Some accounts say that it was the servants of the king who proposed Dymphna as the replacement, others say that it was the king himself who first considered her. Either way, there was a grave lack of discretion of judgment on his part to consider his own daughter. Psychologically, he was possibly suffering from what is known as transference, a condition in which the absence of a close emotional companion results in the transference of those bonds and affections to a similar entity. This transference can happen in other situations, such as when a father goes off to war and the son is left alone with the mother, she begins to assimilate the son to the father. Normally, it results simply in emotional attachment, but in severe cases in which there is extreme lack of control, it can lead to consequences as serious as incest.

The realization for Dymphna that this prospect was rising in her father's mind was a horrible shock. As agonizing as it was to experience the pain of her mother's loss, the grief was now twisting her father's mind even more than could be imagined! There was no solace she could offer her father since all acts of attention or charity she showed him did nothing but increase his desire for her. He was incapable of rising above his desires and could not interpret what she was offering as heartfelt compassion, only desire and lust. His only means of gaining some stability from his brokenness was to exert power and control over another. It was unimaginable that her father considered taking his own daughter as a love companion, and worse, to be a means of filling his need for intimacy. Dymphna was crushed. She did not know what to do. She was paranoid, anxious, and afraid. She was afraid of the very man who was her father, or at least what he was becoming. The weight of this stress was burdensome, and Dymphna knew that it would lead her to some very difficult decisions. If she agreed, she would become involved in a physically and emotionally manipulative (not to mention disordered) situation, that would most certainly lead her father into grave sin. If she resisted, she would put herself in danger of enraging her father and possibly causing him greater anguish than before. This situation put extreme pressure on the young girl, so she went to the one person she could go to: her spiritual father.

Fr. Gerebernus was a wise and kind priest. Not only was he the one who baptized Dymphna, but he was also one of her caretakers. His priestly, loving heart was a welcome haven for the young, traumatized girl. The priest knew that God was planning great things for this young girl. She had grown in beauty and grace and was already imitating her beloved Savior in her charity. He knew she had also made a secret vow of virginity, vowing herself to Jesus alone.

The good priest saw there really was only one safe and secure option: to flee. He knew that because of the king's efforts to seek a wife, the eyes and ears of the king were everywhere. They had to flee far away, as far as they could. So, he instructed Dymphna to come with him in the dead of night to the docks and they sailed to a far-off land. It is uncertain if Gerebernus knew their destination beforehand or if they were simply to set off and go as far as they could. Regardless, Dymphna, Gerebernus, and a few other assistants loaded up their small boat and fled Ireland, never to see it again. It was a long trip, but the humid air from Ireland pushed them away with great speed. Eventually they landed in the lush, forested region of Antwerp in what is present day Belgium in a small area known as Gheel. They located a small chapel dedicated to St. Martin and it was here that they resided, seeking refuge in the forest.

However, their peace was short-lived. The hope had been that separating Dymphna from her father would not only remove the near occasion of sin but also give clarity to the mind of the king. This hope was in vain. In fact, far from dulling the passion of her father, her absence made it grow even more and twisted his already twisted mind. He was powered by an almost inhuman and monstrous force.[147] His desire was set on his daughter and his eyes were so closed to reality at this point that nothing would stop him from getting what he wanted. The king sent scouts out and they discovered a small town in Antwerp where they believed the child had gone. They entered an inn there and paid with Irish money for recompense. The innkeeper noted that a young virgin living in the nearby village had used similar coins. After further questioning the scouts discovered that the girl was accompanied by an old priest. They knew they had their prize. Word was sent back to the king who quickly rushed to the location.

You can imagine the horror that passed through Dymphna when she realized that her father was coming after her again. What seemed at first like broken confusion and a delusion on his part, was now seen as something far more powerful and dangerous. However, she was determined to stand strong. She did not run this time, she stood against the force of evil, for her house was built on the firm rock of Christ. Much of her father's passion had now passed from sadness to desperation, from desire now to anger. His dislike for the faith was now a hatred. The first thing he did was seize the priest Gerebernus and hand him over to his men to be executed. This punishment was not only for Gerebernus'

---

147 . It is not known exactly what condition the father suffered from, but there is some belief he may have also been possessed, that at some point in his grief and pain he allowed the devil to have access to him in his weakness. Demonic possession and mental illnesses are not the same thing though sometimes they manifest in similar ways. This book does not to go into depth on the distinctions but there is a very big difference between the two, and those that suffer from mental issues are not to assume possession. However, possession can manifest certain similarities which need a trained eye to discern them. This is why Dymphna is also a patroness for those who are possessed.

profession of faith but for taking his daughter away from him. Dymphna, he would save for himself.

The man that now approached Dymphna was not the same man she had known as her father; he had changed and been twisted into such a strange and demented creature. The once strong king had become a broken man, and now that broken man had become a lustful monster. He stood before his daughter with a sense of satisfaction and accomplishment. He had her right where he wanted her, and it was impossible for her to escape again. However, Dymphna was not the same girl that he had known before. Her faith and life experiences had matured her. Her devotion and love for her only spouse, Jesus, had turned her from a child into a woman. She had grown in virtue and emotional firmness and was not afraid anymore. There would be no more escape stories because she would not run anymore.

Her father made the first move: he invited her back home to take her seat as queen and to receive all the riches he could give her. All she had to do was marry him, to be his love and give him the companionship he lost with her mother's death, a companionship that they both were lacking. He saw her as a victim and tried to get her to play the victim role. She would not be a victim to his desires; in this encounter, she was the stronger of the two. She did not need his riches or wealth, for she had all she needed. She had love; she had a lover richer and more beautiful than anything this world could offer. He was a strong support for her at all times and she would not leave Him. It was her Lord and Savior who also was her bride. Her father was shocked; he was shocked not only that she refused his offer but also that she professed being a Christian and being married to Jesus. His astonishment was short lived because now he was infuriated. He would not be denied his desire and he could not stand that Christianity would take both his wife and his daughter. All his wounds fueled his anger. If he could not have his desire, no one would. In a fit of uncontrolled madness, he drew his sword and rushed at his daughter.

Dymphna experienced a rush of emotion. It wasn't fear, it wasn't sadness, it wasn't anger. It was compassion. She could see that beneath all his anger and lust was a broken man looking for love. He desired that which everyone desired and which Jesus, her Spouse gave so freely. However, she knew her father was blind and lost, a poor man who never saw the treasure of Jesus. She pitied him; she loved him and forgave him for what he was about to do. As he drew his sword and approached her, she also felt a surprising emotion: joy. She rejoiced that she would soon see the one she loved and who she knew was waiting for her. She was going to die for the one who died for her. She took one final look at her father as he drew his sword, his eyes glowing with rage. She knelt and prayed for him. She prayed for the healing of his wounded heart and mind. She knew that deep down this man was still her father and that he was living in an internal hell. She prayed for God to have mercy on him and that he would ultimately find peace in the Lord. She knew that so many people became victims just like her father, tortured by their own minds. As she began her final approach to Jesus, she wished to be near to all those who suffered from mental issues. Behind each one was a suffering human being who longed to know love. With that, she bowed her head, the sword struck her tender neck, and her body fell to the ground.

At this moment, the king regained some of his sanity. He saw no longer an enemy or an object of desire; he saw his daughter. He realized now what his passions had done and how, far from giving him the consolation he needed, they left him ever more alone and took the life of his own daughter. The mighty king now crumbled, crushed again by the weight of his sorrow and oppressed by the burden of his own guilt. Having no morals or higher god, he also had no sense of forgiveness and mercy. He was overwhelmed by the sorrow of his own doing. It is uncertain what happened to the father after this point. The hope is that his dear child, who was now in heaven because of his actions, interceded for him and he repented.

The bodies of Dymphna and her priest companion were both buried by the inhabitants of the town. Shortly after, hordes of mentally ill began to flock to these tombs asking for prayers. The tombs were made of a beautiful white sandstone that is foreign to the region and legend has it that angels buried them.

Peter finished his dictation of Dymphna's *Vita*, which carried the story and martyrdom of this young girl far to the ends of the Catholic world. According to the traditional process, the bishop formally moved her body to the new church of St. Dymphna where it was housed with great honor. Soon, to make the tombs more accessible, Bishop Guy moved the relics into the church for people to gather and seek prayer. They were given the honor of an altar in the church, showing the people's reverence for them as true martyrs and worthy of honor and prayer. The insane, the depressed, the possessed, and all kinds of others were brought to the church and received healing and hope. Even after Bishop Guy's efforts to aid devotion and the number of pilgrims, there was little that could be done to relieve the volume of people pressing into the town. The rush of pilgrims was so great that many people found they still had to wait several days to get to the tombs. During this time, they prayed a nine-day novena and took up residence in the locals' homes before finally being moved to a sick room adjacent to the church to prepare for their spiritual encounter. The locals showed their faith and charity through the care they offered these pilgrims. The citizens of Gheel still continue this loving practice that has become a foundation for how common psychological care is offered to the sick. [148] The community was built up in faith and with new companions, while the sick were given spiritual, mental, and physical care in loving families. Many of the ill recovered but stayed in the area because of their attachment to the community!

Since then, Dymphna has become one of the most recognized and revered saints. She has shown a great power of intercession, particularly for those who struggle under the burden of mental illness, not just by providing a cure to their disorder but also by relieving them of their sense of isolation and loneliness. Many Catholics have been inspired by her life and example and have trusted themselves to her prayers. There are a variety of novenas that are made to her for those who struggle with different mental illnesses, her medal is given to many people who feel oppressed or in despair, even her relic has been known to cure many people who up to that point felt hopeless. It is this very palpable accompaniment that Dymphna has offered the Church since the 600s that make her one of the most beloved saints in the world.

Friends of St. Dymphna

Angelle Jeansonne

This first testimony came to me from a friend I knew through working with Steubenville. She lived not too far away from where I was assigned as a priest and when she heard of my story of St. Rose, she shared her own story.

A while back I was trying to assist a friend and kept coming across St. Dymphna. She was not the saint I was particularly

148. In 1850, the care of the mentally ill passed from the church to the government without the intervention or involvement of the saint. It had been seen how successful the practice of the group homes were and incorporating the mentally ill into society had worked, so it became a model of secular care. A full hospital was built and several thousand mentally ill form a community there now. Though St. Dymphna is not directly invoked by them, her watchful care and intercession still accompanies them.

looking for. I did not like that she was noted as the patron saint of incest. That word alone made me uncomfortable, and I thought it would make others feel the same. (I love my patron saints and Google makes it so easy to find one. I also can never spell her name right without looking it up and I'm not even sure I pronounce it correctly!)

Basically, I tried to move past her because it was easier not to focus on this topic. In the end I found a prayer card and medal of hers that didn't spell out incest and I introduced her to my neighbors who are beyond anxious and have lost numerous babies during pregnancy. I had to order a medal and it was cheaper to get a bag instead of just one. A different neighbor walked with her adult child who always struggled with her faith and anxiety. It was too perfect to not pass along a medal to her as well.

Fast forward: the biggest wake-up call has been this past week at the Sunshine bridge in Convent / St. James. I found out that a good friend's husband attempted suicide there. She's a Christian as well as their children. Her husband had a difficult upbringing: at the age of seven he was told by his mother that God did not exist. He struggled to make sense of Jesus and his religion. By the Grace of God, after several hours standing on the bridge, he returned over the railing, although he still wanted to jump. He eventually passed out on a platform and rescue teams secured him. He is now in a very secure facility in Marrero.

After attempting to counsel his wife I introduced her to St. Dymphna. Only then did I realize Dymphna's father was a pagan while her mother was Christian. I knew she had seen the images on social media of her husband's attempt, and so I found myself also searching for related articles. That morning I found out that two weeks before another man successfully jumped from the bridge after he had impregnated his fourteen-year-old daughter. The word I hated jumped out in my mind: INCEST! Now, I began to see Dymphna was placing herself right in the middle of a terrible situation to be an intercessory bridge. I became part of a group that posted news concerning this bridge and I posted about Dymphna and some prayers to her. I invited people to pray to her, especially as they cross the bridge. The other day I was invited to an Industry of Faith luncheon that I've never attended and there was so much talk of anxiety, depression, etc. She's the perfect saint for our world right now, even though she is so unknown.

Vanessa Contreres

The next testimony was submitted to me from a woman in California who heard about my work on this book.

About a year and a half ago, I was struggling with depression. I was pregnant. I should have felt over the moon about being pregnant just I had felt in my previous pregnancies. This pregnancy felt different. I wanted to hide away under my bed covers and cry. There was a hopeless darkness that I felt. A friend of mine reached out to see how I was doing. I told her I felt awful. I explained my symptoms to her. Next thing I know, I receive a small package with a St. Dymphna pendant inside. I didn't know who St. Dymphna was. I'd never heard of her. So I looked her up. St. Dymphna: patron of mental illness. I will admit I didn't feel immediate consolation after having received the pendant; until I found myself locked in my room feeling helpless, even more so as my husband and I had argued about my depression and how he did not understand it. That's when I remembered my St. Dymphna pendant and prayed for her to intercede for me. I also grabbed hold of my rosary and made an effort to go through each mystery. I felt an inner peace when I had finished and decided to cling to prayer in the times I most needed peace.

A few months ago, I was on Instagram and read a post from someone I follow that stated how she believed saints choose us. Someone commented on that post about a website that randomly selects a saint for the person seeking a saint. I got curious and checked the website out. I clicked and St. Dymphna was randomly selected for me. Not a coincidence.

Two months ago as I was shopping at a Catholic store for my seven year old who will be receiving her first holy communion soon, I also had the pleasure of finding a St. Dymphna prayer card laid out on the counter by the cash register.

I'm a firm believer that nothing is coincidence. We are meant to be exactly where God wants us be.

After many weeks of prayer during my pregnancy I found the peace I needed. I am no longer suffering from depression, and I owe it all to God and St. Dymphna, who interceded for me.

Stephanie Vonders
Wichita, Kansas

The following testimony is related through the organization "Treasures of the Church" which is a traveling ministry that bring various relics of saints to different churches and parishes. They organize expositions of relics in which people are able to come and see and venerate the relics of various saints. Many come seeking great healing and walk away with miraculous events. More information is available at their website: www.treasuresofthechurch.com

Twenty years ago I was diagnosed with an obsessive compulsive disorder: Trichotillomania (or "hair pulling"). It has affected my life in every aspect imaginable. At times it became so difficult to deal with I wanted to die. I had severe depression and anxiety and I tried almost every medication out there to gain control of this disorder. My teen years were especially hard. I prayed for a healing through St. Dymphna, the patron saint of mental illness, for twenty years; I even chose her as my Confirmation saint name.

During the exposition my daughter told me St. Dymphna's relic was there. I became emotional, because I have always wished I could visit her tomb. I went to the relic, knelt down, and I placed her relic upon my head and began to pray. "Heavenly Father I beg you one last time, PLEASE through the intercession of St. Dymphna grant me a healing of this horrible thing." I made the Sign of the Cross with the relic on my head and got up. We went home that evening and I maintained my hope.

Now, almost two months later, I have not pulled my hair! Previous to this, I had not gone a day without pulling for twenty years. I had come to the point in my life where I had almost given up, but thanks be to God, He relieved me of this burden!! I received a healing through the intercession of St. Dymphna.

Good Saint Dymphna, great wonder-worker in every affliction of mind and body, I humbly implore your powerful intercession with Jesus through Mary, the Health of the Sick, in my present need. (Mention it.) Saint Dymphna, martyr of purity, patroness of those who suffer with nervous and mental afflictions, beloved child of Jesus and Mary, pray to Them for me and obtain my request. Amen

"St. Philomena, Wonder Worker"
by Normal Faucheux
digital copy provided by Normal Faucheux: Sacred and Religious Art, LLC

ST. PHILOMENA

As I was putting this book together, I mostly had to just put an ear to the ground and hear the rumblings the saints were making on earth. I shared the story of my friendship with St. Rose and then watched an unfolding of other stories and testimony come about. I included the saints in this book who came across my path in God's providence; the discretion was largely on their part. However, there was one saint that continued to be on my heart: Philomena. I had not received a direct or personal testimony about her, nor was I personally devoted to her. However, the parish I was at as I wrote this book, St. Frances Cabrini in Alexandria, has an annual mass in honor of her. Seeing the devotion of the people that attended this mass and who knew Philomena warmed my heart to her.

I knew that amongst all the saints Philomena stood out. She is considered the patron saint of miracles due to the great number of miracles that come from her intercession and the fact that all the information about her life came through private revelation to a sister; it is said that she was canonized solely because of the miracles that occurred through her relics. For a book about the presence of the saints in the Church, she seemed a shoe in to be included.

However, Philomena is a saint shrouded in a bit of mystery and controversy. She is not included in any of the Church's long lists of martyrs, even though she was said to have died in the early Church. She was reportedly "de-canonized" in 1962 and her feast was taken off the calendar. Some people argue that she was never actually canonized in the first place. With all this controversy, I felt a bit hesitant about taking her on for this book.

One night, as I was lying in bed, I felt a little bit restless. To be honest, some of that restlessness was coming from the composing of this book. I didn't know if I wanted to open a can of worms and write about Philomena; I felt it might be a bit too much to take on for this book. Then I heard a voice. I thought it might be St. Rose but it was a different voice, a soothing female voice. To be honest, I don't remember exactly what was said, but I know that I was filled with confidence that I should not be afraid to write on Philomena and that it would all work out if I just focused on writing a story about her. I rested peacefully and took up the task of writing about the little virgin martyr.

Sometimes God calls us out of our comfort zone; often He also works outside the expected zone. One of the things Philomena teaches the world is that we can't cage God. In C. S. Lewis' *The Chronicles of Narnia,* Jesus is represented by Aslan, a good lion who remains untamed. No matter how close and familiar we become with God, no matter how much we feel we start to understand theology and dogma, God will never become just a cog in our hands; He will always have an elusive nature that beckons us to sit in awe of Him. Philomena, as the patron saint of miracles, shows that the things of heaven and the saints of God exist in a greater reality than we do now. Faith in the supernatural should never lead to apathy or complacency. Philomena emphasizes what all the saints proclaim: our faith is not just an object we can collect and own, but it is a personal, powerful entity that we journey with. She wants us to hold onto the truth that we will never fully encompass heaven. Rather, heaven holds us and as we try to capture its concept, it captures us. Philomena shows that heaven can always wow us, and miracles do indeed happen.

Patron Saint of Miracles

Miracles have always captured the attention of man and engaged his imagination. The very word "miracle" comes from the latin word *mirar* which means "to look at." Miracles demand our attention. Miracles are God's way of shaking man from his sleep of disinterest. As much as God is a God of order and harmony, every so often He likes to throw us a curve ball, just to remind us He is still God. Miracles are not occurrences that disrupt or disturb the natural order or break the laws of nature, but rather are a sequence of events or actions that occur above the natural order and could not be performed simply by agents of this world. Because of the physical nature of the agents in the particular situation, they could not perform the action that occurs without the outside assistance of God. Miracles can be explained as follows:

> Theologians in general continue to explain the concept of miracles as follows: a) the miracle is operated by God as *principal* cause, and it occurs in the world; b) is worked *outside* of the natural order, that is in a superior mode to the power of nature; c) *outside or above* but not *contrary* to the natural order, because the miracle is not a violation of the laws of nature; it is moreover an exceptional fact determined by a special divine virtue that intervenes in the created things, producing a superior effect to their natural power; d) in the operation of a miracle, God can make use also of a creature . . . as an *instrumental* cause. [149]

Miracles, at their heart, are external signs of God's power, goodness, and providence. They grab our imaginations to form a more perfect image of the person of God in His power and goodness beyond simple cause and effect logic. God is at work in miracles, working inside the natural world in a way that is helping it to work outside of its natural limits without contradicting them. This point means that God cannot make a circle a square, or an animal seek to kill itself, or a person violate their free will. Miracles reveal that God is not just another force of nature, nor just another creature of this universe. He is God, and He is incredibly close to His creation but is not a part of it.

Moreover, we see that God can not only perform a miracle upon a creature, but that creature can even be a cooperative instrument of God in performing a miracle. Such an example is what we see and hear about in the bible of various humans healing and raising the dead. They are an active agent with God who is the main source of the power of the miracles. Humans becomes like a protagonist in a story where not only does the author move the story along but so does the actions of each character who is working with the author. Miracles show again and again the great overlapping of the spiritual and physical world. They make the presence of God and His supernatural presence more and more palpable and reveal that there is a reality greater than just what can be seen and touched.

Humans are subjects of God's miracles, primarily because God wants to show His power and goodness not for His sake but for ours. Many miracles take place in the human sphere; some of the most notable are humans being healed of various

---

149. My translation: "I teologi in genere continuano a spiegare il concetto di miracolo come segue: a) il miracolo è operato da Dio come causa *principale,* ed è fatto nel mondo; b) è operato *fuori* dell' ordine naturale, cioè in modo superior alle forze della natura: c) *fuori o sopra* ma non *contro* l'ordine naturale, perché il miracolo non è violazione delle legge della natura; è piuttosto, un fatto eccezionale determinate da una speciale virtú divina, che interviene nelle cose create, producendo un effetto superior alla loro naturale Potenza; d) nell'operare il miracolo Dio può servirsi anche di una creatura...come causa *strumentale.*" Le Causa dei Santi, 108.

sicknesses or diseases. Among this kind of miracles are those found in Scripture as part of Jesus' ministry to the poor, namely that He healed the sick. The raising of the dead is another amazing miracle that occurs upon the human subject and that we find in Jesus' life and ministry. All these miracles point to the glory of God as well as Jesus' plan and power for salvation within the human life: if Jesus can do such things in the physical realm, then why can't He do the same in the spiritual life? There are also miracles in nature that God has performed such as the famous halting of the sun for Joshua, the parting of the Red Sea, the miracle of the dancing Sun at Fatima, and the transformation of Eucharistic hosts into human flesh, most remarkably in Lanciano, Italy. Many of these miracles were performed in the face of an unbelieving crowd to draw people back into belief. [150]

People can also be the channels of God's works as instruments. We see in the book of Acts many of the same miracles performed by Jesus as taking place in and by His Church. Because the Church is the body of Christ, the same Spirit that was at work in Jesus can be at work in its members. Miracles again have God as the principal cause but the human agent as an instrumental cause. They both work together but always with the end of giving glory to God and leading people deeper into faith. Normally, miracles by their nature are rarer occurrences. However, as we discussed in Chapter 3, miracles through a saint's intercession point to

---

150. An important note must be made on this point: the devil also can create visible signs to tempt and deceive people. Many saints such as St. John of the Cross said that a person's entire faith should not be based solely on visible manifestation, being that these occur purely in the realm of the visible and don't necessarily call forth a higher action of faith. St. John of the Cross encourages people to be more dubious in the face of these, especially when it encourages a belief that is not a universal and public belief that God has revealed to His Church. Christians must always first walk and believe by faith and not by sign and only allow the miracles to help and assist in confirming what is already believed. A miracle should NEVER encourage a separation or deviation from something that has been universally believed and accepted

their closeness to God and their care and concern for us.

Philomena marks one of the most unique saints in this regard of miracles. Not only are miracles in no short supply through her life, but miracles after her death are the principal way in which this saint has been known! All that has been truly and fully known of her comes from revelation and miracles through her intercession and relics. This unique reality of her veneration also comes into play in the unique way she became honored as a saint. For most saints, we first view their earthly life as a formation of their spiritual life, but not with Philomena. We begin our study centuries after her death and find that her spiritual life in heaven became the causative force for the discovery of her life on earth. She stands as a beautiful reflection on the saints that, it is their lives in heaven that has the greatest impact on the Church and that their lives of virtue on earth have not ended in death but rather become all the more wrapped up in the current mission of the Church. Even though Philomena's earthly life came first, her life in heaven is the true anchor of her identity. All saints are called to the same truth: our life and call to be in heaven must be the anchor of our life on earth and everything that we do on earth should be animated and in sync with the life of heaven. Keeping our focus on the life in heaven gives direction and purpose to our life on earth.

The Discovery of Philomena

It was May 24, 1802. Deep in the Catacombs of Priscilla in Rome, archeologists were doing some work around the Greek Chapel in the central area of the Catacombs. This location was a prominent one, housing some of the oldest and most well decorated painting in the catacombs and the history of Christendom. As repair and remodeling work was being done, the workers came across an unopened tomb. It was not uncommon to find unopened tombs in the catacombs but as the excavations continued, something surprising was found: a tomb stone. It was very rare to find a marker for the bodies down there, much less one that had writing on it. This marker was three marble slabs that had two anchors, three arrows, a palm and a flower with the words: "LVMENA-PAX TE-CUM FI". This discovery merited the intervention of one of the priest caretakers, especially since there were clear symbols that identified a martyr. The following day, May 25, the niche which had been well sealed was opened. Rearranging the tiles, it was found that the message inscribed was "PAX TE-CUM FI-LVMENA" or "Peace be with you Philomena". Philomena was not a martyr that had been known up to that time and only means "lover of light". The anchors, arrows, and palm branches not only gave hints that the person was a martyr but also potentially how they were martyred. Even more surprising, inside the tomb was a small glass vile containing dried up remains of blood, which would only have been conserved if the person was revered as a martyr.

Due process called for this "relic" to be brought to the Relics Treasury in the Vatican for proper veneration and research. Philomena's relic was given to the care of Msgr. Giancinto Ponzetti, custodian of Rome's cemeteries and relics of martyrs. Not far away in the town of Mugnano del Cardinale, a young priest names Francesco de Lucia had the great desire to have a martyr's relics in his church. It was a call on his heart to help lead people closer to God and encourage them in their own walk of holiness by venerating and praying to a martyr's relics. Alas, this dream seemed far off. In June of 1805, the young priest accompanied a priest friend of his, Msgr. Bartolomeo De Cesare to Rome along with a special delegate from the King of Naples to greet the Pope and give the Holy Father his best wishes. They were all heading to Rome for a special occasion: De Cesare was preparing to be ordained a bishop at the end of June. On their journey, De Lucia made his wish to have "a saint with a name" known to his soon-to-be bishop. De Cesare was very excited about this desire. He saw that the stars were aligning and that the young priest's desire for a saint might be fulfilled. What better person to ask for a saint's relics than the Pope himself!

As De Cesare entered the Papal Court and offered his best regards to the Holy Father, he made the urgent request of the young priest known to the Pope. Surprisingly, the Pope was moved and agreed to grant the request. The relics he chose were the newly discovered urn of Philomena. However, there was one small issue: technically relics of martyrs can only be given to a bishop. Providentially, De Cesare was being consecrated a bishop in a few days! So, the Holy Father imparted the relics of Philomena to De Cesare who in turn entrusted them to De Lucia for his church. On June 30, De Cesare was consecrated bishop and then on July 1, De Cesare, De Lucia, and Philomena left Rome to begin their journey to Mugnano De Cardinale.

On the way down, the motley crew stopped in Naples for a few days to rest and visit close friends. While there, gossip began to spread about the arrival of this curious saint. People began to flock to visit and offer their prayer intentions. The crowds were so great that they moved her relics to the local church for public veneration, which was her first appearance to the world. Eventually, on August 9, they were able to move the relics to Mugnano and on August 10, 1805 Philomena found her resting place in the chapel of Our Lady of Grace in Mugnano, Italy.

The Revelation of Philomena

Just like all the saints, Philomena's life in heaven has continued to have an impact on the physical world and the visible Church, but she is unique in that her life in heaven revealed her life on earth. Philomena shows again and again how the events of this world do not hinder the life of heaven and the active role that heaven plays in this world. As we have said, the saints become more alive and more active in heaven, and the life and message of Philomena is a perfect example. Philomena had already begun to work and perform miracles even before anything about her life was known. But the mystery would be short lived.

In 1833, the devotion to Philomena had spread far and wide in Italy, especially amongst the religious. In Naples, not far from Mugnano, there was a retreat center where a mystic and ascetic sister lived named Sr. Maria Luisa of Jesus. She had given her life to prayer and penance and had come to know of the discovery and miracles of Philomena. The archeologists had examined the tomb and had made certain evaluations about how she had died, her prominence in the church, her purity of life, and her fortitude at the moment of death. However, many of the specific details of her life, character, and the exact circumstances of her death were unknown. Philomena appeared in a dream to Sr. Maria Luisa to give details of her life. Sr Maria saw a young, beautiful girl who seemed to resemble the images and statues of Philomena that were becoming popular. This young girl opened the story of her life in great detail for the world to come to know her.

> I am the daughter of a Grecian King and my mother was of royal blood too. However, they did not have children and therefore prayed a lot and offered gifts to their false gods. . . . They embraced Christianity and soon after my mother gave birth to me on the 10th of January. I was named Lumena, because I was conceived and born in the Faith, to which my parents had become greatly devoted. I was

> named Filomena, daughter of light, which enlightened my soul with the grace when I received Baptism. [151]

It's clear that the first great miracle that Philomena was a part of was the conversion of her parents. In the early days of the empire, there were many pagans and it seemed that her parents, of Greek descent and royalty, were pagans who had been revered in the area. The faith was presented to them by a local priest who made the promise that conversion to the Faith would end their barrenness. God destined Philomena as an instrument of the manifestation of His power. Already Philomena was participating in the life of heaven and the power of God's miracles. Her very birth was a miracle!

Sr. Maria Luisa continues to recount how Philomena and her family made it to Rome and the circumstances of her life, her devotion, and ultimately her martyrdom.

> My father had to speak to the powerful and proud Emperor Diocletian to discuss peace between the reigns. My mother and I went with him. During the meeting, while my father tried to make the emperor see how unjust the war declaration was, the emperor kept staring at me and then he said: "Do not trouble yourself anymore; all your distress is over; you shall have the power of the whole empire to protect you as long as you give your consent and let me have your daughter as my spouse." [152]

---

151. Msgr Giovanni Braschi, *Saint Philomena Testimony of the Light of Christ*, (Cultural Book Sanctuary of Saint Philomena, 2011), 128.
152. Braschi, 129.

As a king, Philomena's father was caught in a war that he was unprepared for. He appeared with his family before the Emperor to negotiate peace. Much as king Herod in the Scriptures, the Emperor Diocletian was willing to grant anything to satisfy his lust. It seemed a small price to pay for peace in his reign, but the king was not aware that Philomena had made a vow of virginity to Jesus and thus she refused the offer. As much as her father pleaded and threatened, she would not give in: "God and my virginity are more important than my Kingdom, and my Home is heaven!" [153]

Her father was not as strong in his will; he eventually handed his own daughter over to the emperor for the sake of momentary peace in his reign. The emperor tried to kindly allure the young princess to do as he wished. She refused. He offered her gifts. She refused. He threatened her. She refused. Finally, he threw her in the prison in his basement and mistreated her and tempted her. She remained faithful and strong through the graces Jesus gave to her. Eventually, she received a heavenly promise during this trial.

> After thirty-seven days, the Queen of Heaven, surrounded by dazzling light, holding Her Son in her arms, appeared to me and said: "My child, you will bear this imprisonment only another three days, and after another forty days you will be free from this horrible place. . . . You will be exposed to terrible tortures for my Son." At this news I trembled, I saw myself being tortured to death, but the Queen of Heaven exhorted me by saying: "My beloved child, your name is Lumena like my name and that of my son: my son, your spouse, bears the name of light, star and sun;

153. Braschi, 129.

> my name is Aurora, Star, Moon or Sun: I will stand by you."[154]

We are given a very human image of Philomena: she is scared. She was a thirteen-year-old girl being told she will have to endure horrible pains. As with us all, pain and suffering was something to be avoided and even scared of. However, she was comforted knowing not only that she was not alone but that she would be given the strength to endure. It is never any of our wills to suffer, nor is its God's will. However, God gives us the strength to endure what nature fails to hold up under. Jesus draws near to us in suffering. It shows that God's compassion is not just an emotion but a true desire to be with the one that He loves who is suffering. Philomena was reminded of the humble reality of human nature, but that grace and God's strength would be given her. Mary sent Gabriel the archangel (who was said to be Mary's guardian angel) to watch over her.

The time eventually came for her to embrace suffering. She was taken, tied to a pillar naked, and then tortured by the soldiers. Her young body, full of wounds and blood was now exposed to the elements. The Emperor commanded that her body now be taken back into the prison and left there to die. As Philomena waited for her spouse to come and take her home, two angels appeared and healed her body, making her more beautiful than she had been before! However, the emperor attributed this event to the pagan god Jupiter's wish that Philomena become Empress. Thus, he resumed his seduction, but Philomena remained strong in her faith and determination.

> Then he became furious as a lion and ordered an anchor to be tied round my neck and that

154. Braschi, 130.

> I be thrown with this and left to die in the water of the river Tiber, so that my person and any recollection of me be lost forever. At that moment Jesus showed his supremacy by sending two beautiful Angels to cut the rope and the anchor fell to the bottom of the river, where it still stands today covered by earth. [155]

Hence this attempt at martyrdom shows the meaning of the anchor that was inscribed upon her tomb. This great sign was enough to move several people to the faith, but it was not enough to sway the emperor. At this point he considered her a witch and he desperately tried to shoot her with arrows on various occasions. On the first attempt the arrows struck her, but God miraculously healed her, then on the second attempt, the arrows froze in the archers bows. Finally, he tried one last time.

> He ordered the use of searing arrows heated in a furnace, believing this would destroy what he called my magic; but again my Spouse freed me from this tribulation. The arrows redirected themselves against the archers and six of them were killed. [156]

Not quite what the emperor expected. Finally, it was time for Philomena's crucible to be ended and receive the glorious end she awaited.

> Fearing the worst, Diocletian ordered I be beheaded. My soul rose triumphant and glorious to Heaven to receive my Spouse and

---

155. Braschi, 131.
156. Braschi, 131.

> the crown of Virginity, for which I suffered so many torments. This fortunate day for me was August 10th at 19:30 local time. And it was for this reason that the Almighty arranged for my translation to Mugnano on the 10th of August with all its glorious support from heaven. [157]

Providence had the last word in two areas: that Philomena would indeed marry a great ruler and herself become a ruler, but when she was moved to her final place of honor was the day when she was also finally brought to her place of rest in heaven. Now, it is true that these events are not recorded in any official register from the past, nor has her legend been recorded and observed from the tradition of earlier Christians. Philomena is unique among the saints since she came from heaven, the final goal of life, to reveal the story of her life on earth and how she got to heaven. The Church calls this private revelation, which means that it can be used to support and encourage the faith, but it is not part of the general revelation of God's saving mysteries such as the sacraments, the teaching office of the Church, and the office of Pope, among others. This revelation was given to Sr. Maria Luisa to help her and others in their devotion to Philomena.

The honor of Philomena

Even before Philomena's revelation was officially given, devotion to her spread like wildfire. For many saints, devotion arises from an admiration of their life and virtues, and people are edified by learning about their lives on earth which leads to a connection with them in heaven. Not with Philomena. She shows that, as with all the saints, they sometimes act

---

157 . Braschi, 131.

independently, even almost despite our attention or lack thereof. They are still active members of the Church, with desires, hopes, and gifts of God to share. They are not just manifestations of our conscience, or good examples that we can meditate on, or a wishful desire for something better; they are someone wholly other than us. Philomena reminds us of the wild liveliness that the saints possess in heaven and that far exceeds what they had on earth. What we lacked in knowledge of her earthly life; she has given us with knowledge of her in heaven.

Firstly, since she had spent a few days in Naples before arriving at the church of her final resting, it was in Naples that the first set of miracles took place. One of them involved a woman who had a cancerous growth on her hand. As the woman was preparing for an amputation, she went to the chapel to ask for a cure. After taking the mysterious relic of this unknown martyr and placing it on her bandaged hand, she went to the doctor for the procedure to be done. When the doctors unwrapped her hand, they found it completely cleared up!

Her transfer to Mugnano did not slow down the spread of her works. Philomena was attributed with multiple miracles such as healing a crippled boy, giving sight to a blind girl, even raising a boy from the dead! On another occasion it was said that a fire had escaped from a fireplace and was devouring the entire house. As the fire grew larger, it began to spread and threatened the entire village. At this moment, a priest ran and threw a paper image of Philomena into the fire and within minutes the fire was extinguished.

To recount all the reported miracles would take much time and many volumes. To this day miracles occur on a regular basis through her intercession with great variety and occurrence. Some are very moving and powerful, others exaggerated and fantastical. It has been the duty of the Church to authenticate these miracles. Here I will mention more of the authenticated miracles that have also been held up for people's edification.

The first that has been authenticated was in 1823, the miraculous sweating of her statue. The archbishop of Naples in 1806 had given to the Sanctuary a wooden statue that contained inside of it a small relic of Philomena's bone. It was a custom with many saints to take their statue in procession on their feast day. However, this year something very different took place.

> On August 10, 1823, during the procession, the statue became heavier. The next day, the statue sweated fragrant '*manna*' for three consecutive days. Regarding this, there are two public records; one signed by the Vicar Foraneo and by 17 priests of the clergy of Mugnano, the other by the Mayor, the Chancellor, and from the Members of the Council.[158]

This scene evokes the image from the Book of Exodus when manna—a white, flaky bread-like substance—appeared on the ground after the dew evaporated and was used as food for the Israelites in the desert. With Philomena, this "manna", which was a sweet, soft bread, seemed to have sweated from her statue and remained there as a sign of God's continued care for His people, just as He gave them manna when Moses cried out to Him. This event established Philomena as another great intercessor offered to the Church in her journey through the modern world.

The next big miracle also concerned a statue of Philomena. In 1925, a devoted woman had commissioned a statue of Philomena by a famous sculptor to be done out of paper

158. Braschi, 27.

mâché. As famous as the artist was, he was not a believer and so when he made the statue of Philomena, he gave her a very morbid, almost corpse-like appearance, rather than the joyful, living, victorious image that a martyr had. The pastor of the church, as well as all people who saw it, agreed, and felt that it was inappropriate, so they stored the statue in the sacristy and had it covered. One day, when another priest was coming in to get ready for mass, he removed the covering and was shocked by what he found. He went to the pastor and together they went in to find that the Philomena statue now had a beautiful, lively rose color added to it. However, no one had been in there to modify the statue. It was amazing because it was completely dry, as if someone had done it a long time ago and was spread all over as if the statue were alive. The statue was examined to see how this could have happened. The same materials used in the statue were placed in the same conditions to see if a similar reaction occurred, only to find that the result was not the same.

Even if this event does not seem incredibly monumental, what was so interesting about it is the amount of verification and witnesses there were. There were about eight witnesses to verify the change, which took place within a few moments. The artist himself, who was not a believer, was not only convinced that the change took place but was upset because it had happened so quickly and was clearly not a result of his own work. Two sworn judges were commissioned to judge the statue with extreme prejudice. There was no presence of a natural cause to the change, its speed in changing as well as the persistence of the change and the impossibility to reproduce it are all compelling. All of this information was compiled and adjudicated by Cardinal A. Ascalesi around August 27, 1926.

It had also been verified and ascertained that the relics of Philomena self-multiplied. In 1834, Bishop Anselmo Basilici was asked by several various churches to receive relics of Philomena. However, the relics that had been originally received from the catacombs were very few and thus distribution was very difficult. Miraculously, the relics multiplied enough to fulfill the requests of all the bishops who asked. This event was also verified by the delegates sent by the Holy Father who deemed it a truly supernatural event.

Among the authenticated events there were several healings as well, such as a Franciscan sister on the point of death who suddenly recovered and a young girl who for ten years had suffered terrible, incurable illnesses and was instantly healed when people prayed to Philomena. However, one of the most influential was the miracle belonging to Pauline Marie Jaricot in 1835.

Founder of the Society for the Propagation of the Faith and The Living Rosary, Pauline was a well-known and respected lady in the Church. However, for several years she had suffered with severe sicknesses that were painful and debilitating. It had been remarked to her that the raising of the dead was more likely than her being cured. It was extremely frightening for her, as she recounts:

> But what scared me most of all, and made me tremble every moment with the possibility of imminent death, was an aneurysm of the heart, with which I had suffered for many years, and that especially for the past fifteen months caused me a deadly heart palpitation that took my breath away and forced me to stay nearly always in bed. The doctors considered my life like a daily prodigy because the blood that palpitated in my heart, would strike back in my chest, where a sore had generated, which would constantly make me sick with rotten blood, which gave off an intolerable smell even for myself, and I had

> developed an enormous obstruction in my liver that caused an enormous swelling of my whole body, from the soles of my feet to my neck, as everybody could see. [159]

It can be imagined that this experience was as humbling as it was painful. Pauline was essentially bedridden and could hardly raise her arm to feed herself. She and many of her close companions began to invoke the intercession of Philomena for the healing this most terrible situation. There was a slight improvement and Pauline was able to at least get out of bed into a chair, but she was far from cured. However, one of the greatest experiences that Pauline said she received from Philomena was not the physical cure, but the loving attention and companionship that the young martyr saint offered her. As she said: "You have been my protecting Angel and my support for my whole painful journey. You have been like a helpful cloud, keeping covered from the harmful heats of the fervent season, which threatened deadly effects." [160]

Pauline knew that she needed to go to the shrine to visit her dear advocate. Philomena had been with her through so much of this suffering, it was time for Pauline to go and offer some thanks and homage to her dearest of friends. Pauline truly did not have the intention to ask to be completely healed; she was thankful for the mobility she had received and was willing to accept whatever came from God's hands. She had already received a powerful aid and felt satisfied with this recovery if it was from God. However, Philomena had different plans.

Upon her arrival at the sanctuary, she was so excited and filled with joy at being able to greet her saintly friend and protector, and this filled the other pilgrims with charity and

---

159. Braschi, 35.
160. Braschi, 36.

compassion. The great mass of people who were present there began crying out to the little virgin martyr for Pauline's healing. "From the night of Saturday August 8, until Monday the 10th, I was brought to the church twice a day, on my chair with armrests, and the people who were at the feet of the Saint V. and M. were asking with fervor for my healing."[161] One of the great fruits of the saints is that they not only draw us into greater companionship with the saints in heaven but with others. The growth of the Church and the growth of charity is the burning flame of their hearts.

Finally, the charity of Philomena and the prayers of others paved the way for the grace of God to touch Pauline:

> At last Monday evening, at the moment of the blessing of the Most Holy Sacrament I felt unusual strength in me, and with ease I wanted to kneel down. I felt the urge to try and walk, and to go out of the church without my chair. I had it brought after me for precaution, in case my weakness would return, but to my amazement I managed, without it or any support, to walk up to my hotel. [162]

Strength had returned, pain had disappeared. It also was not something that was short-lived; she continued to grow stronger and stronger and walked on her own every day to the Shrine for mass and devotions. She had no problems walking, kneeling or anything that a normal person could do, even dancing! All of these marvelous events are attributed to the charity of Philomena. Above all Pauline saw that it was the hand of God at work, a God who loves to show

161. Braschi, 37.
162. Braschi, 37.

His grandeur in diffusing His goodness and power through a variety of instruments and companions,. God was pleased to work through Philomena and is even more glorified in how He can use even the humblest of girls sentenced to the most horrible of fates to work some of the greatest wonders. The charity of the saints becomes augmented in the embrace of God and makes them want to lift and give hope and charity to all the small and humble people of the earth who pray and make pilgrimage. The saints are true brothers and sisters and wish to work in great ways to make the people here below into saints as well and form a unity of charity in the Church.

After Pauline's healing, her relationship with Philomena did not come to end; no, she did not see Philomena as a genie to grant her wish. She truly was brought into a friendship with Philomena that remained into eternity in heaven. The saints are the best friends because their relationships only grow stronger, even after death! So Pauline and Philomena left Mugnano, closer than when they had arrived. As a token, Pauline was given a small relic of the saint. Pauline took her dear friend with her back to her homeland of France and wanted to share the love and devotion of this wonderful little saint. Friends have no greater joy than to share the love they have for their friends with others and to draw others into friendship too. In France, Philomena found another dear friend who journeyed with her, worked miracles with her, and eventually joined her in heaven as a fellow saint. This relationship was one of the most famous and important ones of all.

The Curé of Ars and Philomena of Rome

France has been known as The Eldest Daughter of the Church since French culture, society, and civilization was crafted with no little influence from the strong presence of the Faith. France in turn has given some of the most beautiful architecture, writing, and saints back to the Church. Much of the Church's great theology developed in France, and countless saints and doctors of the Church owe their education to the University of Paris. Even at times when the secular rule and the ecclesiastical rule were much closer and bonded, France had a special relation with the Church as the place of the crowning of Charlemagne and the heart of the Holy Roman Empire. Many of the great kings of France were canonized, many of the crusades were preached in France, and much of the monasticism of the West came from France. Against this backdrop of faith, the French Revolution stood out with ever more grewsome horror.

A fruit of the Enlightenment and man's desire to be free from older thoughts and ideals, the French Revolution was considered one of the biggest black marks on history. The root of the revolution was sparked by a great economic collapse that took place in France resulting from bad governance on the part of King Louis XVI. In response, there was widespread revolt, and the various classes of society were destroyed. The majority, which belonged to the lower class, asserted martial law upon the rest of society. The king was ultimately put to the guillotine and in 1789 the fall of old France began. 1793 began the horrendous time of the Reign of Terror, a period in which all that was the foundation of society, from the monarchy to the Christian religion, was sought out to be eradicated. People wanted to put God to death in France to get rid of what they saw as the cause of the corruption in the world. Priests were hunted down and killed, religious were arrested and sentenced to death. Many of the beautiful old churches were burned and destroyed. The Revolution spread far and wide not only throughout Paris, but all of France and ultimately laid the foundation for some of the horrible events of communism.

The world that John Marie was born into in 1786 was cold and dark. The great living tree of the Church in France had been chopped down to its roots. But as again and again has taken place throughout the Church's history, the saints are the new growth that sprout up and bring life back to the Church, because they themselves are the Church at its fullest and the Church exists most fully in them. John Marie Vianney experienced the faith during this time much like how his future friend Philomena had experienced it in the early Roman days of Christianity. The faith was persecuted, masses and prayers were said in hiding and in a whisper, sacred objects were buried, and priest were fugitives. It may have been some of these encounters that drew John Vianney to the vocation of the priesthood, and it may have been this experience that gave him a greater connection with his soon-to-be virgin martyr friend.

The French Revolution finally ended in 1799. John Vianney was finally able to enter seminary around 1802 without fear of bloodthirsty revolutionaries. He was ordained a priest in 1815 and was sent to be the pastor of a small country town of Ars. As he set off on his journey, he was told, "There is not much love for God there." From 1818 until 1859, John Marie worked tirelessly in prayer, confession, preaching, penance, and charity, serving the small flock that was given to him. Though the community only consisted of about 250 persons, John dedicated all his energy to saving them. It was not numbers that he was worried about or focused on, for even one soul won over to God was worth more praise and rejoicing than 99 saved souls (Lk 15,7). John, like many other saints, saw the precious value in every single soul and treated them and loved them as if they were the only person in the world. The more John Vianney acted in this way; the more people were drawn to him. Countless people flocked to his church for his masses, to go to confession to him, to seek some healing. France was beginning to see the light reappearing through the darkness of the Revolution's residue. God was using John as an instrument to bring grace back into France, but John wished to remain hidden and humble.

It is not known exactly when and how Philomena's and John's lives first crossed. Some say that John had been going around asking for alms to help him with the building of a school and had thus come to the home of the Jaricots to ask for funds but walked away with a relic. Others say it may have been Pauline's mission to spread devotion to Philomena and that she had an intention and drive to give the relic to the holy Cure. Still other sources said they had known each other before Pauline's cure and when John Vianney visited her after her return, he begged her for a relic, and then he refused to give it back! It was certainly at the hands of God's providence who drew His beloved saints together and gave John a "scapegoat" for all the wonders taking place in Ars, to preserve his humility and to give him the great support and love of a heavenly friend who was as anxious about saving souls as John was.

The friendship between John Vianney and Philomena was a true and perfect friendship of mutual love and respect centered around a common goal: saving souls. As with all the saints in their attitude toward us, Philomena loved John very tenderly and sweetly. Her love was increased because of his great love for the Lord, which was the central axis around which they both turned. John loved Philomena as his *sa chère petite Sainte*, "sweet little saint." They had a deep love for each other based on the things of the spirit, which is the foundation of all the truest friendships, as is highlighted by the other saints and their friendships. It was true, pure, and firm and able to endure for eternity, showing that friendship with the saints is the greatest of all friendships.

John Vianney and Philomena showed the perfect blend and interaction of the Church: visible and invisible, heavenly and earthly, spiritual and temporal, triumphant and militant. Both were united in one single purpose. The ministry of John Vianney skyrocketed: pilgrims from all over came to wait in line for hours to go to confession, crowds of people gathered for mass, sick cripples came for healing, poor were taken care of, sinners were converted, the good were made saintly. The interaction between the two was very beautiful: John Vianney offered every prayer intention, every praise, every good report, every need to her; Philomena listened attentively to him, refused him nothing, marveled greatly at his humility and holiness. She kept him humble and hidden, he kept her known and venerated. He was the foot soldier on the ground doing the great work, she was the great heavenly intercessor, winning grace and answering intercessions. Who was the real author of the good taking place? Ultimately it was the Holy Spirit at work. Man is again and again invited to be simply instruments of God's power and grace. The more generosity man shows to God, the more God can act in that person's life and soul. With these two, gathered in the name of the Lord, truly was the Lord present (Mt 18:20). Neither of them could claim to be the source of the good works because it was God who worked through them; only John Vianney had the advantage of being able to speak openly and thus blame it all on Philomena! This only opened wider the gates for God to work through them.

It has been said that Philomena even appeared to John Vianney because he was able to recognize pictures of her as being either authentic or not, as being a good representation or not. He fell ill after long hours of confessions and was bedridden and considered on the point of death. The people rushed to the altar of Philomena and began to pray unceasingly for him. He went through a few ups and downs, recovering and then coming close to death. However, the Cure said that God seemed to have changed His mind through Philomena's intercession. He lived and dedicated an altar to Philomena. Countless other cases of healing took place in Ars, especially at the Philomena altar, to the point that the altar was filled with crutches and small tokens of thanks.

When John's life came to an end, after years and years of amazing ministry, he was able to finally join his dear friend in heaven where their friendship bore its great fruit. The love and charity they showed each other, as well as the fame of the miracles, spread the devotion of Philomena far and wide. After the time of John Vianney, several other saints grew to have a devotion to Philomena as well. St. Frances Xavier Cabrini (1850-1917), the missionary of the Sacred Heart who founded many great schools and institutions in the United States, Nicaragua, Italy, Panama, Argentina, Spain, Brazil, France, and England, used to carry around with her, in her small meek suitcase, a small statue of Philomena on all her missionary trips and sought her intercession. Padre Pio was also said to have been very devoted to Philomena since he was a child. To this day, the Shrine in Mugnano continues to receive many powerful testimonies of healings from Philomena, not only at the Shrine itself but from people all over the world who write and offer their praises and thanks for the little wonder worker.

The "Canonization" of Philomena

One of the unique and controversial points about Philomena is her canonization. Basically, she did it backwards. Through the many miracles, there seemed to be a "divine confirmation" of her presence in heaven; she had a huge following of people who recognized and were inspired by her holiness and thus a true fame of holiness. However, what she lacked was the historical, verified documentation of her life and martyrdom. The only evidence that testified to the reality and veracity of her life and martyrdom were the writings on her tomb and the visions given to the mystic.

We must remember that being canonized a saint is a juridical proclamation of the Church about public devotion to a Servant of God that is based on but distinct from the theological reality of them being in heaven. The efficient cause of canonization is a declaration of the Holy Father in the form of a ceremony of canonization. It can be verified that Philomena lacked a formal canonization ceremony. So how did she get canonized? Essentially, in 1834 around September, a decree was put out by the Congregation for the Sacred Rites allowing the Diocese of Nola (where her relics are kept) to offer public honor to Philomena in the form of mass and divine office on August 11. On January 30, 1837, Pope Gregory XVI issued a rescript, or a formal reply, in which he approved *Officii, et Missae in honorem Sanctae Philomenae,* "Office and Mass in honor of St. Philomena."[163]

ac
Sutrina, et Nepesina.
Approbationis Officii, et Missae in honorem Sanctae Philumenae Virginis Martyris. Instantibus Rmis Episcopis Sanctissimus De speciali gratia benigne annuit praevia tamen revisione ab Emo, et Rmo D. Cardinali Praefecto cum Sanctae Fidei Promotore peragen. Die 30. Januarii 1837. —
Decretum prostat sub adnexo Officio

Original photocopy of the rescript of Pope Gregory XVI approving mass and office for Philomena.

163. I have included in here a photocopy of the original decree by Pope Gregory XVI for reference. This document is stored in the archives of the Congregation for the Cause of Saints.

The pope not only approved for the Universal Church the actions of true devotion to Philomena, which was only right and correct for a saint, but he even called her "Saint Philomena." Though she lacked the canonization ceremony, (which many formal saints lack because of the great presence of the living faith before there was a need for the ceremony), she certainly received the juridical action of a declaration by the Holy Father. Certain sources state that Pope Gregory had a private audience with Pauline Jaricot after her return from being healed by Philomena and declared the miracle to be of the highest order. There is even a humorous story that he asked her to stand up and dance since that was something that truly was impossible before her healing! Hence, there is a strong basis for believing that Pope Gregory knew of Philomena and her reputation, verified a first-class miracle through her intercession, and made a public papal decree with the effects of canonization attached.

However, the plot soon thickened. In 1961, Pope John XXIII published a decree of the Church that stated: *"Festum autem S, Philumenae V. et M. (11 augusti) e quolibet calandario expungatur"* "The feast of St. Philomena Virgin and Martyr (August 11) is removed from all calendars." For many persons devoted to St. Philomena, this declaration seemed to be a very harsh and stern blow. Many were also confused: did the Church de-consecrate a saint? What did Philomena do wrong? This declaration above all seemed to snuff out public devotion to the wonder-worker saint. With various thoughts and criticisms that have surrounded this decision, a balanced evaluation is needed to work through the false accusations and assumptions.

Firstly, St. Philomena was *not* de-canonized. The Church does not say that a person is not a saint. Firstly, if they are in heaven, this is an unchangeable truth; it is a reality that cannot be affected by simple declarations. To canonize someone, it means there is enough certainty and proof that they are in heaven that the Church can approve public shows of honor. The Church can say that someone is in heaven due to proofs of intercession and holiness of life, but the Church cannot say that someone is not in heaven, since only God can judge a soul. Canonization, as was covered in detail in Chapter 3, deals more with a public celebration of devotion and the listing of a certain Servant of God among the persons honored by the Church in public worship. The removal of the feast of St. Philomena (even note the wording: she was still referred to as saint in the document), was not the removal of the title of saint, but rather the removal of the feast from the universal calendar of the Church.

Secondly, the context of the decree by John XXIII is very important.[164] The long and the short of it is that Philomena was not singled out and removed as a sort of punishment in any way. The removal of her feast day was within the greater context of other feasts that were remembered but becoming multiplied out of popular devotion. Such feasts included the Memorial of the Crown of Thorns, the Flight into Egypt, the Humility of Mary, and several others. The Church was not removing these feasts because they were not real or worthy of honor. The Church was removing the feasts because the multiplication of celebrations was damaging the universal honor and devotion to the central mysteries they were attached to. Hence, many feasts were removed so that the central celebration of these feasts would be more exalted. Obviously, people are still able to, and rightly should, recognize and honor these realities. The statement removing Philomena from the universal calendar came directly after the listing of these feasts. What the mind of the Holy Father seemed to be saying was that the feast of Philomena

---

163. The entire document can be found in the Church's listing of yearly decrees the Acta Apostolicae Sedis: https://www.vatican.va/archive/aas/index_sp.htm March 29, 1961 (AAS LIII/3 pg 168–180, of special importance: 174_.

celebrated by the universal Church was (and as her entire presence in the life of the Church testifies) a fruit of devotion and pious learning about this saint. Hence, her feast and many other feasts were removed to prevent the redundancy of duplicating feasts and the possible decrease in devotion to the central mysteries.

However, there was more sound reasoning as to why her feast was removed from the general calendar. The presence of her feast on the universal calendar makes its celebration somewhat binding on the entire Church. However, Philomena is a saint who has never been found in the Roman Martyrology (the lists of the Church's saints from times past), and most everything known about her life on earth comes from private revelation. The historical reality of this saint, that is, the details of her life, which lends itself to the powerful example that the saints are for the Church, is not as supported as it is with the rest of the saints. Hence, the Holy Father seemed to be removing her feast on account also of a lack of the historical precedence and recognition from the faithful given to her life on earth. The lack of the critical presence of her earthly life makes the entire proof of her sainthood rest upon the reception and devotion of the Church through intercession. Removing her feast was not saying she is not a saint, nor that she could not be celebrated in private devotion (some even argue that she can still be commemorated with the liturgy by those who wish). It was taking away the mandatory nature of her celebration, based largely on the fact that her earthly, human life was not as well verified. This final criterion, the historic reality of the saints and their celebrations, is one of the principals currently in the discernment process for having a celebration on the universal calendar that the entire Church universally and yearly commemorates.

The Lesson of Philomena

Philomena is one of those reminders that we may never completely explain everything about the spiritual realm, and that God is still a mystery, not a mystery we are meant to be withheld from, but one that can only be understood through entering. God will always be greater than our minds and designs. We can't put limits on God: He will always be greater than our limitations. Philomena, the patron saint of miracles, is a testimony that miracles are not a thing of the past. Miracles have a wild, elusive power that we cannot grasp but only accept. We are invited to surrender to the works of a God, who is not a thing of this world that we can put a leash on and tell Him when and how to act. Philomena doesn't fit into the normal box of saints because the Church herself does not fit into any normal box. She is a reminder that our faith is radical, personal, and greater than our own designs. Fact, truly, will always be greater than fiction since the imaginations of our mind don't hold a candle to the realities of God and heaven.

I'm reminded of my first trip to Alaska. My parents and I went in September of 2018 and we were blessed to catch a very active showing of the Northern Lights. As much as I tried to stop and take pictures, there came a point when taking pictures just failed to catch everything and I had to sit back and absorb the somewhat mysterious power around me. No explanations or scientific research could match the beauty of nature at work.

When it comes to the supernatural, sometimes we must do the same. It is important to not try and become masters of the mysteries, but rather companions. We are called to have the heart of a child, a heart that can be caught up in awe and wonder. We must remember that there is something greater than us out there. What the saints continue to show us is that when we stop trying to capture the mystery and start to let ourselves be captured, we discover a new reality to share in. Philomena, daughter of light, will continue to show us that the show goes on. She is a light in the Church showing how personal our faith can be and that in heaven we are forever apart of a reality that is not static and stale but wonderfully alive and vivacious. May Philomena not only continue to show us the wonders of God, but also allow us to wonder at God again.

To thee, O Great St. Philomena, we turn in our afflictions, for thou art truly worthy of the title, "Powerful with God", who stimulates the faith and courage of the faithful, Pray for us! ... Philomena, whose name is glorified in Heaven and feared in Hell, Pray for us!

THE JOURNEY CONTINUES

In July of 2021, I was appointed pastoral administrator of a small Catholic Church named St. Jo-seph in the town of St. Joseph, Louisiana. It is a very quiet, rural town nestled on the delta of the Mississippi River, adjacent to the beautiful oxbow Lake Bruin. The families there are very simple yet devout; they love the Lord and they love their community. It was an honor to have this church as my first community.

Arriving at this church, I did not go alone: St. Rose came with me. She would be an inspiration, intercessor, and sister companion for me in my new parish. Being that Rose loved to garden, I figured she would love this area with all its farms and forests and natural life. As a pastoral administrator, I had all the duties and responsibility of a pastor, including leading the devotional life of the community. Since I had just arrived in July and August 23 is Rose's feast day, I wanted to offer something special for Rose and the community. The town had a large and lush community garden filled with several garden beds that grew all sorts of fruits and vegetables and complete with a large colony of Monarch butterflies! I found a blessing for seeds and seedlings for the new year which would impart fruitful and healthy growth to the small seeds that would soon be planted. I figured this would be a great blessing for Rose to be a patron for. So, on August 23 I gathered with a small group of my parishioners and some of the locals in the garden with a statue of St. Rose as they all brought various seeds to be blessed. Standing around the statue of Rose, I prayed the beautiful prayer of blessing for seeds and sprinkled Holy Water on the gardens and the gardeners who were present. It was a fun and enriching opportunity for all.

Fast forward about a month or so, I found myself in a bit of a rut: I was musing over some mistakes I had made, and how I let my pride get in the way. I was trying to hold God, my life, and my parish under my control and I realized that my spiritual life was taking a toll. I thought I could control everything and that I had stopped relying on God as much as I had. Well, if that was true then the current slump of spiritual desolation and guilt was also my fault. I felt a bit ashamed of myself and I natural felt that I had disappointed God. I turned to St. Rose, and I needed someone to lean on. As much as my guilt wanted to tell me I didn't deserve a sister like her, I felt her voice crying out in the distance, "But we don't love because you earned us, we love because you need us to!" As much as it was a voice of reassurance, it was hard to shake the shame. I made another plea to Rose; I asked her to give me a token of her love, a reminder that even in my sin and failure she would not abandon me. Moreover, I was totally surrendering to her: the way, the timing, the complete manner of the sign I surrendered to her. I did not want it to be something that I was in control of anymore. If she chose to wait, I would accept it; if she wanted it to be small, that was fine with me. Even if she decided not to give me any sign at all, I would accept that too, just asking that I could have a sense of trust over and above my own failures.

Three days later, I was back in Alexandria for my weekly trip into town for some work in the diocese office. While there, I needed to drop something off at my former parish of St. Frances Cabrini where I had been serving as parochial vicar and where much of my relationship with Rose had grown. When I was in the church office my former pastor was just coming in to enjoy lunch. I was running errands, so I didn't have much time to stay and visit and I certainly did not want to hold them up. As I was giving my greetings, the pastor told me, "St. Rose made it into the church." I paused to figure out what he meant. Then I remembered: before I had left, I gifted the parish a framed image of St. Rose like the one I had received in Lima. I had to go check it out: I ran over to the Church, opened the door, and walked into the nave of the church. I turned to the left and there next to the American flag in the back was Rose. She looked so beautiful. I smiled with satisfaction at seeing her there and I turned to leave. Then I paused. Was this my sign? I turned back around and walked up to her. She looked so bright and lively. I reached up and touched her face. I immediately felt my sense of guilt and desolation melt away like snow. I gave her a smile, a prayer of thanksgiving, and then I went on my way.

Later that evening, I was back in my parish for our evening mass and our weekly faith formation. It was a good night and a nice turn out. After the talk, as people were talking and walking around the church, I noticed one of my parishioners was hanging around waiting for me. She was a kind woman, someone who just recently had rediscovered her faith and was coming back into the Church more. She was also very active in the community and was one of the people in charge of the community garden. She walked up to me and gave me a hug; I could tell she had something to tell me. "So, I just found out I'm pregnant," she said a bit bashfully. "How great!" I replied and gave her a hug in return. "Yeah, I actually found out the day we did the blessing at the garden," she told me. Wait a minute: that was St. Rose's feast day, and we had done a blessing for seeds and new growth! I was seeing something beautiful take place. Someone else walked up, overhearing the good news. "So was this God's plan or your plan?" they asked her. "Oh, definitely God's plan.", she replied. 'Definitely God's plan' was right, and I felt I had received a double portion of the joy I had asked for.

In John's Gospel, Jesus said, "No longer do I call you servants, for the servant does not know what his master is doing; but I have called you friends for all that I have heard from my Father I have made known to you" (Jn 15:15). The saints became the friends of God and were given knowledge of God's great delights. We are also called to be friends of God. The saints who share in God's knowledge share friendship with us as well. As this book comes to an end, it also comes to a beginning: a new friendship we are all called to. Maybe you have a favorite saint or a special devotion but never saw them as a figure in your current life. I invite you to take a new look at your saint friend. Perhaps you have never had a devotion to the saints. Maybe there is a saint following you and you aren't even aware. I have written this book not with the hopes of giving a history but rather a future, one that is filled with compan-ionship and support.

In choosing how to conclude this book, I noticed that an Epilogue is normally considered a closing section that takes place outside of the setting of the rest of the book, usually at some point in the future. The real anchor of this book is not in the past, nor even necessarily in the present. It is in the future, in the joys of heaven. The saints journey with us not so much to ease this life, but to guide this life to heaven. It is there that all joys will be complete and we will share each other's companionship forever. The love they have for us, mirroring God's love, desires to be with us. We have come to know them as we walk beside them and they support us, but our gaze turns together to the common goal we are looking toward: heaven. We become familiar with heaven now by making friends with the inhabitants of heaven. It gives us an acquired taste for the joys to come.

Finding Fellowship

Maybe you're asking yourself at this point: how do I find friendship with the saints? Or, is there is a special saint journeying with me? Maybe you want to walk closer with a specific saint or think there already is a specific saint in your life. Maybe you have no real thought about how to begin a relationship with these coheirs to heaven. Fear not. It's not a daunting task. It's a delight for the saints to share this road with us and when we give them permission by our willingness and openness in our activity, they are allowed to enter more into our life. So where to begin?

Take and Read

Read up on the saints. If there is a specific saint you feel that maybe you are called to or you're drawn to, read up on them. Sometimes just learning some basic biographic information can be helpful. Maybe they share a birthday with you, maybe an important event in your life was marked by their feast day, maybe something about their birth or their life connects with yours. You can start off in very general ways and look at basic chronological information. There is a great deal of basic information available. Then, it is good to delve more in-depth: find a good biography of the saint and read it. Again, you can either read the lives of a collection of saints or pick up a good biography of a specific saint. This book hopefully gave you some good starting points on a few saints but there are a great variety of other biographies out there. Many saints have written beautiful works and coming to know them and their writing not only gives you more insight into their lives but also gives them permission to walk with you. Next, look up information about patron saints. Each saint is a patron of a certain sphere of influence in this world. Because the love and devotion of this world caries over and increases in heaven, they have a special care and concern for many endeavors we find ourselves taking on. Learn who is the patron saint of what, especially of things you partake in or experience in this life. You may see that a certain saint is the patron of your occupation, of something you've been through, of a struggle you want to overcome.

Imagine Your Friends

Next look into various saint devotions and artwork. Consider adopting a certain devotion to a saint through a novena or specific prayers to them or prayers that they prayed. Prayer is how we put our faith and understanding into action; it gives the saints permission to work in our lives. Consider finding some holy cards or medals of saints and begin to wear them or keep them in your room. These physical elements are silent yet tangible ways to invoke their intercession. Most medals are stamped with the words "Pray for us" and this prayer is prayed constantly as you wear them. Images and medals also are visible reminds of the saints and work as sacramentals, or channels of grace, in our lives.

Saintly Roulette

If you still don't necessarily feel certain of one saint, don't fret. Consider turning to Mary, Queen of All the Saints, asking her to pray for you and guide you. St. Faustina had a tradition in her community that on New Year's Eve they would take the names of a whole bunch of different saints, write them on strips of paper, put them in a basket, and then at the end of mass they would say a Hail Mary and leave themselves to the complete guidance of the Lord as they chose a saint to journey with them that year. I did this tradition with my youth group as well as with a group of married couples on a retreat and my parish and the outcome was incredible! Some very powerful connections were made, just from the simple luck of the draw! Consider making that a tradition with your family, friends, or even your church parish.

Step out

Finally, journey with your saint. Turn to them, pray to them, invoke their intercession. Ask them to share some of their graces and merits with you. Ask them to spiritually adopt you. There will be great variety in how the saints make this palpable to you, but in the end remember it is all for the glory of God and all to lead us closer to Him, so we should not get too caught up in finding the saint and losing sight of the Lord of all saints. As we have seen, the saints are always oriented to the Lord and if we see them as companions, they can't help but point us to Him. Keep their medal on you and touch it in hard times as a reminder of their closeness. Place their picture in a prominent place and celebrate their feast day with a special devotion. They will never be outdone in generosity! When times get hard and you feel you have failed, trust in their merits. In a very special way, during mass, when heaven and earth are united, ask your saint to be with you. When you receive communion, and thus enter into communion with the Body of Christ as it enters into you, not only know of your closeness physically to Our Lord Jesus but also to your saint. You receive all of heaven! Ask your saint in that moment to be very close to you and to help you grow in the love they have. Don't be afraid from time to time to ask your saint for a small token of their love for you, some way of seeing how they are present, and then leave the creativity up to them! Above all, try to be a saint yourself. In so doing they will want to help you and will show you the road and the end we seek.

As a kid I used to ride horses and one of the important things we had to remember is that wherever their head is facing, that is where they are going to go. Riding a horse and holding the reins is a training in turning the horses head in the direction you want it to go. In many ways, the same is true for us: we will go in the direction we face. When the saints are at our side, they keep us from turning our heads away and keep us moving forward. The more saints we surround ourselves with, the more reminders we have of heaven when we turn our head. So let us take up this journey to heaven; let us journey with the saints who have already finished the journey yet never tire to walk with us. Let us all walk together, no longer strangers, but now as friends.

AFTERWARDS

My hopes are that this book has been an aid to you in your own faith journey. I have grown in my own relationship with the saints and feel that ending this book has opened a new horizon. The stories I have cited in this collection are but a few of many stories. Hopefully, they will inspire many more! I know there are many companion stories out there, waiting to be discovered, and more to be started. If this book has either helped you to form a relationship with a saint who is journeying with you or helped you to realize a saint has been journeying with you already, I want to hear!

This book is hopefully only the first of many. If you would like to share your story with me, please don't hesitate! It can be a story of a saint, an angel, St. Joseph, or Mary! Please send all stories to frtreynolds@diocesealex.org God bless you!

BIBLIOGRAPHY

Bible
Revised Standard Version Catholic Edition. Scepter Press Princeton, 1946.

Catechism
Catechism of the Catholic Church. 2nd ed. Vatican: Liberia Editrice Vaticana, 2021.

Church Documents and Decrees
Acta Apostolicae Sedis. March 29, 1961. https://www.vatican.va/archive/aas/index_sp.htm

Apostolicam Actuositatem, Decree on the Apostolate of the Laity. Vatican II, (Vatican City, 1965).

Lumen Gentium. Dogmatic Constitution on the Church. Vatican II, (Vatican City 1964).

Mater Sanctorum. Instruction for Conducting Diocesan or Eparchial Inquiries in the Causes of the Saints. (Vatican City, 2007).

Papal Documents
Pope Benedict XVI. *Deus Caritas Est.* Vatican: Libreria Vaticana Editricia, 2005.

———. *Spe Salvi.* Vatican: Libreria Vaticana Editrice, 2007.

———. "Address to the Community of the Roman Major Seminary for the Annual Feast of our Lady of Trust," February 20, 2009. Vatican City State.

Pope Francis. *Maiorem hac dilectionem* Motu Proprio. (Vatican City State, July 11, 2017.)

Pope John Paul II. *Evangelium Vitae.* (Vatican City, 1995).

Books
A Benedictine Monk. *In Sinu Jesu.* Angelico Press, 2016.

Alphonsus, Sister Mary, O.ss.R. *Saint Rose of Lima, Patroness of the Americas.* Charlotte, NC: Tan Books, 1982.

Aristotle. *On Man in the Universe.* Roslyn, NY: Walter J. Black Inc, 1943.

Benito, Jose Antonio "Tercer Concilio Limense" *Obispos participantes en el III Limense. Semblanzas: Santo Toribio Alfonso de Morgrovejo.* Facultad de Teologia Pontificia y Civil de Lima/Universidad Pontificia de La Santa Croce. Lima, 2017

BIBLIOGRAPHY CONTINUED

Braschi, Msgr Giovanni. *Saint Philomena Testimony of the Light of Christ.* Cultural Book Sanctuary of Saint Philomena, 201.

Caridi, Cathy. *Making Martyrs East & West.* DeKalb, IL: Northern Illinois University Press, 2016.

Congregatio de Causis Sanctorum. "Le Cause dei Santi: Sussidio per lo Studium." Quartra Edizione Libreria Editrice Vaticana, 2018.

Dubay, Thomas. *Fire Within.* San Francisco, CA: Ignatius Press, 1989.

Enright, Robert D. . *Forgiveness is a Choice.* Washington, DC: American Psychological Association, 2001.

Franciscan Friars of the Immaculate. *Padre Pio: The Wonder Worker.* New Bedford, MA: Our Lady's Chapel, 2009. Preface by Fr. Andrew Apostoli CFR.

Gallonio, Antonio. *The Life of Saint Philip Neri.* Translated by Jerome Bertram. San Francisco, CA: Ignatius Press, 2005.

Hebert, Fr. Albert J. *Saints Who Raised the Dead.* Rockford, Il: Charlotte, NC: Tan Books, 2004.

Joly, Henri. *The Psychology of the Saints.* Roman Catholic Books, 2006.

Kheriaty, Aaron. *The Catholic Guide to Depression.* Nashua, NH: Sophia Institute Press, 2012.

Ligarda, Rosa. *Santa Rosa de Lima Escritos de la santa Limeña.* Facultad de Teologia Pontificia y Civil de Lima, Lima Peru, 2016.

Lewis, C.S. *The Four Loves.*

Lozano, Neal. *Unbound: A Practical Guide to Deliverance.* Grand Rapides, MI: Chosen Books, 2009.

Nault, Jean-Charles, O.S.B. *The Noonday Devil: Acedia, the Unnamed Evil of Our Times.* San Francisco, CA: Ignatius Press, 2015.

Pope Benedict XVI. Jesus of Nazareth: *Holy Week: From the Entrance into Jerusalem to the Resurrection* San Francisco, CA: Ignatius Press, 2011.

———. *Jesus, the Apostles and the Early Church.* Huntington, IN: Our Sunday Visitor, 2007.

BIBLIOGRAPHY CONTINUED

Sarah, Cardinal Robert and Nicholas Diat. *The Day is Long Spent.* San Francisco, CA: Ignatius Press, 2019.
Sheikh, Bilquis. *I Dared To Call Him Father.* Grand Rapides, MI: Chosen Books, 2003.

Spirago, Francis. *The Catechism Explained.* Post Falls, ID: Mediatrix Press, 2020.

St. Thérèse of Liseux. *Story of a Soul.* Study Ed. Translated by John Clark O.C.D. Prepared by Marc Foley O.C.D. Washington, DC: ICS Press, 2005.

St. Philip Neri. "The Maxims and Sayings of St. Philip Neri. Daily Devotions." West Monroe, La: St. Athanasius Press, 2009.

Websites

www.treasuresofthechurch.com
www.santiebeati.it
www.mariagoretti.com

Other

Preface I of Saints. "The Glory of the Saints." The Roman Missal. English Translation according to the Third Typical Edition. London, The Catholic Truth Society, 2010

CPSIA information can be obtained
at www.ICGtesting.com
Printed in the USA
JSHW081410201222
35008JS00003B/6